PERUSING FOR

PIONEER PATHWAYS

The Wonderful and Entertaining Life of
James D. Spain- An Autobiography

With foreword by James A. Mitchell

ISBN: 978-1-71668-518-7

IV

In memory of my loving wife, Pat, with whom I have shared a wonderful life and will miss forever. She supported and inspired me for most of my life.

Also, in memory of my mother and father who played such an important role in the accomplishments of my life. I only wish they could have known and appreciated their role in my final outcome.

A very special thanks to my daughter, Lisa. Without her special editorial help and encouragement, during the last three years, this book could not have been completed

FOREWORD

I first became acquainted with Dr. Spain as a student in his biochemistry class in 1964. Dr. Spain is himself a 1951 Chemistry graduate of Michigan Tech, and served Michigan Tech for 29 years as a professor, pioneer cancer researcher, innovator, and leader.

He was born Feb. 3, 1929 in Washington D.C. He spent his youth in Arlington, Virginia, Chicago, Ill, Jacksonville, FL and New Orleans, Louisiana. Like many of us who studied chemistry, Dr. Spain's attraction to chemistry began with a chemistry set and the resulting chemistry lab he set up in the family basement. Also, like most of us during the junior high and high school years, he was fascinated with reactions that "go boom".

As a student at Michigan Tech he studied chemistry under Dr. Bart Park, Dr. Bradekamp, and Dr. Royal Makens. He studied biochemistry and bacteriology under Dr. San Clemente. He enjoyed gym class with Verdie Cox and skiing with Fred Lonsdorf. He was member and president of Phi Lambda Upsilon, the Chemistry Honor Society.

He obtained his master's degree from the Medical College of Virginia and his PhD at Stanford University, conducting pioneer cancer research. He was awarded a position at prestigious MD Anderson where he continued his pioneering cancer research.

In 1956, a chance encounter with his favorite Michigan Tech chemistry professor, Dr. Royal Makens, led him and his wife Pat back to Michigan Tech as a Professor of Chemistry and a 29-year career of groundbreaking research, innovation, and leadership:

He introduced cancer research to Michigan Tech.

He initiated a more comprehensive course in biochemistry.

He initiated a course in instrumental analysis.

He invented precipitation chromatography.

He added gas chromatography to the instrumentation course.

He founded the Department of Biological Sciences.

He started the first Limnological or Oceanographic graduate studies at Michigan Tech, which has morphed into the Michigan Tech's Great Lakes Research Center (his family motorboat was Tech's first research vessel).

He pioneered the application of computer software to chemistry and biology education and research.

He published a 350-page text on the application of computer technology to the biological sciences.

He started and directed an Instructional Computing Center at EMU.

He wrote and formed a company to sell ChemSkill Builder software, which was marketed by McGraw Hill. (The first practical computerized homework instruction in general college chemistry capable of transmitting secure student records to instructor.)

I encourage you to share Dr. Spain's delightful story and relive with him the years in which Michigan Tech broke out of its undergraduate college cocoon and blossomed into the vibrant research and innovation University which it is today. You will be glad you did!

James A. Mitchell
MTU Chairman 1997-2000
1595 Galbraith
Grand Rapids, Mi 49546
Jamitchell@mitchelliplaw.com

x

Table of Contents

Prologue _____ XV

Chapter 1 The Early Years (1929-1940)_____ 1

Chapter 2 Florida (1940-1946) _____ 25

Chapter 3 New Orleans (1946-1948) _____ 51

Chapter 4 Student Years at Michigan Tech (1948-1951) ___ 67

Chapter 5 Patricia Welburn Mann _____ 91

Chapter 6 Marriage and MCV (1951-1953) _____ 97

Chapter 7 Stanford (1953-1956)_____ 117

Chapter 8 MD Anderson (1955-1956) _____ 141

Chapter 9 Copper Country_____ 149

Chapter 10 The New Professor (1956-1962) _____ 167

Chapter 11 Fish Stories _____ 195

Chapter 12 Adventures of the *Pat-Sea* (1966-1984)_____ 213

Chapter 13 Department Head (1962-1968) _____ 233

Chapter 14 Limnology and Oceanography (1968-1978) __ 257

Chapter 15 Computer Pioneer (1965-1994)_____ 285

Chapter 16 Life Changes (1982-1985) _____ 303

Chapter 17 Clemson (1985-1994) _____ 319

Chapter 18 Golf (1949-2013) _____ 339

Chapter 19 Guitar Picker (1948-2010)_____ 361

Chapter 20 Electronic Homework Systems, Inc.(1994-2010)375

Chapter 21 Conclusion (2020) _____ 413

About the Author _____ 423

PROLOGUE

As the final days of the year 1900 were coming to an end, a branch of the Spain family gave birth to a boy in the back of their covered wagon just outside of Purdy, Missouri. This baby boy was to be the ninth generation of the Spain Family since their arrival from England. Their family had been called "Spain" for many generations before that, when they had been washed ashore from the terrible storm that destroyed the Spanish Armada.

This branch of the Spain family had been following the pioneer path to Kansas where they had heard that there were opportunities in the wheat-growing town of Hutchinson. They arrived in Hutchinson a few weeks later and took up residence there. As soon as they could, they had their first son baptized as James Dorris Spain. He had been given this unusual middle name after his mother's best friend Doris. She began calling her son "Dorri" for short. The father was able to find employment and other members of the Spain family later joined them in Hutchinson, so things were going quite well until Dorri's father caught a serious disease and died. By this time Dorri was fourteen and had completed the eighth grade. However, he was obliged to find work to help his mother and older sister, Nora, take care of two younger siblings, Fred and Flora. His first job was with

Western Union Telegraph company as a delivery boy. A few years later, his mother married a man named George Julian and as soon as he thought his family could do without him, Dorri responded to his urge to move west and headed to California.

On arrival at his destination, Los Angeles, he spent some time looking around and taking whatever job he could get. Since he was a rather handsome lad, he was able to pick up some bit-parts in films and hang out with some of the movie people. During this period, Harry Houdini, the famous magician, and escape artist, was in the town, working on movie serials and playing in some of the local theaters. One of Houdini's interests at this time was exposing the tricks used by fake spiritualists. These ideas influenced young Jimmy, (as he was beginning to call himself) and would also have a powerful impact on his future son as you will see.

His jobs with the movie industry began to peter-out because of a strike. Fortunately, the Al G. Barnes Circus was wintering over in LA and he met up with one of the circus people that he had known from years earlier in Hutchinson. He found that the circus company had a position open for an advance man. This position would allow him to meet people on the road and help plan for the arrival of the circus in town. At first, he wondered if this was the kind of job for him, but then he decided to give it a try for a week or so with one of the men, till he got a feeling for the ropes. As it turned out it was a perfect opportunity to develop his personality and learn skills that would serve him throughout most of his adult career. It was here, at the suggestion of his boss, he began to call himself "Pretty Prairie Jim". This seemed to provide the perfect "ice breaker" and was not that far from the truth. He had plenty of opportunity to develop his social skills, as he had to visit well over one hundred towns during the summer of 1919. I am sure that he must have learned plenty of "traveling salesman" jokes. He was successful in his job, as he was hired for a second year with an increase in salary. However, late in the summer, he was to receive a letter from his mother, asking him to return home, because of an illness. So, as his job was almost complete, he talked with his boss and arranged to get back to Hutchinson as soon as possible.

It was great to be back in town. He couldn't believe how much Hutchinson had changed during the seven years he had been gone. There were more buildings, more people, more good-looking women, and definitely more friendly women! He found that the wealth of stories that he had accumulated in movie-land and on the road with the circus, combined with his newfound personality were endlessly fascinating to the ladies.

By combining these same skills as a head waiter at the new Bisonte Santa Fe-Harvey House Hotel and Restaurant, he was able to get a semi-lucrative job. So, he decided to stay home for a few years. All was going well, until one of his lady friends, who had several kids by a previous marriage, was making some serious plans for their marriage. Since this woman also came from a family with a rather questionable reputation, Jimmy decided it was time to change careers again and join the United States Army.

The records for enlistment in the U.S. Army for this period have been lost, but we assume that he made his way to the nearest recruitment station and from there to the training center, at Fort Funston, Kansas. The next time we have any record of him was when he was assigned to Fort Washington, Maryland, just outside of Washington, DC., where he attended the Salvation Army dances and among other women, met Frances and Jane Pitkin, two sisters from Clarendon, a small town just across the border in Arlington County, Virginia. After meeting Jimmy at a few of these dances, Frances and Jane decided to invite him home for a Sunday Dinner. It turned out that Jimmy was an instant hit with their parents.

Jimmy liked the two sisters and the mother and father, (and particularly the mother's cooking), so he decided this might be a good place to settle down. Consequently, he set about getting himself honorably discharged from the U.S. Army and began looking for a job in the hotel business, since his experience, prior to the Army, was at the Harvey House in Hutchinson.

At this time, Washington had just completed the Mayflower Hotel, one of the largest in the city and what would become the hangout for several future presidents. Jimmy applied there and was given a job in the food service area which ultimately led to managership of the Coffee-Shop. This good fortune must, I believe, have had something to do with his experience with the Harvey House chain of restaurants! However, as future career changes will attest, his personality must have also played a major role in this as well.

With this impressive job description and a year or so of courtship, Jimmy Spain and Frances Pitkin were married and within a year had produced the beginnings of the tenth generation of Spain's in the United States of America. One has to wonder what sort of person he will become.

CHAPTER 1

THE EARLY YEARS

(1929-1940)

I was born in Washington, DC on February 3, 1929 and christened James Dorris Spain, Jr at St. Georges Episcopal Church, in Arlington, Virginia, where my mother had been brought up and her family had gone to church. My mother and father were living in an apartment on Connecticut Ave, near where the National Cathedral was being built. Consequently, my mother had plans for me to enter the Cathedral Boys Choir School.

However, this was not to be, as the year was 1929 and it was not too long before the Mayflower Hotel had to cut back on its higher paid staff. My dad found his next job at the Duke Hotel in Durham, North Carolina, where we lived for about one year. As the depression deepened, he took a job at the Eseeola Lodge in Linville, NC., giving my mother and me our first experience with living in the mountains, an attraction I've had for most of my life. Finally, we simply had to give up and return to my grandmother's home in Arlington. It was here that I had some of my first remembrances since we lived there off and on during the early years of the Depression.

My grandmother's house was located at 802 N. Jackson St, in the village of Clarendon. Clarendon, Arlington County, was located right across the river from Washington City. It was part of the original District of Colombia, which was laid out to be ten-mile square, part in Maryland and part in Virginia. The portion that was in Maryland was designated Washington City, as it contained the Capitol, the White House and essentially all of the government buildings. The portion in Virginia was first called Alexandria County and later changed to Arlington County, after Robert E. Lee's plantation home, Arlington. The county contains several small towns, the largest of which is Clarendon. The house on Jackson St., of course, belonged to both my grandfather and grandmother. But I think of it as her house because she did most of the running of it. It was a boarding house and on occasion also a rooming house. She served dinner seven days a week to about four boarders and sometimes had two roomers, as well. All this may have started during the depression, although my Granddad seemed to have a perfectly good job running the Studebaker automobile service garage in Clarendon.

My grandmother came by her avocation naturally, as her father had owned a hotel and dining room at Chautauqua Lake, New York.

Her mother died when she was young, leaving her to run the dining room. After several years working for her father and helping to manage the hotel, she was said to have run away from home to visit someone in Virginia. During this trip, she met my grandfather, a dashing young bicyclist from Manassas, Virginia. Following their marriage, they lived in Washington and had two daughters, Jane, born in 1903, and Frances, born in 1906. When Frances was about five, they moved to Clarendon, then they had a third daughter, Elizabeth, in about 1915. Their house was a two-story, concrete-block construction with kitchen, dining room, living room and foyer on the first floor; and four bedrooms, bath and sleeping porch on the second floor. It had a beautiful, screened porch that wrapped around two sides and a basement that was called "the cellar", where my Granddad had a wood-shop and Gramma had her laundry, including an electric clothes washer made of copper. This was also where she kept the fruits and vegetables that she canned in zinc or glass-topped Mason jars. Of course, Gramma's primary domain was her kitchen, where she baked hot rolls, apple pies, cookies, and all the other goodies that young boys love. It was standard fare to have hot rolls and baked beans every Saturday night and fried chicken on Sunday. The traditional Thanksgiving, or Christmas Dinner was turkey and dressing, cranberry sauce, mashed turnips, creamed onions, mashed potatoes and gravy, green peas, rolls, mince pie and pumpkin pie.

A significant portion of my early training in etiquette seemed to occur at my grandmother's dining table. Of course, we all sat down for dinner at six o'clock, when the boarders arrived. Gramma sat at the end of the table closest to the kitchen and Granddad sat at the opposite end. I sat just to the right of Gramma and next to me was "Aunt Vernie", not really my aunt, but one of Gramma's oldest friends and a long-time boarder. Aunt Vernie was a very lovable spinster lady, who was my self-appointed guide to good manners, as my mother was usually seated further down the table near Granddad. Aunt Vernie taught me several things, but the one that sticks in my mind is that "no one eats until the polite grandmother begins to eat." This rule was particularly true for desserts since my grandmother served the desserts and was thus the last seated. Aunt Vernie also had some after-dinner tricks, which were my earliest introduction to magic. The one that I remember was that, in which the "magician" sticks a small piece of paper on her fingernail. While chanting "fly away, fly away, fly away home", the fingers of both hands are popped up and down on the edge of the table and the piece of paper magically flies from the finger of one hand to a finger of the other. The secret is that there are two pieces of paper and more than one finger on each hand to show. This was simple, but to a little kid, it was impressive.

Each night before dinner, I would wait for Aunt Vernie, sometimes walking up the street to meet her. Every now and then I would visit her at her apartment a few houses up the street. There we would play games and look at books. All the boarders were interesting; most of them being teachers, but Aunt Vernie was my favorite. One of the appeals of Aunt Vernie was that she was only a little more than four and a half feet tall.

One of my other favorite people was my real Aunt Jane. However, she was off working at the Navajo Mission in Fort Defiance, Arizona, most of the year. She would come back for vacations and bring with her various Indian artifacts, such as blankets, pottery, and statues. She also brought pinion nuts that came from the pinion pine trees. These were tiny little nuts that were fun to eat, but hard to get the meat out of. It is hard to believe that the Navajos could get much food value from them. Aunt Jane was an artist and would spend hours giving me my early training in drawing and painting. Later, when we moved out of Gramma's house for good and Granddad was ailing, she returned to help Gramma and became the first art teacher for Arlington County's elementary schools.

I don't remember much about my Aunt Elizabeth, as she was off at nursing school during much of the time that I was at Gramma's house. I think she was either busy with her studies, or off with her social life. She disappointed the family by dropping out of nursing school to marry Robert Athey from Clarendon and they had three children: Robin, Michael, and later Susan Elizabeth. As the depression wore on, Robert got a job with the CCC and the young family moved to Roanoke, Virginia. During the time Elizabeth was in nursing school, her best friend was a red-haired girl called Ermoye Stoll. Ermoye was so likeable that she was "adopted" by Gramma and Granddad and visited numerous times over the years. She also became a close friend of Aunt Vernie.

During the time when we were living with Gramma, my dad made a little money going door-to-door selling jigsaw puzzles. Finally, he decided that he just had to get a job, so he hitched a ride on a freight train to Chicago, where he got a job as an elevator operator at a hotel (this was before automatic elevators). It was here, that he became fast friends with a baseball team by the name of the House of David. These guys were a bewhiskered band of barnstorming ballplayers, that piqued my dad's interest in baseball in a way that lasted for the rest of his life.

My dad considered this job as being sufficiently lucrative to have my mother and I ride the bus out to join him. There, we lived in a two-room apartment, probably in the same hotel. I can remember that we were quite happy and went several places, once even seeing the Chicago World's Fair of 1933. As Christmas was coming up, we celebrated by going to downtown Chicago to one of the big movie theaters. This was especially impressive to me as it included one of the early *Mickey Mouse* films. However, my mother was lonely for home, so when Gramma wrote saying there was a job opening at

McGruder's Specialty Grocery Store in Washington, we all headed back to Arlington, having great expectations. The excitement was short-lived however, as Dad discovered the pay was significantly less than he had been making as an elevator operator. So, for several more months, we lived with my Gramma and Granddad.

I remember only a little about Granddad, whose full name was Egbert Amasa Pitkin and called Bert by his best friends. He had been active in athletics as a young man, bicycling, weightlifting, and boxing. He still had a boxing bag hanging in the basement when we lived there. He had an early kind of easy chair (Morris Chair) that was in the corner of the living room. I remember Granddad scolding me severely once for prematurely exposing myself while rushing up the stairs to the bathroom. Thus, I was a little afraid of him. However, he taught me to use some of the tools in his workshop and showed me how to whittle. One time I remember cutting my thumb rather badly, while whittling in the basement when Granddad wasn't there. Gramma had to rush me to the doctor's office to get it sewed up. Another time, he showed me his Smith & Wesson revolver, but I was never allowed to touch it. All in all, I think that I must have loved him very much, as I remember crying a couple of years later, when we drove away on our move to Florida. He died about a year later and I never did see him again.

During the fall, after our return from Chicago, I went to kindergarten near the village of Lyon Park. All I remember is the Christmas party where we practiced in our toy-soldier uniforms with blue construction paper hats. In the afternoon, the building had been cold, then in the evening it was boiling hot, so I became sick and threw up in the middle of the whole thing. This later turned into pneumonia and I was in bed in my mother's room (actually, Aunt Jane's room, but my father and mother were sleeping there while she was away). The doctor gave me a new drug, called "sulfa" and said that it had pulled me through, but I really think it was the mustard plaster that they kept sticking on my chest. Wow, did it burn. I think that it was later that year that I had my tonsils out and spent still more time in that bed. Needless to say, I didn't get much from my year in kindergarten. But I guess it hasn't held me back too much

It was the following summer that we were able to rent my Great Aunt Emma's four-room house that was just across the street from St. George's Episcopal Church. This was the church that my mother's family had attended ever since coming to Arlington. By this time, my dad had been put in charge of the liquor department at McGruder's Store and began learning the basics of the industry that was to employ him for the rest of his professional career. So, our return to Arlington was one of those twists of fate that one's life takes, which in retrospect determines the entire course of future events. If I had stayed and grown up in Chicago, it is unlikely that I would have gotten to know a certain Patricia Welburn Mann, whose mother and grandparents also attended St. George's Church.

We lived in Aunt Emma's house during my first three years of elementary school, attending Mathew Fontaine Maury Elementary, a couple of blocks away on the other side of Wilson Boulevard. I discovered, many years later, that Mathew Fontaine Maury was America's first great oceanographer and that Wilson Boulevard was named for President Wilson who used to take this route frequently to get to his golf course in Virginia. It is interesting that these two topics (oceanography and golf) were to occupy a significant portion of my time in later years.

I have a couple of remembrances from this school that I will relate. Both had to do with my artistic talents, or lack thereof. The first had to do with my Aunt Jane, who as I mentioned earlier became the traveling art teacher for Arlington County Schools. Hence was my teacher on numerous occasions, where most of the time she kept our relationship at a low key, not to embarrass me. So, I am sure that I learned a lot of good things from her. But, on this one occasion she wanted the class to tear a piece of paper exactly in half by first folding it, then pulling it apart in a way that she had demonstrated. Apparently, I thought that I knew better and failed to get a straight tear. She looked at me with a frown on her face and said: "Sonny

Spain! Haven't you learned to tear paper properly?" Obviously, I was extremely embarrassed, as I remember it to this day. It was the only time I can remember her being cross with me in my entire life.

My other artistic faux pas was when the teacher caught me passing around a piece of crude pornography that I had produced. Hopefully, this never went any further than the trash basket, as it certainly would have embarrassed the family. In an unrelated occasion, I had received a whole dollar for some reason; perhaps it was my allowance for the next month, or perhaps it was a gift from somebody. Anyway, I went to Spinna's Store, located next to our school, and proceeded to spend it all on trashy little junk toys and candy. When I carried the bag of stuff home, I discovered that there really wasn't anything in the bag that I wanted. This was a great learning experience about the spending of money that is perhaps the reason I am so parsimonious to this day.

As I said earlier, we lived right across the street from St. George's Episcopal Church. Of course, I went to Sunday School like a good boy should, but my greatest learning experience came not from the Sunday School teacher, but from the janitor. Since the church had a sidewalk running all around the side and front, I spent a fair amount of time roller skating, or riding a tricycle on it. Since there were few other kids in the neighborhood, I would often talk to a man named Zebedee, who was the janitor for the church. He would sit on the back stoop of the choir room and talk to me about this and that. As a result of our relations, he taught me some of the most valuable lessons of my life. I didn't know what color he was, or what difference that would make. I was just a kid. He was just a nice old man. After I got to know him better, I would tag along as he did his chores and sit around talking to him as he fried up his lunch and ate it.

One day, when I was helping him by carrying two old wooden collection plates, the edge of one of the plates broke and they both fell clattering to the floor! Now I was in a pickle, as I'd heard that the priest was a gruff old German, named Father Miller, whom I expected would parcel out dire punishment. I didn't know what to do, but Zebedee must have said: "the sooner we tell him, the better". So, we found Father Miller in his office and Zebedee encouraged me to explain what had happened. Father Miller looked at the broken plate and said, "Son, you weren't at fault, as it had already been repaired once, along the line of the break". So, I was exonerated from my clumsy behavior. This seems like a small thing as I look back on it, but the experience shaped my future behavior more than any other that I remember. Thank you, Zebedee, you taught me some of the most valuable lessons of my life.

There were a few kids in the neighborhood and one that I remember especially was called Little-Virginia, as her mother's name was Virginia. Her name was treated as if it were all one name like

Mary-Ann or Bobby-Joe. When her mother called her, it was "Little-Virginia, it's time for lunch.", etc. Little-Virginia wasn't all that little, as she was taller than I and fairly plump. She lived in a big house, across a fence and lawn next to our little house. Once I was invited to lunch by Little-Virginia's mother. My mother cleaned me up and sent me around to the front door of their house, as this was a major social event. When the plate of lunch was placed in front of me, I discovered that sweet potato was one of the featured items. Well, sweet potato was one of the things that I had always resisted eating, probably saying such things as "I don't like it." But now, I was a guest and I had been taught to eat what was put in front of me. So, I tasted it and wow, was it good! I ate it all and probably had "seconds". When I got home and excitedly reported my discovery to my mom, she must have said: "I hope that you have learned something from this." And, in fact I did, as I can't think of very many things I haven't liked since that day.

During this period, we had a visit from Patricia Mann and her mother, Mary-Mac (Mac is short for McLouth, which was her middle name). Mary-Mac had gotten to know my mother when they were in the Girls Friendly group, as teenagers in St. George's Episcopal Church. I think that I must have first gotten to know Pat back when her mother had invited some of the Girls Friendly group to their summer camp at Harold Harbor, near Annapolis, MD. She was about a year younger than I, but we seemed to get along OK, as we have a memorable picture taken on the beach when we were 4 or 5 years old, that her grandad liked to call "Mug-Wumps".

So, I was glad to see her again and we went out on the porch, where I showed her the "movie" that I had made by cutting out the Prince Valiant comic strips and pasting them together to make a big fat role of "film". These were wound past a square opening, made in a shoebox, to provide the "movie" effect. She seemed impressed, despite the low level of technology involved. I also showed Pat my pet turtle. Although this animal was only about two inches across, it somehow bit her finger, and left a scar on her memory that remained for the rest of her life.

We followed up this visit by a visit to her house, which was actually her grandparent's home, located about a mile further down Wilson Boulevard, in a little village called Ballston. The house was the large rambling type built around the turn of the century. It housed her grandfather's office, as he was a doctor of long standing in Arlington County. We did a lot of exploring around the property and had our picture taken by their birdbath.

13

I was beginning to like my fellow "Mug-Wump" more each time I saw her.

It must have been about this time that I began developing an interest in science and magic. This must have built from stories and discussions with my dad based on his experiences in California in which there was always a simple explanation for everything, whether in magic, science, or religion. Thus, my folks had always bought me toys that involved magic or construction. I suppose that it started with magic, went on to Lincoln Logs, Tinker Toys and Erector Sets. These toys gave me a lot of opportunity to explore the relationship of form and function, as well as develop dexterity. This was not just one toy at one Christmas; I remember several versions of these learning toys that carried on over many years of my youth. Eventually, I got an electric train and a microscope. Since these are unlikely toys for little girls to play with, there is no wonder that relatively few females of that time ended up with successful careers in science and engineering. The "ten-cent" stores, like today's dollar stores, offered many inexpensive books on topics that included the history of science, the stories of great scientists, etc. and I had several of them. The radio shows, such as *Little Orphan Annie*, *Jack Armstrong*, and *Tom Mix* often had themes that related to science, or had give-away items such as decoder rings, three-dimensional pictures, invisible ink, simple chemical experiments, such as vinegar and baking soda. I began getting catalogs of magic tricks and related stuff that I studied by the hour. My folks started me collecting stamps and this got me involved in organizing things of a common nature. It also got me thinking of selling things as I would put together packages of stamps, which I imagined would be for sale to my friends.

Later, I began making model airplanes. These were not like the model airplanes that one buys for kids today, in which you get a couple of plastic parts that you can put together in half an hour or so. No, these planes were models of the planes from the 1920's, many of which were constructed of stringers of wood put together to make a frame, then this was covered with silk or muslin and painted. Hence, the models were also constructed using a similar design. We were given a box of balsa wood that was marked to indicate the parts to cut out, some tissue paper, wheels, engine block and instructions. It was up to the kid to cut out the parts, maybe 50 or so, glue them together according to the pattern provided, using model airplane glue, then cover this frame with tissue paper, spray it with water to make the paper shrink to form the completed plane. Typically, it would take several days working full time. Obviously, a father would have to help get this all started, depending on the age of the kid. Some kids had model airplanes hanging all around the ceiling of their room, but I only had one or two. Thus, my interest in science and engineering developed more in other directions.

I think that my Mom was a major influence in all these activities, although I can't really remember either my mother or father pushing me to do anything or go in any particular direction. It must have been very gentle nudging over a long period of time. Mom had been a schoolteacher and must have helped with homework, but only when needed. She also encouraged me by buying books that I wanted. When living in Aunt Emma's house, Aunt Jane gave me a subscription to *Nature* magazine. I remember because one magazine featured spiders of all different types and it scared me at the time. Mom also had experience in art, so encouraged me in that direction as well. One year, she had me try piano lessons, but my musical talents were still dormant, and it didn't really take. Money was too scarce to try to force anything on a kid who wasn't really ready.

Dad tried to encourage me in the area of athletics, although I had the feeling that he had never done much himself, probably because he had to go to work at such an early age. Perhaps for this reason, he wanted so much for me to get involved. He would try to get me to play catch with him and all the other things that fathers do. Even when we were in Durham, several years earlier, there is a picture of me hiking a football with him at the Duke University stadium. When we lived in Aunt Emma's house, his major interest was baseball. He had even come to know some of the players on the Washington Senators team. One day, he proudly brought home a baseball that had been hit out of Griffith Stadium, where the Senators played. My dad bought it from a kid who had picked it up. So, I proudly took it out to play with and see if I could find someone to show it to. To get to the playground near the school, I had to cross Wilson Boulevard that had just been recently paved with brand new storm drains. Of Course, luck would have it, I dropped the ball and away it rolled straight down the storm drain. I tearfully returned home to explain what had happened, but I'm afraid this experience killed my dad's enthusiasm for trying to develop any athletic talents in his son. We didn't do much of an athletic nature until several years later.

During this period, my dad was developing his social qualities by studying the book "How to Win Friends and Influence People" by Dale Carnegie, and also by becoming an actor with the Barn Theatre over at Bailey's Crossroads. This personal development ultimately led to a position with Calvert Distillery, makers of several prominent brands of whiskey. He probably started as an Assistant Sales Manager for the D.C. area and worked up to Sales Manager. This provided enough money to buy a new home for the family. So, we moved to a little, white painted brick house on Fenwick Street, about a half block south of Arlington Boulevard. This is now a limited access freeway, but at that time, it was just a four-lane highway on the other side of our vacant lot. I can remember on the night after the closing on the house, we went out for dinner to celebrate. The restaurant selected for this occasion was the White Castle in Clarendon, where we had a great time eating their juicy hamburgers.

Our summer activities included going to a resort in Maryland called Breezy Point Hotel. This was a collection of old wooden-buildings, clustered around an open-air dining room, the main attraction of the resort. Actually, the hotel was out in the country, quite a way from the water. To get to the water, one had to go down a trail to an oyster boat that would take you out onto the Patuxent River, where you could swim off the back of the boat. As I said, the main attraction was the food. The hotel had several excellent cooks that really put on a spread. The big day was Sunday when the entrée was fried chicken followed by homemade ice cream. It was fun to hang around the kitchen to watch the ice cream being made. Also, I was fascinated by a homemade flytrap, where flies were drawn in by a dish of syrup or vinegar and caught as they flew up from the surface. One of my other activities was to go down on the dock and catch crabs by enticing them with a piece of chicken neck on a string. When the crab gave a jerk, you would pull it up slowly to catch it in a net. I don't remember what we did with it then.

We also liked to drive up into the mountains, perhaps spending the night. The ultimate goal was to go on Skyline Drive, which was still being built by the WPA at that point. Perhaps, this was an interest left over from the time our family had spent in Linville, NC. Years later we were still taking trips like that. One time I remember we had planned to go up on Skyline Drive the following morning and when we awoke there was a dense fog that cancelled our trip.

The money that my dad was now making made it possible for us to take two major trips during the summer of 1938. One was to drive out west to visit my father's family in Missouri and Kansas. Before that time, I don't remember seeing any of his relatives. I think my mom was in much the same boat. Our trip was a relatively slow one, as the roads were all of the two-lane variety, through country towns, backwoods, etc. We stayed in tourist cottages as there were no motels to speak of and certainly none like we have today. Restaurants were all of the small-town variety and thus took time to order food and eat. Some had really poor fare; you never could tell ahead of time. Finally, we got to Aunt Nora's, who lived on a farm in Missouri with her husband and young daughter, Leota. It was exciting for me as I had never been on a farm and I got to sleep on the porch under the open sky. The porch roof had been lost in a tornado some time previously. The first night I slept out in the pitch darkness, I started hearing an unfamiliar noise "munch, munch" and I pulled the covers over my head. The noise got louder and louder and I was about to dash inside, when I realized it was just a cow munching grass about a foot or so from my head. I felt brave that I had not run, but for a time it had scared the hell out of this city boy! Another farm incident that almost got me was my first ride on a horse. I guess Nora put me on it, then led the horse out into the yard and thought that I could manage. About that time, the horse decided that it would prefer to be back in its stall and began galloping for the barn. Through the barn door it went with nary a break. The door wasn't very high, so little Jimmy got scraped off the back of the horse and went plump into the mud.

Fortunately, nothing got broken, but my interest in horseback riding had definitely been dampened. A positive highlight of this visit was that every morning Aunt Nora made biscuits and milk gravy for breakfast. My mom and I probably wondered a bit at first, but soon came to like it, and my dad loved it. We had never had this delicacy before and he had none since leaving Kansas, fifteen years earlier. Note: this was before biscuits and gravy caught on at restaurant chains across the country, in fact, there were no restaurant chains! If you read *The Grapes of Wrath*, by Steinbeck, you will realize that biscuits and gravy were standard fare for people from this part of the country. My mom got Nora's recipe and eventually learned to have it on a regular basis, using Bisquick to make the biscuits.

After a few days, we continued our travels to Hutchinson, Kansas, my dad's hometown, where we stayed with my dad's Aunt Alley. Her house was right in town not far from the State Penitentiary. This made an impression on me, as one day somebody escaped, and they blew the siren for quite some time. We were also near the tracks of the Acheson, Topeka & Santa Fe Railroad, where there were a lot of trains going by. But most impressive was the dust. This was during the Dust Bowl and each morning we had to scrape dust from the windowsills, even though the windows had been closed tightly during the night.

We toured the paper mill that made packing boxes from wheat straw and the Cary Salt factory that purified salt from the deep mines under the city. I was particularly interested, as this was my first experience with a chemical factory. One of the products of the salt factory was the salt lick used for cattle. I remember having a sample salt lick that I took back home and licked on occasion (not a very good habit). After visiting with various Spain relatives on farms outside town, we headed back to Virginia. One thing I discovered on this trip was that my dad was called "Dorri" by most of the people in Hutchinson, as his middle name was also Dorris.

The other trip we made was when my dad took me to see the New York World's Fair. This was great fun for me, as the theme of the fair was how science was providing all the modern conveniences of the future. So, for a budding scientist, it was great stuff. I really can't remember much of what we saw, other than being on the New York Subway and going directly to the gates of the fair. I brought home lots of souvenirs that I kept in my room for the next year or so. When we returned, it wasn't long before my mother had a surprise for me, as I was going to have a baby brother.

While my mother was in the hospital, my Aunt Flo came from Missouri to stay with me. She was a lovable person and great fun to be around. One of the things that we did when she was there was to go to the Pirates Den restaurant in Washington. It was owned by Errol Flynn, who had starred in films like *The Sea Hawk, The Prince and the Pauper,* and *Robin Hood*, so I looked forward to seeing him. He had been there at the opening of the restaurant, which my dad had attended, but was not there the night we went. When Aunt Flo left for home, she asked what game I wanted her to send for a present: Bingo or Ping-Pong. I got the names confused and said Bingo. When it arrived, I was greatly disappointed, as I was looking forward to hitting the ball back and forth across the net.

I was also disappointed with my new brother, as I had never heard anything that made so much noise. I guess I just wasn't used to being around babies and of course, I was no longer the only child. My brother was named George Julian Spain, after my father's stepdad. That summer, we went one more time to Breezy Point and then left for our new life in Florida.

CHAPTER 2

FLORIDA

(1940-1946)

In 1940, my dad was made Florida State Sales Manager for Calvert Distillers. So, Mom, Dad, my baby brother, George, and I moved to Miami in August of that year. We drove as far as Columbia, SC and then, leaving Dad in Columbia to carry out some business, the rest of us flew on down to Miami. This was our first experience on commercial airlines and so it was quite exciting and memorable. My mother had flown in biplanes when she was a young woman, so she was particularly excited about flying all her life. The first leg of our trip was in the Lockheed Lodestar from Columbia to Charleston. Then we got on American Airlines DC-3 that took us on down to Miami, probably stopping in Jacksonville. This ride got pretty bumpy, once we got into Florida and both my brother and I were quite sick. After landing in Miami, we took the bus over to Miami Beach and rented an apartment in a hotel on Washington Ave., south of Lincoln Road. This is in the area that is now called South Beach. We were about one short block from Lumas Park and the Atlantic Ocean, so every day we would go trouping down to the beach. Very shortly after arriving, my mother hired an old beach bum to teach me how to swim, more or less.

It was a great life; we went to the movies at the theatre across the corner from the hotel, once seeing the original version of *The Mark of Zorro*. On occasion my mother and I would walk up to the big new theatre on Lincoln Road where they even had free orange juice. Although only 11, I was given freedom to walk all over the place, as no one worried about kids being picked up by perverts in those years, although I'm sure that it did happen. I remember walking all the way to Biscayne Bay and out onto some of the islands that are part of the causeways to Miami. Sometimes, I brought back coconuts and other tropical things that I had picked up along the road. One of my recollections was of Mom, George and I going out to dinner at a seafood shack, several blocks south on Washington Ave., to what was then the low rent district, where we had a red snapper dinner with fries and cold slaw for 25 cents. This price was pretty unbelievable even at that time.

When school started, I was able to walk to school, as it was on the next street over from Washington Ave. During the Jewish high holidays, I remembered being one of the only kids who came to class. The teacher took this time to show me some science demonstrations, particularly one to form neat patterns of iron filings on a piece of paper, with a magnet placed under it. Our apartment was on the second floor overlooking an alleyway behind the shops. One of which was a soda shop that served as a high school hangout. Every evening, the jukebox, just inside the backdoor, was blaring away with the latest Benny Goodman and Tommy Dorsey records and I would go to sleep listening to this great music that undoubtedly provided the foundation for my later interest in jazz and blues.

During the winter months, we moved to a house looking out onto the ocean at Neptune Beach, near Jacksonville. I was told the reason for the move was because Dad's main business had shifted north, but it was more likely the result of a wintertime rent increase on our hotel apartment at Miami Beach. In any case, it proved to be a rather cold and damp decision. At Miami Beach, the Gulf Stream is just a few hundred yards offshore, while at Jacksonville it is at least twenty miles offshore, which makes a major difference in temperature, quality of water, weather patterns, etc. We had many storms out of the northeast during the winter and it was not uncommon for us to have sea-scud ("meerschaum") blowing over the seawall and flying in windrows across our front yard. All we had was a space heater to keep the house warm, so it was pretty cold and miserable. In addition, our shoes, leather suitcases and books became overrun with mildew and other fungi. I lost many of the books that I had valued. Also, we were introduced to the Florida cockroach. In short, we probably should have stayed in Miami Beach (or simply moved to a

27

less expensive home in Miami). Since the Jacksonville Beach schools were not of high quality, I was sent 23 miles away to the Bolles Military Academy, about five miles south of Jacksonville. I have few remembrances of school that year, other than my having to wear a uniform and spending a lot of time on two different busses. A city bus took me from the beach eighteen miles into South Jacksonville and a yellow school bus took me down along St Johns River to Bolles. Each afternoon the whole process was reversed. It sure would have been a lot nicer to walk around the block to the school at Miami Beach. Of course, when the weather warmed up, things became a whole lot more enjoyable.

During this period, the star of our family was George, particularly during the summer, when the sun had bleached his hair yellow and it was long and curly. Since he also had a beautiful tan, he looked like some kind of a movie star. He also was a good kid, so that when we would go to a restaurant, the waitresses would flock around to talk to him. It was something to behold. I don't believe that I was jealous of him. It was more like we were all proud to have him bring such attention to our family. Of course, he spent a lot of time on the beach digging in the sand and floating in his inner tube out in the ocean. That's where he got all the tan. I suppose that it is about this time I began to tease him, but I can't remember any specific instances. There certainly was no reason, as he looked up to me with a lot of respect and called me Brother, as he still does sometimes.

28

At the end of the summer we moved into a house in South Jacksonville, so that I could catch the bus to Bolles down at the end of the block. About all I remember about this house are the huge yellow pine trees in the front yard. We did not stay there very long however, because my mother began worrying about the health of her parents and talked Dad into moving back to Washington. Since I was doing well at Bolles, they enrolled me on campus and left me there when they returned north. I had a reasonably fun time during the remainder of the year. I was "into" magic, so had various tricks that I pulled on the kids. Two of the main targets for my tricks were the nephews of Cuban President Juan Batista, who were a year or so younger than I. Once, for example, I made a wooden slot machine with some sort of wheels that turned around. Since I had to hold the machine down with my hand, I also had control of the payoff. I don't know how much money they put into the thing before finally figuring out that it was a gyp. I suppose I paid them back. I also had a special ring with a piece of metal designed to hold a cigarette behind your hand, so that it could be made to appear and disappear when you bent or extended your fingers. My advisor/teacher, Captain Nellimark, confiscated this trick as he felt it to be "too sophisticated" for a kid my age. He enjoyed using it himself, after that. I was still making model-airplanes from balsa wood, tissue paper and glue. I can remember liking the smell of glue, but I never heard of anybody sniffing it to get high. In fact, I wouldn't have even known what the word "high" meant, nor did anybody else, as far as I knew. By now, I was making planes of my

29

own design, weird things with little wings, big body, etc. They weren't much for flying, but fun to make. From a military standpoint, I was in Company C, that is, just the little guys. Companies A and B were for high school kids. We did have a class in military science and tactics and did drill with our cut-down rifles. As a result, I can still do some of the stuff real soldiers do. One of the things that caught my fancy was bugle calls. Our major activities were all instigated by specific calls; reveille, taps, etc. Consequently, I got a kazoo and learned all the common bugle calls. I guess that was the extent of my musical training during that period, although I do remember attending a dance, where the band played all the good old music, I had learned back in Miami Beach. I got a kick out of standing around and watching the band play.

Once at spring break and then again at the end of the year, I took the train from Jacksonville to Alexandria, where my folks picked me up. I must have had previous experience riding trains, so this was not a big deal. It was pretty much like riding a bus, except that you had a chance to walk from one end of the train to the other, even the lounge car in the back. These trains were loaded with service people, as this was the beginning of World War II, and the trains had soldiers and sailors going to and from assignments. Two main railroads served the East Coast: the Atlantic Coast Line and Florida East Coast Railway. The primary means of transportation in America at that time was the train. The train made stops in Savannah, Columbia, Raleigh,

Richmond and perhaps a few in between. I got on the train in the evening and got off the following day. I just sat up in the chair car for these trips. When I finished my school year, I moved back to live with my folks in the white brick house on Fenwick St.

This house was only about a mile from Ft. Myers, the cavalry fort that provides honor guards for parades in Washington, DC. At that time, there were no gates or guards, so I could ride around the fort on my bike, sometimes, watching polo games, etc. On the other side of the fort is Arlington Cemetery, although I rarely got that far from home. There was a nice black dog that used to play with George and me at the time. I don't think that it was ours, it must have been a neighbor's dog. The side of our house had a steep grassy slope that we would roll down with the dog running back and forth. It was great fun. Unfortunately, I began teasing my brother again and on occasion came very close to hurting him. This is not anything that I am proud of and have regretted it for many years.

During summer evenings, the other kids my age and I used to have great fun playing "kick the can". This is the game like "hide and seek" except that it starts all over again if one of the hidden kids can get back to the can and kick it before the "it" kid can tag them. The game gets more and more fun the darker it gets. One night I came home so hot and red-faced, that Mom gave me a glass of "smoke" (ice cream and ginger ale) to cool me down. It was so good that I gulped it down into my hot stomach, with the result that in about five minutes, it came back up again. We didn't do that anymore.

Mom, George, and I would still take the occasional trip to the mountains. One time we made it all the way down to Gatlinburg, Tennessee. This was a special trip as it was a quaint little village in those days; just a bunch of little shops and small motels that ran along beside a little river. It must have been summertime and it was nice and cool at night, which we all appreciated, since of course, there was no air conditioning anywhere at that time. We went into Smokey Mountain National Park and drove up to the top of the mountains, taking pictures along the way with Mom's black and white Kodak camera. The following day, we stopped for one more night at Maryville on the way down the mountain. This was an even smaller town in a country setting. We were lucky to see all this at that time, as it was destined to be ruined by the vast numbers of visitors who over-run the area now with all of the development that has followed.

In the fall, I started school at Thomas Jefferson Junior High School in the eight-grade. This was great as I began getting some courses in science. However, most of my science learning was at home. By this time, I had gotten two different chemistry sets, and had accumulated other stuff on my own. My folks had allowed me to set up a little chemistry lab in the basement. I think that this was the time that Aunt Jane had given me the old chemistry book that she had used

32

in college. She always contended that her book was the beginning of my interest in chemistry, but I think that it goes back before that.

During my first year in junior high school I had a major problem with an ingrown toenail, probably because I had failed to take care of it properly while at Bolles. This problem was so bad, that I had to go around all over the place in shoes with a cutout toe. This, of course, added to my embarrassment about things in general and prevented me from participating in gym and other aspects of athletics, not to mention the effect on my social life.

I had a buddy who lived a couple of houses down the street whose father worked for McGraw-Hill Book Co. We had both read William Beebe's book about diving to great depths in the ocean with a bathyscaph. So, he and his sister planned and built a diving helmet out of a garbage can. It had two notches for the shoulders and a faceplate of glass that had been glued in place with some tarry kind of material. This contraption was supplied by air through a garden hose and hand pump, much as was shown in the movie *Wake of the Red Witch,* starring John Wayne. (Note: this is the movie where the star dives down to the deck of a submerged ship and has a fight with a giant squid, while the villains try to cut the air hoses). My friends tested their contraption toward the end of the summer at a beach in Maryland. I don't think that it turned out to be very successful. I had another friend who lived further down the street who was also "into" chemistry. He was sure that he had a way of making rubber, but it turned out that his starting material was a bottle of glue that, on closer examination, had a Latex base. Thus, my friends always seemed to be science oriented in one way or another.

During the period that we were in the Fenwick St house, I began developing a strong interest in world politics. In the early stages of World War II, I admired Germany for the tremendous efficiency of the German Army and Germany's accomplishments in science and technology. If one focused only on such accomplishments, the Germans seemed to be (and actually were) way ahead of the US at that time. The superhighways (autobahns), the modern architecture of buildings and bridges, the blitzkrieg attack by the army and the advanced nature of the air force seemed to give much to be admired. They were, of course, way ahead of the US in chemistry, having developed synthetic dyes, synthetic rubber, etc. At that time, almost all the chemistry literature was written in German! (Even six years later when I went to college, it was felt extremely important for chemistry students to take at least two years of German.). I read such novels as *A Toast to Tomorrow and A Drink to Yesterday* that dealt with a high-ranked German policeman, who was actually a British "mole" during the early stages of World War II. I had a huge map drawn out on the back of a piece of linoleum in the attic where I played war games with all my toy soldiers. When the Germans attacked the Russians in the Crimean Peninsula, I followed those battles closely, emulating them on my battle map. After Pearl Harbor and the US entered the war, I began to realize that I was on the wrong side and began to reorient my thinking. If you look back at those times before WWII, you should not be shocked at my early leanings, which had no relationship to those of my parents.

I think that it was about this time that my Aunt Elizabeth, Uncle Bob, and family moved to Dundalk, Maryland, just outside of Baltimore, where we used to visit on occasion. They had a nice house with a yard that backed up on one of the estuaries of Chesapeake Bay. Uncle Bob had an interest in sailing and had bought a Star Class sailboat. Unfortunately, at the time I saw it, he had gone aground and ripped off the keel. His plan was to replace it with a piece of I-beam that he had gotten from the nearby steel mill where he worked. However, before he was able to do this, he got sick with leukemia and spent the next several years battling this disease. Whenever we would make this trip, I would play with Robin and Michael who were a year or so younger than I. I always envied their home on the water.

Our summer vacations were spent in a cottage over in Maryland on the shore of Chesapeake Bay, at a place called Plum Point. Here, I would wander down the beach generally looking for what I could find. I later realized that this was a type of searching called perusing. One day an old man saw me looking and said, "Are you looking for shark's teeth?" Whereupon I asked what they were, and he said that they were all over the beach. I, of course, hadn't seen one yet. He said, "Come on, I'll show you." So, we walked along perusing*[1] the beach, and he would say "There's one" and I would look and there it was. Shortly, I got my eyes tuned to what a shark's tooth looked like and began picking them up one after another. At the end of our stay there, I had collected a whole jar full, one being almost two inches across. These were fossil shark's teeth that had been lost by sharks long before Chesapeake Bay was even formed. It turned out the man was a paleontologist who had worked for the Smithsonian Museum in Washington. He vacationed at Plum Point each year, as it was just down the beach from a place called Scientist's Cliffs, a place where numerous fossils were found. My friend took me down to see where some scientists were carefully removing the skeleton of a baby sea mammal from the cliffs. I didn't get to see much of it, as it was covered in plaster to protect it until they could get it back to the museum, but it was fun to be around such things.

The following year my interest in boats caused me to construct a kayak-like sailboat in the basement of our home on Fenwick St. The construction was based on my own design, following much the same

---

* Peruse: A type of searching that may either be casual, or intense. We see both of these types of searching exemplified in this situation. For further discussion see page 211.

approach as building a model airplane. It had strips of wood going along a wooden frame; all covered with some sort of cloth, probably an old bed sheet. This was then painted with some leftover blue paint that we had in the basement. The mast was some leftover piece of wood (a mop handle?) and the sail was another used bed sheet. I probably could have found a proper design to hold a boy my size and weight, with proper instructions how to make it waterproof. But I discovered that is not what I like to do. I like to do things my way, according to my own plan, where the fun is in the making, not so much in the final outcome. For example, I can hardly remember how this boat worked, although, I can remember building it quite well. As I look back, I realize that this is a pattern that I have followed my entire life. If you continue with this saga, you will see more examples to come.

During the ninth grade, I became interested in girls; actually, in one girl whose name was Marty. This was really my first chance to associate with the opposite sex, as prior to junior high; I had been at Bolles, which was strictly a boy's school (at that time). I remember taking Marty to the movie up at Columbia Pike. The movie was *Tonight We Love,* about a concert pianist who played Tchaikovsky's "Piano Concerto in B-Flat Minor". I still love that song. This was the movie where I tried to get up my nerve to put my arm around my girl's shoulder. As I remember, it never happened, but I worried about it through the whole movie. We also went to parties at various kids' homes, all very well chaperoned. One of the highpoints of one party was playing spin the bottle. I worried too much about that also. I really liked Marty, but our friendship came to a screeching halt at the end of the school year, as we moved away for good.

My mother got a hankering to go back to Florida, so my dad finally gave in and gave up his job with Calvert Distillery, as they couldn't put up with such indecision. So, Dad took a position with Brown-Forman Distillers, who had headquarters in Louisville, Kentucky. Dad wasn't too happy about having to do this, but my mother said: "Once you get Florida-sand in your shoes, you can't stay away". This proved to be correct, as she remained in Florida for most of the rest of her life.

We drove back to Florida in the spring, as soon as I finished school. In fact, we didn't even stay for my graduation from Thomas Jefferson. This was the first of three graduation ceremonies that I was to miss. We spent the summer at Neptune Beach in a new house that my parents purchased. It was interesting in that it had "pecky cypress" walls that had lots of holes where spiders would build their web houses. A great feature for me was that the previous owner had left lots of books, including *The Complete Works of Mark Twain*. I spent a lot of time that summer reading these books. In addition, we went to the library in Jacksonville, where I checked out all the books that they had on analytical chemistry, the field that I was "into" at that time. The most interesting stuff I copied by hand, as there were no Xerox-type copy machines at that time. A funny thing happened a year or so later when the FBI visited my dad. They were investigating all people who had checked out books on chemistry. We didn't know it at the time, but this was during the Manhattan Project when they were very paranoid about anybody who might be spying on the construction of the Atomic Bomb from uranium. Later, we had a good laugh about that. Apparently, no one had looked at the age of the individual checking out the chemistry books. It just shows how thorough their investigation was at the time.

I did spend time on the beach as well, building sandcastles and swimming with my folks. The beach there had lots of activity; in addition to flocks of pelicans, skimming the waves, we also had numerous bottlenose dolphins that cruised just beyond the wave-line. Often, they were only a few yards away from us when we were swimming. In addition, the Navy PBY flying boats were patrolling constantly for German submarines (U-boats) that had torpedoed tankers and cargo ships just offshore. In fact, one of the problems with the beach was the tar-like material from sunken ships. Often it would get on our feet and require dry cleaning fluid to clean it off. Once there were some German spies who came in on a U-boat and landed on the beach between Ponte Vedra and St Augustine. The FBI picked up these spies, but one never knew if there were others who came in undetected.

That fall, we moved to NW 58ᵗʰ Terrace in Miami, a long way from Miami Beach, but near a good high school called Thomas Edison. There, I went to 10ᵗʰ and 11ᵗʰ grades, taking chemistry, biology, and Spanish, as well as typing (presently called keyboarding). I'm sure glad I took that. During my sophomore year, I got a job at Shell's Super Market, one of the first of its type in the country. I was a bag boy, putting stuff on the shelves when not needed for bagging groceries. We made pretty good tips carrying groceries out to cars. It was a menial job, but it did give me an introduction to what work was.

My buddy at school had a father who ran a boat rental place over by Biscayne Bay. Often, my buddy and I would bicycle over there and take one of his dad's boats out for a trip on the bay. At that time, they were building islands in the bay by pumping sand and silt from the bottom and discharging it behind concrete bulkheads. This is the way most of the causeways and islands are still formed in that area. We thought that the end result of this process of island-building would be a bay full of islands with one very deep hole in the middle.

We had a fun time bumming around the Bay. However, it was on the return from one of these trips that I almost tangled up with a streamlined train. I was about half a block away from the crossing when I heard the train blow its horn. Like all kids, this excited me, so that I began to peddle faster and faster to be there when it passed.

Then, I realized that I was almost to the crossing, slammed on my breaks, slipped down, and was sliding on the street towards the train, which was now ripping through the intersection at about 60 miles per hour. Of course, I stopped before sliding under the wheels, or I wouldn't be telling you this story, but it sure scared the hell out of me to be so close to such a huge machine streaking down the track. That was the first of two near-death experiences involving trains. I sure hope that they don't come in threes.

Our house on 58th Terrace had only two bedrooms, so that initially, my brother and I were sharing a bedroom. As I said earlier, I had been teasing my brother and generally causing problems as a result. My folk's solution was to buy me an 8'x 8' house of sheet rock that was constructed in the back yard among the banana trees. Steel bands hooked it to a concrete foundation, so that the hurricanes wouldn't blow it away. I had a bunk bed and a lab bench so that I could move my chemistry stuff away from the main house. At that stage of my life, about all I can remember doing was the permanganate and glycerol reaction. This involves putting some finely ground potassium permanganate in a glass pill bottle. Next, I would put several drops of glycerin on the permanganate, quickly screw on the top and then run. In a little less than a minute, the mixture would begin to react, heat up and explode, throwing glass in all directions. One time I remember doing this on the doorstep of my "lab", splattering purple permanganate all over the door and wall. This color eventually wore off. This sounds like a stupid thing to do, but I never got hurt. All my "experiments" during that period were of this type. It was not until the following year, that I began doing something a little more constructive.

My dad had a friend who worked for the Bailey Meter Co. who was impressed with my interest in the subject of chemistry. So, the following summer, he was able to get me a job with the Jacksonville Power Plant. The position was to change the daily charts produced by the Bailey Meters, but also to collect water samples and analyze them for alkalinity, hardness, etc. Wow! This was my first chemistry job, for which I was paid $35 per week. So, I began taking the bus from Neptune Beach into Jacksonville and transferring to the bus that went out to the power plant at the north edge of the city. This was about an hour-long ride each morning, plus another hour coming home, but it was well worth it. The job wasn't that easy, as it entailed going all over the plant, climbing up and down ladders, across catwalks, under pipes, through steam, etc. to get to the thirty or so meters that were scattered around the power plant. Usually, the clocks that moved the charts needed winding and the ink-pens needed cleaning, in addition to changing the charts. I think that OSHA would have some question about a 16 year-old-kid doing this job, but there was no OSHA at that time.

After my chart collecting in the morning, I did some record keeping and filing of charts. In the afternoon, I did my water collecting at various locations and brought the samples back to the lab for analysis. Here I developed skill in titration for alkalinity and chloride. After some more record keeping, I had some time to consider how the plant might solve the problem of boiler scale. Obviously, I never was able to provide a solution to this problem, still a major one in the industry, but I spent a lot of time thinking about it and doing a few experiments. On several occasions, I went to lunch with my boss, which I really enjoyed, as I got to listen to all the worker-talk. At the café, were guys not only from the power plant, but also from the paper mill that was located right beside the power plant. To this day, the smell of sulfite paper mills gives me a very positive feeling. It wasn't new to me, as the same smell used to be all over the Jacksonville area, especially when the fog went down along the St. Johns River to Bolles School.

At the end of the summer I had accumulated a considerable sum of money and thus began buying chemical equipment and supplies for my little laboratory in Miami. I was able to get all the standard glassware, including burettes and pipettes. However, because of the war, I was unable to get an analytical balance. Somehow, my lab just didn't have the priority.

So, by the time I returned down south, I could start setting up my lab. I had a jug of distilled water up above my funnel-shaped sink and a waste jar below. I had been able to obtain concentrated nitric, sulfuric, acetic, and hydrochloric acids, so I was able to make up solutions for various kinds of titrations, etc. One thing that I had been unable to get was silver nitrate, needed for chloride titration, because silver was a war priority item. So, I decided to make my own by dissolving a couple of silver quarters in nitric acid. At that time, silver coins were about 90% silver 10% copper. So, the solution I obtained was green because of the copper and I wanted pure silver nitrate. My plan was to put in an iron nail to displace the pure silver and re-dissolve it in nitric acid. This all worked fine until I was evaporating the purified silver nitrate in an evaporating dish on a tripod and happened to tip the evaporating dish all over my apron, which I was fortunately wearing. However, by reflex, I wiped at the silver nitrate with my hand to get it off the apron and got it all over my hands. Despite my rush to wash it off, the concentrated silver nitrate had already reacted with my skin. Within minutes, my hands had turned from gray to glistening black. There was nothing I could do. My hands just continued to get blacker and blacker, and no amount of washing would do a thing. So, until the skin finally wore off some weeks later, I went to school with these shiny black hands. This was a tough experience for a kid who was not very socially confident in the first place.

My social life at Edison High was what you might call "lacking". I really can't remember any instance of going out with a girl while I was living in Miami. Dad and I did go to see several football games during those two years. Our football team played most of its games in the Orange Bowl stadium on the south side of town. Our big rival was Miami High School that was in Coral Gables. Since the Orange Bowl was their home stadium, we had a lot of trouble beating them.

Once during this period my dad and I went to see the real Orange Bowl game on New Year's Day. It was an exciting game, as it was won in the last second by a long kickoff return down the sidelines, although I can't remember who won and who lost.

My Dad encouraged me in my scientific studies by giving me the 29th Edition of *Handbook for Chemistry and Physics*. This 3.5-inch-thick tome I have used off and on for over 60 years, so that it was tattered and torn when I finally consigned it to the paper drive.

While we were in Miami, I only remember going to the beach a couple of times, as the beach was not very attractive for a couple of reasons. First, it was not the fine smooth sand that we encountered up in Neptune Beach, which was good for making huge sandcastles. Miami Beach, on the other hand consisted largely of coarsely ground coquina shells. And, unlike Neptune Beach, the water was clear and

45

sparkling blue-green from a distance. Unfortunately, it also contained a lot of Sargasso weed with all the microscopic critters that inhabit these weeds. For a budding biologist, this could make for fascinating study, but at the time, this was not my cup of tea. Also, on occasion, the sea was overrun with beautiful blue-purple critters called the Portuguese Man-of-War. These consisted of a floating balloon-like body from 1" to 3" across with stinging tentacles dangling as much as five feet behind. The body is easy to see as it is filled with some gas to give it a sail-like appearance, but the tentacles are less obvious. When there was a man-of–war infestation, there could be hundreds of purple bodies washed up on the beach. When these are present, most people just stay out of the water. However, when we first went to the ocean, there were only a few visible and we went right into the water. It wasn't long however, and my little brother began screaming at the top of his lungs and we couldn't figure out what was wrong with him. Finally, we saw a tentacle around one of his legs. My parents washed him off good, but he kept screaming. Then, he began getting red splotches on the skin of his legs and having trouble breathing. In short, he was going into serious anaphylactic shock. So, we grabbed up our stuff, ran for the car and drove as fast as we could to a drug store a mile or so down the beach. Fortunately, they had seen this before and knew what to give him right away. He, of course, recovered, but that was about all we wanted of the beach for that day and probably for the rest of the year.

It was a year or so later, when I somehow got inspired to make an underwater breathing apparatus from a gallon jug, some rubber tubing, and a face mask that I had from somewhere. The idea was to hook up the jug with a stopper with glass tubing rigged so that water could flow in and air would flow out into rubber tubing going to the face mask. A weight was attached to the handle of the jug to pull it down into the water and keep the mouth down. It looked like a masterpiece of engineering but lacked any real analysis from the standpoint of total air capacity. However, I was dying to give it a try in the ocean, so one day I talked my mother into taking us over to the ocean, some 5-10 miles distance. As I got into the water, everything looked good and no men-o'-war were evident. With my jug full of air, I swam out to about 6-8 feet of water and began my dive. For the first few feet, everything looked good, but by the time I got to the bottom, my jug was more than half filled with air. Suddenly in front of me were several feet of man-o'-war tentacle. Whereupon, I panicked, began backing away and trying to get to the surface all at the same time. The jug and the weight were abandoned, as I began thrashing around trying to swim to the shore. What had been light and easy to swim with when filled with air, were heavy and cumbersome when filled with water. I ended up with a head filled with sea water and the full knowledge why the gallon jug is not a common means of providing air for underwater swimming.

Those years, we would spend our winters in Miami and our summers in Neptune Beach near Jacksonville. I think that the last summer we had some pretty good waves that could be ridden into the beach by various means. The most obvious, of course was the surfboard. When I say surfboard, you are probably thinking of the 6-8 foot long boards made of plastic and fiberglass that they use today. But this was in 1945, and such things were not used along the Atlantic coast. What we had was a wooden board about 3' by 1.5' and less than an inch thick that could be put together by almost anyone with some lumber and a few tools. In fact, I think that I found mine lying on the beach, where it had washed up by the tide. Obviously, they were not designed for standing on, but rather for lying on and sliding across the water in front of the wave. If you catch a good wave, you could slide along right on to the beach. However, it could be exciting and a little dangerous if the waves were really big. The worst thing that could happen to you was to fall over the front of the wave and have the board jam into the sand, leaving you hanging like a sheet on the clothesline with a thousand pounds of water crashing on your back. If you learned to keep the front of the board up so that this didn't happen, this could be a lot of fun.

The other way to ride the waves was to bring a mattress cover to the beach and wet it with water. Then it could be filled with air by simply holding it up to the wind and tying it off at the end. The air would not escape because the holes would be blocked with water and you could lie across it and ride the waves into the beach. The only difficulty here was that the constant chaffing action of the wet cloth and sand against the skin of the chest would leave you with badly chafed skin, especially on your nipples.

After two years in Miami, my dad became the Southeastern Sales Manager for Brown-Forman and was transferred to the New Orleans office. Hence, the following summer was spent largely getting ready for this move. For the next few years, my folks didn't return to Florida. But, as my Mom would say, once you get the sand of Florida in your shoes, you are bound to return.

CHAPTER 3

NEW ORLEANS

(1946-1948)

My Dad was appointed the Southeastern Sales Manager for Brown Forman Distillers sometime in the spring of 1946. Since the headquarters of the S.E. division was in New Orleans, our family was planning to move there. However, since we had a summer home in Neptune Beach, near Jacksonville, we elected to spend the summer there and come over to New Orleans in the fall just before school started. I was to enter my senior year in high school and my brother, George, was to enter elementary school.

I tried to get my summer job back at the Jacksonville Power Plant, but didn't have any success, either because it was already filled, or for some other reason. As far as I knew, I had done a good job; I had certainly tried hard enough. Perhaps, the personnel department had discovered how young I had been and found that I was breaking some rule or other. At any rate, I found myself looking for some other kind of chemistry-related job. I tried at the Jacksonville Paper Mill and also at the Turpentine Factory, but to no avail, I think because I just looked so immature. Since I had been so lucky the previous year, I didn't even consider accepting anything out of my "professional" field of chemistry. Since money did not seem a factor, I spent the summer reading books, enjoying the beach and keeping my mother company, as my Dad was busy in New Orleans.

The three of us drove over to New Orleans sometime in the late summer, arriving in the early evening. My dad had an apartment in the French Quarter, located on the ground floor looking out on to one of the typical French Quarter gardens. However, this must have been too small for us, as we found ourselves spending the night in a friend's apartment just above the Old Absinthe Bar, across the street from the Old Absinthe House. This was an historic old building with windows going from floor to ceiling and famous balcony with cast-iron railing. I think it was Saturday and as a result, was not the quietest place to spend the night, since there was no air conditioning and our balcony windows needed to remain open. Of course, there were crowds moving up and down the street until early morning, so we didn't get much sleep. I think the next day we moved to a room in the Roosevelt Hotel and began a search for more permanent housing.

My folks bought a nice little white house in the northeast section of town, only about a block from the Fairgrounds (a famous New Orleans racetrack). Our neighbors on one side were French, the husband being a chef at one of the famous restaurants downtown. I don't remember the neighbors on the other side except that they had a beautiful daughter, whom I never got to know because I was so shy. I think that she got married about the time we moved away, so perhaps it was just as well. Essentially all our neighbors were Roman Catholic, who attended the St. Ignatius Loyola church about two blocks away. All the male kids went to Jesuit High School; the few girls went to a convent school. There was one other Protestant guy; we both went to the public school on Canal Street, called Warren Easton High School. Many years later I discovered it to be the school from which assassin Lee Harvey Oswald would also attend. It was an old school built in the '20s, with sagging wooden floors, old blackboards and not much else. It was only attended by boys (at that time, all schools in N.O were segregated by sex) who didn't have enough money to afford the Jesuit High School, and a few Protestants like me. The students appeared to be of mixed races, although I don't remember seeing any actual black students. The mix of people in N.O. is more like a northern city than that typically observed in the south. With lots of Italians and Irish in addition to the Cajuns, it made for an interesting dialect. Consequently, the school wasn't much to speak of. I remember that my homeroom teacher used to sell jewelry and other stuff (?) on the side. My physics teacher used to give an assignment and sit back with his feet in one desk drawer and spit tobacco juice into another, which was lined with newspapers. Amazingly enough, we did have a few good teachers, one in particular, taught math to me and a few other kids who were college-bound. I don't remember a football team, or any other team, or social activity. There was hazing of new students, but I missed most of it, as I was home sick the first few weeks. In the end, I never even attended the graduation or participated in any graduation activities. I took the city bus there and back each day and put in my senior year. I haven't heard from them since.

This is not to say that my life was devoid of social activity. Our neighborhood was loaded with guys my age, all of whom went to Jesuit High. My folks' big mistake was not being wise enough to send me there as well (However, who knows how this might have changed my life). These were really clean-cut guys, raised by strict Catholic families. We used to hang around the drug store, drinking nickel sodas prepared at the soda fountain. In the evening, we would all take off down the avenue in a group, going to the latest "Gashouse Gang" or "Three Stooges" movie. Once, we were stopped by the police because of the size of our group, but as soon as they talked to us, they saw we meant no harm and let us go. In the afternoon, we frequently had a touch football game in the vacant lot across from our house. Since I was tall, I often got to play the quarterback position. This was great for me as I had never had friends like this and never really participated in sports to speak of. For this reason, these were important years for my social development. Because of the nature of the high school and my general shyness, my relations with the opposite sex were rather limited. A few of the guys in the neighborhood had sisters, but they were usually off somewhere else. Perhaps they were not allowed to socialize with the Protestant guy. I did have one date with the daughter of my mother's hairdresser, but that was a disaster. I agreed to take her to a roller-skating rink. This seemed pretty safe as I was sure that I could skate, having done a lot as a kid on the sidewalks in Arlington. However, when I got out on the rink, I found that skating on a wooden floor was a different thing entirely and ended up having a miserable evening looking and feeling like a dork.

As I approached graduation, it was time for me to decide where I was going to attend college. I always knew that I would go, but neither of my folks had pushed me in any particular direction. Since I had been oriented toward chemistry for as long as I could remember, I decided to check the library for American Chemical Society approved schools. I had also had enough of the south, both because of the heat and humidity, and the race situation, so I wanted a school north of the Mason-Dixon Line. The resulting list included MIT, Cal Tech, Illinois Tech, Carnegie Tech and Michigan Tech. So, I applied to all these schools. MIT thought enough of my grades to have me interview with an alumnus, who turned out to be the Superintendent of New Orleans Public Schools. So, I got dressed up and went down to the impressive office building for N.O. schools and was ushered into the superintendent's expansive office. He smiled, shook my hand, and asked where I was getting my diploma. When I replied Warren Easton High School, he almost laughed in my face and said: "I don't think you can expect to go to MIT from Warren Easton!" at which point, my interview was rather abruptly terminated. It was hard to believe that he would blame me for a school for which he was responsible.

Cal Tech, in their ignorance about the quality of WEHS, sent an exam for me to take at the public library. Shortly after this was returned, I received a letter of regret. Illinois Tech and Carnegie Tech each sent post cards saying they were overcrowded with veterans returning from WWII. (Because of the GI-Bill, great numbers of veterans were able to attend college, who would otherwise not have attended). Michigan Tech was crowded as well but sent a catalog and a nice letter suggesting that I go to a local college and try again next year. The catalog showed pictures of skiing and ice skating, so I decided to find a local school and try Michigan Tech the following year. I had no way of knowing that this casual decision would have such a fortuitous impact on my entire life.

The best "local school" in New Orleans is Tulane University, on St Charles Ave, seemed to fit my needs. Since I was staying at home on the other side of town, I took the city bus to Canal St., where I transferred to a streetcar, then transferred again to a trolley bus for the final leg of the trip. Even then, the cost of 14 cents was a great buy

56

because of the efficiency of the N.O. transportation system. Tulane had a powerhouse football team at that time and as a freshman, I was expected to wear my green beanie to every game. This I did for the most part, as the seats were "free" and I began to enjoy football. The Tulane stadium was also the site of my gym classes, with the locker room located under the stands. It was also the site of the Sugar Bowl game on New Year's Day.

I was a day student and I had a lot of time to kill so I hung around the student union where I learned to play pool, among other things. I had a good year at Tulane and got good grades. I made friends with several pre-med students, but they almost got me into trouble. Because I knew chemistry and they needed help with chemistry, I made the mistake of providing it once during one of the quizzes. Shortly after that, a confidential note from one of the Honor Student Committee members stopped that in a hurry and I never got involved with cheating again. Many years later, when I was a teacher, this experience gave me an insight into the cheating problem that was useful in dealing with students who strayed from the straight and narrow.

Since we had sold our house in Neptune Beach, we remained in New Orleans through the hot summer, where I played poker out on the screen porch with the guys. I kept busy earning $1/hour for keeping the lawn mowed. I also helped my Dad with some of his

Brown Forman marketing ventures. Regularly, he would take 8mm movie pictures of the various advertising gimmicks that he had planned. He also took pictures of the Mardi Gras float that was sponsored by B.F. This gave George and me a chance to see the parades and be in one of them as well. I helped by editing the short snips of different subjects into a single film, along with titles, so that he could show it at company sales meetings. Another venture we worked on was part of a campaign to re-introduce a whiskey called King Red Label, which had been withdrawn during the war supposedly to save on red dye. Dad had placed signs all over town, including a huge one on Canal Street, saying "Red's Back in Town". These were designed to build curiosity, as it did not say what "Red" was or mention the whiskey in any way. Part of his campaign included putting stickers on pennies also saying, "Red's Back in Town!" So, he hired me and my buddies to put stickers on thousands of pennies. All went well for a while, until the pennies started gumming up the money sorters at some of the big banks. Then the Treasury Department landed on my Dad for defacing federal currency and we had to stop. I assume he was let off with a warning and perhaps a small fine.

I mentioned above that we did take part in at least one Mardi Gras parade. Mardi Gras refers to the "Fat" Tuesday before the start of Lent, but the Mardi Gras season starts a couple of weeks ahead of the actual day. There are at least 10 parades and I attended several them during the two years I lived in N.O. Each parade is sponsored by a krewe, or club, with names like Bacchus, Zeus, Hermes, and Zulu. These clubs were assigned a particular night when they could put on the parade, often with floats that had been used for decades. Each parade was followed by a costume ball, which was attended by the krewe, their wives and special friends. My mom and dad were invited to at least one, that I can remember. This was a big deal and they got all decked out in a tux and a dress that my mother bought for the occasion. On parade nights, the guys in the neighborhood would go downtown to see what we could see. The parade route typically went down Canal St. and out St. Charles Avenue. It was certainly an experience, as we got to see all kinds of weird people both on the floats and off. New Orleans people are a little odd to begin with, but during Mardi Gras, they really let their hair down. You are liable to see almost anything.

My chemistry experiments were at a low ebb during this period, as they had to be done in my bedroom, a converted sunroom on the back of the house. Here I made an analytical balance out of balsa wood, razor blades and glass. I had always craved one since I had tried to buy one for my lab in Miami and the war effort made them unavailable. This worked out fine, but another experiment almost ended in disaster. For some reason, I wanted to make some ammonium nitrate, perhaps because I had some leftover nitric acid and ammonium hydroxide. Anyway, I mixed these together in the proper proportions and produced a solution of ammonium nitrate. Then, to get rid of the water, I put the mixture in a round-bottomed flask and heated it with an alcohol lamp. It bubbled away as the water was driven off and then for some reason, stopped bubbling after an hour or so. Finally, I gave up although it was still a clear liquid (I was expecting it to form white crystals). I left it sitting on the table in disgust. When I returned, the entire liquid had turned into solid. Apparently, what I had observed earlier was approximately one cup of molten ammonium nitrate. Later, I began to think, what would have happened if this had been jarred or in some way activated to "go off", this being the same stuff that blew up Texas City during the war and more recently, the Federal Building in Oklahoma City. Since this was now solidified in the bottom of my round-bottom flask, there was no way to get it out without breaking the glass. I think that I must have quietly disposed of this potential disaster. Hopefully, it made it to the dump without being jarred in the wrong way.

One other experiment was to try to prepare opium. We had many oriental poppies around the yard, and it seemed like a natural thing to try to extract some opium, for what purpose, I have no idea, except to see if it could be done. So, I gathered the fresh seedpods after the flowers were gone and put them all in a kitchen pot. I mashed them up with some water and let them ferment, which seemed like the thing to do. Then I forgot about it for a number of days. But, when I returned to check the progress, it had turned into an absolute stinking

60

mess. These investigations into pharmacology ended when I had to throw the entire experiment in the garbage, including my mother's kitchen pot.

As I said earlier, my granddad had introduced me to his Smith & Wesson 38 revolver and after he died, I inherited it along with the 6 cartridges. I assume that my mother knew of my having it, but at this time, it is hard to believe. I also had received his army holster and had cut it down for quick draw action. This treasure was stored away in my bottom drawer and on occasion, I would show it to a visiting friend. Once there were about three of us kicking around without anything to do and we decided to go out to a vacant lot near Lake Pontchartrain to fire off some rounds. This we did, without cleaning the gun first or anything. I assume that we took turns, blasting away at tin cans or something. Fortunately, we survived without mishap, but looking back, it certainly was a crazy thing to do. The good news was that the 6 rounds were gone, and it wasn't long after that the firing pin got broken. Now it's a good gun, which is the way it remains to this day.

While we were in N.O., I learned to drive a car. Soon, I was driving all around with my buddies from the neighborhood. I didn't drive much downtown, except to take my dad to work on occasion. This was a tricky thing to do, especially when going through the

French Quarter, due to the streetcar named Desire. The streets were really narrow, so when you got on the side that of the streetcar was on, there was just barely enough space for a car to go between the streetcar and the gutter.

All the time we were in N.O., I never had any accidents, but I sure came close on a couple of occasions. Once my buddies and I were driving down the main street that went toward Lake Pontchartrain and I came up to a red light. Well, I thought I would show off, so I whipped through a gas station on the corner, came out on the cross street and was turning left to continue on the main street, when the light changed, and somebody just about creamed us.

Another time at night, we were racing some other car. I thought it would be cute to ditch them by going through City Park. We went on a road that went back into the less inhabited areas and as we went over an arched bridge that hid us from view, my plan was to shut off the lights, pull to the side of the road and stop abruptly. All of which I did, except that the grass was very wet from the dew and the car slid in an uncontrollable fashion across the grass towards a clump of trees, all in complete darkness. It was only at the last second that the car stopped, and we were able to recover our breath. Despite these experiences which suggest that parents should not trust their kids with the family car, we really need to relearn this every generation.

One other car incident didn't involve reckless driving but did almost get us in trouble with the police. It was Halloween, and we were out to pull some tricks on people. Someone had gotten a bobby pin and a piece of string that had been rubbed with wax. We drove onto a dead-end street and parked across from a clapboard house. Then, one of the jokesters sneaked across to the house and pushed the prongs of the bobby pin under one of the clapboards. After sneaking back, we began to pull our fingers along the waxed string. This caused the bobby pin to vibrate against the wood and set up a strange machine-gun-like noise within the house. It wasn't long before the lights turned on and someone came out on the front porch to see what was causing the noise. We lowered the string and slumped down in the car. After a few minutes, they went back in and turned off the lights. This process was repeated few times. We were all doubled up and practically gagging, trying not to make any noise with our laughter. About the fourth time, a police car slowly pulled into the end of the street and drove up to the front of the house. We dropped the string out of the window and got down as low as we could get. We were no longer laughing as we realized that the string led directly to our lair. The police went to the door and talked with the man of the house, but apparently neither they, nor the police could figure what was making the strange noise or exactly where it was coming from. Eventually, the police left and after a period of time, we slowly drove down to the end of the street with the lights off, made a U-turn and got the heck out of there.

One of the few constructive things that I did was to develop an interest in music. I guess it was simply living in New Orleans, although I don't ever remember going down to the French Quarter until we were just about to leave town. I did see Louis Armstrong once at the City Auditorium. One of the things that we did was to have a street band at one point, where I made a "gut bucket" base from an old wash tub, a stick, and a piece of cord. This made some reasonably good sounds. I don't remember where we played, but we did have fun practicing. I also learned to play my mother's old ukulele. She taught me many of the songs that she knew from her youth. But my main instrument became the snare drum. This came about when I went with my family to a party across Lake Pontchartrain at an estate near Covington, LA. My dad's assistant "Stumpy", also attended. Stumpy was the life of any party he attended, as he played a full-sized ukulele, and sang such songs as "You are my Sunshine", "Five Foot Two", etc., many of which I sing to this day. He was so accomplished, that on some songs he would flip the ukulele into the air, catch it with one hand and go on to the next line of the song. He obviously had a great impact on me. During the party, I began banging on an ashtray or something and he was very impressed. He said (in his best Texas accent), "We gotta git that boy a snar' drum". So, I took it to mean that he (or somebody) was going to get me a drum. When time went by and there was no snare drum, I began to ask about it. Finally, at Christmas, my folks gave me an old used drum and a pair of brushes. From that point on I began to accompany some of the Dixieland jazz records that my Dad had. I also played along with the radio, which had lots of good New Orleans music. So, that was my thing for the final months in town. The following year, I was accepted at Michigan Tech, where my musical interests would grow in an entirely different direction.

CHAPTER 4

STUDENT YEARS AT MICHIGAN TECH

(1948-1951)

I arrived at Michigan College of Mining and Technology in September 1948, having taken the Copper Country Limited from Chicago's Milwaukee Railroad Station. The previous day, I had traveled from Dallas, Texas, where my folks were living, since earlier that year, my father having been advanced to the position of Southern Sales Manager for Brown-Forman Distillery.

I had not spent much time in Dallas. My recollections are that my mother, Brother George, and I drove there from Arlington, Virginia, where we had been visiting my grandmother and Aunt Jane. What is clearly embedded in my mind was driving into Texas on highway US-80, that we called "eighty-straighty", as it went straight into the eye of the setting sun. For most of this, I was driving, while wearing two pairs of sunglasses in order to see.

When we arrived in the outskirts of Dallas, we stopped at a restaurant and were introduced to the air cooler that was prevalent in the western states at that time. This consisted of a squirrel-cage fan in a large box surrounded by wood excelsior that was moistened by dripping water. Since we had no air conditioning in our car at that time, it felt wonderful. When my folks later bought a house on the north side of town, we found that this type of cooler worked fine as long as the humidity stayed low.

When I got to Dallas, one of my first duties was to register for the draft and to take both the medical exam and IQ test. I was qualified on both counts and proceeded to get my draft card. At the time, men were being inducted into the army for the Korean War, and I had recently turned 19. I continued to have my induction center in Dallas as long as I was eligible for the draft, where they had little interest in me, as they could easily fill their quota with young Texans who were anxious to go into the service. I was able to convince myself that I had a vital occupation and could best serve my country by continuing my education, teaching and research. Whether this is true or not, only God can say.

Earlier in the year, I had been accepted into Michigan College of Mining and Technology, located in the Upper Peninsula of Michigan, 1300 miles from Dallas, approximately 550 miles north-west of Detroit and about 450 miles north of Chicago. The school was located in the Copper Country where America's first copper had been mined commercially from the 1840s' until well into the 20th century. Houghton, where the college was located, is the business and financial center of the Copper Country, which extends about 100 miles diagonally into the center of Lake Superior. These features and others make it one of the most unique and fascinating parts of the United States, so for several months I had been looking forward to my new life, far to the North

About the end of August, I packed the few things that I planned to take to college and was headed north on the train to Chicago, where I boarded the train called the Copper Country Limited, which went non-stop to Milwaukee and then to Green Bay where it headed off into the north-woods of Wisconsin and the Upper Peninsula of Michigan, ending at Calumet. It left Green Bay at about midnight and got into Houghton at about nine the following morning. I was to come to know this route quite well over the next few years as it was the main public transportation in and out of the Copper Country, until about 1960.

I guess I must have walked to the campus when I arrived in Houghton, carrying a small suitcase and my typewriter. It was about a mile to the college. They put me into Douglas Houghton Hall, at the new (east) end. My roommate was Al Sanborn from New Jersey. Across the hall were a couple of brothers Dave and Paul Uitti, from Chicago. Al and I got along ok, but I really hit it off with the Uitti brothers as they were into Chicago Jazz (Lionel Hampton, et al), and of course, I still liked Dixieland and other New Orleans style music. I had not brought my snare drum, but I did have my brushes. So, we began hanging around the lounge where they could play the piano and I was able to use the brushes on a brass ashtray. About all they could play was boogie-woogie, but that was enough to get me going. We began hanging around off and on from that point on.

I was entering Tech at the sophomore level, having completed my freshman year at Tulane. My classes were about as I had expected, except for my major subject, analytical chemistry. For several years, of course, my interest was chemistry, but the branch of chemistry I was most interested in was analytical chemistry. My instructor was Bart Park, a very fastidious person who wore a freshly ironed shirt every day. His technique was to be admired, as he was able to make a titration with an accuracy of a fraction of a drop. My sophomore class was the first course in analytical, and every student looked at Prof. Park with awe and fear. Since I had studied this subject on my own for several years, I thought I would have no problem. Well, in the lab I did fine, but my first exam was a disaster as I got a D! I couldn't believe it. I must have had a bad day. I went back to him and asked if I might have another chance. Amazingly enough he agreed to give me a new exam. I came to his office where he had a tablet armchair off in the corner and I took the makeup exam while he worked away at his desk. The next day when he gave it back to me with a grade of F. It was unbelievable. Slowly, it began to dawn on me that I had to study, not just coast through on what I had learned on my own in high school. I ended up with a D for the course, one of only two in my undergraduate and graduate coursework, both for the same reason, thinking that I knew something when I didn't. Other courses that first year were calculus, organic chemistry, and physics. During the winter term I took industrial stoichiometry, the first course taken by chemical engineers under Dr. Bradekamp, another highly feared instructor. But I had a knack for it and did very well. Maybe I should have gone on in chemical engineering, but for some reason, it never even crossed my mind. Boy, would that have changed things in my life! I was surprised to be invited to join Phi Lambda Upsilon, a national honorary chemistry and chemical engineering fraternity and was one of only two sophomores to join, the other being in chemical engineering. The initiation to this was interesting in that it involved identifying a number of chemicals by smell or touch, while being blindfolded. I think you can imagine some of the possibilities.

The amazing thing was that I didn't really have to do that much studying. I had a very good memory for the material covered in lecture and I didn't seem to do that much homework, other than for the first term of calculus. I had a really good teacher in calculus who expected us to put assigned problems on the blackboard each day, so I worked like a dog. I learned so much that term that the following two terms, when I had an easier instructor, I coasted through with an

A. Thus, I saw lots of movies that year, as there was no TV and the Lode theatre was only about a mile into Houghton. Wow! Was I healthy, as we always walked back and forth. The food at Douglas Houghton Hall (three meals a day) was reasonably good, except when they had Chow Mein. One day when this was served, we started a food riot, where all the "inmates" banged on their trays like they do in the prison movies. Many years later when the dining room manager, Frank Harwood, was a good friend, he still remembered that incident and was quite upset that we had done it to him. However, in general, the food couldn't have been too bad, since I spent all three years in good old DHH.

Once I passed the first day of gym, my athletic life at Tech could only become better. Our gym class was in what is now called the "Old ROTC Gym". It had locker rooms in the basement and a running track all around the top of the gym. My instructor was Verdie Cox, a wonderful person, who remained one of my favorite people until he died. That first day, he decided to get us off on the right foot, perhaps something he had learned in boot camp. So, he gave us calisthenics, 20 of this, 20 of that, etc. for 45 minutes, finally ending up with "OK, do 30 laps around the track and you can get dressed." I could barely climb the stairs to the track, let alone run. But I finally made it, probably the last to complete the assignment. All that I remember is coming down the spiral staircase to the locker room. My legs were like rubber, I could barely stand up. Finally, I ended in a pile of blubber at the bottom. "Wow", I thought, "I'm going to be in great shape after my first term". But it never happened again! From that point on, he would say "OK, go get into a game and keep busy."

The following term was different, as one of the reasons I had come to Tech was to learn to ski. The advantage was that they had a ski hill, run by the school, only a few miles away. Bus transportation was provided to all students to "Mount Ripley". So, one of my first purchases was for some skis. Since I had limited means, I kept my eyes open for a used pair. What I was able to get, was a pair of 7-foot long army surplus skis designed for the mountain troops. So, with some war surplus boots, "bear-trap" binders and cane poles, I was ready to enroll in ski class, taught by Fred Lonsdorf. I learned later that he was an illustrious skier who had served during W.W.II in the famous 10th mountain corps, an outfit that did some of the hardest fighting in Italy. Years later, I was to be his next-door neighbor. Anyway, before long, I could do the snowplow with the best of them and was skiing from the top of "Mount Ripley". Our total means for getting to the top of the hill was the rope tow. So, the first major objective of all skiers was to learn how to hook on to the rope tow without pulling off your gloves or being pulled face-first into the snow. It was many years before they got their first T-bar tow. The big challenge for me was to ski down the outrun slope of the ski jump. Eventually I got so that I could do this. All went well until about the end of winter, when I fell onto my skis and twisted my right leg very badly, thus, ending the ski season. I still get a twinge in that knee every now and then.

When I was to head home for Christmas vacation at the end of the first term, I decided to save some money and share a ride south as far as Jefferson City, Missouri; then, I would take the Katy RR. to Dallas. So, I contacted a guy who had put a note on the bulletin board, and we made a deal. On the day we were to leave about three in the afternoon, there was, of course, plenty of snow on all of the roads. The guy's car turned out to be a convertible, which we soon discovered, leaked cold air like a sieve. Off we went with a couple of other guys. We took a turn on what we presumed to be US-45 and headed south. After driving a half an hour, we came into a village that turned out to be Baraga. We had turned on the wrong road and had to retrace our route for another half hour to get on the real US-45. After a while I went to sleep and when I awoke several hours later, we were well down in Iowa. We stopped to get something to eat and afterwards the driver said that he was tired and was there someone else who could drive. Well, since I was an experienced driver, I said that I would take over. So, we got back on the road, and shortly started on some long straight up and down hills that are typical of Iowa. It wasn't long that I noted that the car had sort of a floating feeling and I was having trouble keeping it on a straight line. About then, a car came from the other direction and I began to fight to keep the car on my side of the road. As soon as the car passed, I must have touched the breaks and wow, it did a complete loop and slammed into the snowbank on the left side. Well, nobody got hurt, but I was totally shaken. When we got out of the car, we found that it was almost impossible to stand on the road even with our snow boots on. It was clear black ice. We had to get a wrecker to pull the car out and after we did, the owner decided to continue with the driving. The driver said: "Spain, haven't you ever driven on ice before?" I guess that I was so dumb that I didn't know there was any difference.

When we finally got to Jefferson City, I got on the train and went on to Dallas for my vacation. I really needed it, as I was suffering from a mild case of PTSD. I was so shaken by the whole thing that I chickened out on the return trip. I felt very bad about this, but there was no way I was going to get back into that car. The train stayed on the track all the way from Dallas to Houghton.

Even though I was only about 19 at the time, we would spend a lot of time in the bars on the weekend. In those days, they didn't watch age nearly as closely as now. I can't ever remember being asked for my driver's license. One of our favorite hangouts was the Town Club in Hancock. Only on occasion when we were visiting Dave and Paul's cousin did we make it up to the Senate bar in Laurium. At all of these places, polka music and country music were played on a 50/50 basis. Since I was familiar with country music and had actually seen Hank Williams, we began to listen to this with more and more interest.

In the Town Club, live music was provided by Lucille and Helen, a couple of gals from Lake Linden. After I got to know them a bit, I was able to "sit in" on the drums every now and then. Since their main forte' was country music, by the end of the first year, my main music interests had switched from jazz to country. Clearly, I needed a guitar. This was reinforced by the fact that the kids called me "Tex" (remember, I was registered at the college as a Texan) and they would say "Hi Tex, where's your guitar".

Following the first year at Tech, I spent the summer living at my grandmother's on Jackson St. in Arlington. Somehow, I got a job at the Arlington Trust Co as a cashier's assistant, tallying checks and adding up the receipts. I think that I made something like $30 a week and fast became convinced that this was not the kind of job I wanted for the rest of my life. Besides enjoying my grandmother's cooking, I made one of my infrequent contacts with Pat Mann, who was home from her job in New York for a short vacation. I think that was the summer that she had a party up at the Country Club around the swimming pool where I met Leila Buck, whom I was rather taken with for some time. Leila was the sister of Henry Buck, who Pat was dating at that time. The other memorable thing that happened was that I went down to the pawnshop in Rosslyn and bought my first guitar. Since I had learned to play the ukulele from my mother while living in New Orleans, I had little trouble picking up the basic guitar cords. Once I got calluses on my fingers so that I could stand pressing down the steel

76

strings, I would sit out on my grandmother's porch and play by the hour. So, by the time I returned to Michigan Tech, I knew most of the common Hank Williams and Ernest Tubbs songs. My Gramma's favorite song was "Hey Good lookin', what ya got cookin'".

In my second year at Tech, my grades continued to be good and I had no more disasters like analytical chemistry. In fact, my interest had now swung to physical chemistry, the primary course taken by chemists during their junior year. The course was taught by R.F. Makens, another very awesome teacher. He wanted complete attention in his class and one time he stopped his lecture in mid-sentence and said, "Someone is winding his watch!" The class, of course, was dead still. After a minute or so, he went on with his lecture, and the watch remained unwound for the remainder of the term.

As a result of things like this, there were many stories about him. The only one that I can remember is the one about hydrogen. This came about because the stock room sink was on a wall opposite from the men's toilets. Dr. Makens went into the bathroom for his morning business one day at exactly the same time the stock room manager, Lyman Richards, washed some waste sodium metal down the sink. If you have taken any chemistry, you will remember that sodium reacts wildly with water to make hydrogen gas and quite a bit of heat. So, when the sodium got down into the drainpipe below the floor, the heat of reaction was great enough to ignite the hydrogen, which went off with a kaboom, blasting water both out of the sink and out of the toilet bowl. This brought Dr. Makens out of the men's room with a considerable amount of water all over his pants and a whole lot of fire in his eyes. He knew exactly the source of the problem and headed right for the stockroom. Surprisingly, Lyman retained his job, despite the stupid thing he had done, he was still there many years later. For a long time, I thought this was just a story until one of my colleagues confirmed that he had been the primary witness.

Because of my increased interest in physical chemistry, I began to like this strange individual who taught my course. So, towards the end of the year, after I had proven myself in class, and also had become the president of Phi Lambda Upsilon, of which Dr. Makens was the faculty advisor, I asked if there was any sort of research that I might do for him. Well, of course there was, and I soon found myself working on a project making some potassium manganocyanide, which he thought would be sufficiently similar to potassium ferrocyanide to crystallize with it in a common crystal lattice. Well, like all projects, things went rather slowly, and I never achieved my goal. However, I was privy to another R. F. Makens story. My work involved chemically combining manganese with cyanide to form the complex salt, potassium manganocyanide. So, I had solutions of potassium cyanide sitting around the lab along with a rubber hose that I was using to transfer it from one container to another (although at this point, I don't know why). One afternoon Dr. Makens came into the lab and began telling me some of his latest ideas about the project. Since he had a nervous habit of diddling around with pencils and things while he was talking, he just casually picked up a hose I had used with cyanide and began flicking it around. He was talking away, so I didn't want to interrupt him, however I was watching the hose, wondering how I could keep him from doing something dumb with it. Suddenly, he began to stick it into his mouth, just as he would a pencil! "Stop!" I said and reminded him that I was working with cyanide. He left the lab in a rather flustered state and I don't think that he ever returned with more suggestions after that incident.

After my sophomore year at Tech, I began hanging around with the Uitti brothers more frequently. Often, we would go to town in Paul's '36 Chevy. This was an interesting experience, as he would try to save money by not using any anti-freeze. This meant that after every trip, he would drain the water from the radiator. Then, before every trip we would take the trash can from the dorm room, fill it with warm water, and carry it out to the car to fill the radiator. This was sort of a chancy thing since it might freeze before we got home, but I don't remember any problems.

After Dave and Sarah got married, we would often go to visit them. At the beginning, they lived in a Quonset Hut on campus, so it was a short walk from the dorm, but when they moved up to the top of the hill in Houghton, it became more of a challenge getting there. Since Paul's car had no snow tires or chains, the usual strategy was to go to Hancock, turn around, go back across the old bridge, and take a running start up Bridge Street hill. This got us over the brow of the hill if we were lucky, but sometimes the wheels began to spin, and the passengers needed to jump out to give it that final nudge on to the flatter part of the hill. Fortunately, this was close to where we were going.

I can also remember taking a trip to Chicago during Thanksgiving. It was at Dave and Paul's house that their Mom introduced me to the "Finnish" pasty. Their Dad said that: "the Cornish people invented the Pasty, but the Finns made it edible". Once, their Dad took us to Jack Diamond's famous restaurant in downtown Chicago. It was one of the best steak dinners I had eaten, up to that time. On the return from one of these trips it began snowing pretty bad, as we drove north through Green Bay and turned from US-41 onto US-441. Dave was driving, with the windshield wipers barely keeping the windows clean and the rest of us were dozing. After about an hour, we came into the city of Manitowoc, about 50 miles south of Green Bay. We had made the wrong turn on to US-441 and were headed back to Chicago. After retracing our trip back to Green Bay, we finally got into Houghton about midnight, driving the last 50 miles on two ruts in the snow.

When Dave's first son was born, he came by the dorm to announce the arrival and pass out cigars. He began teasing me as he knew I wasn't much of a smoker. He pointed to the cigar and said: "I'll give you ten dollars if you can smoke it down to here." Well, I decided to make a quick buck and began puffing away. I went well past the mark he had indicated, feeling proud of myself, but beginning to look a little green. He said, "I'm not going to give you any money, you went way past of the mark I pointed to." I was always falling for stuff like that from Dave, and sometimes, I still do.

Several other things of interest happened during the last two years. Since Dave had moved out of the dorm and Al Sanborn had moved into a fraternity, Paul Uitti moved in with me. By that time, I had gotten a Gibson guitar and Paul had gotten an electronically amplified f-hole guitar. So, we would practice our guitar pickin' on a daily basis, to the consternation of some of our dorm buddies. And, on a few occasions, we took the guitars down to the Town Club and played for beer, or to some amateur show where we could develop our skills. I remember on one occasion, we actually played on the stage of the Italian Hall, site of the 1913 disaster, where 70 people or more died during a panic when they were unable to get out the front entrance. Fortunately, our audience had not been large enough to cause a panic when they left the hall.

During the spring break of our senior year, we took a tour down to Nashville, TN, in Paul's '36 Chevy. This was a great trip, as we went to the Grand Ole Opry at its original venue, the Ryman Auditorium. We followed this by going to Ernest Tubbs' music shop, where the show continued to well past midnight. The following morning, we were driving through some great country and stopped on the edge of a beautiful field to sing "Mockingbird Hill". We continued down to Harlan County, KY to soak up the hillbilly atmosphere.

One time later that term, a friend with an accordion got together with Paul and I out on the back steps of the dorm. We were having a great time playing all the local music until I heard someone in the room above playing some polka music that really sounded great. I said: "Stop, stop, I want you to hear this." So, we stopped to listen for a few minutes and finally asked who was making that music. The fellow upstairs said: "It's you guys! I recorded it." What a wonderful feeling that was.

We celebrated my twenty-first birthday at the Town Club. I believe that this was the time that I had read a newspaper article saying that one could prevent having a hangover by taking a couple of Vitamin B1 pills. So, before we went off to the Town Club, I got myself medicated with Vitamin B1. It was quite a party, with about six of us guys drinking beer. I wasn't worrying, since after all, I was protected. When we finished up and I helped everybody drain the bottles, I headed back to the dorm. Well, the next morning, I was in terrible shape, worst hangover I ever had before or since. I think that I was able to handle half a grapefruit at about 10:30 and a bowl of soup for lunch. I don't have much confidence in the power of vitamin B1 anymore.

Another time, we participated in the homecoming parade. This is back before they had all the hobo cars that they do now. However, we decided to fix up Paul's '36 Chevy to behave like a "hobo car" by taking out the floor-boards, so we could drop various car parts through the hole, whenever the driver made it backfire. After each backfire/junk dropping we would get out into the street, run around behind, and sweep up all the parts. We thought it was a very impressive "float" and hey, we were actually participating in a group activity, which was pretty rare.

We used to love to go to the Michigan Tech hockey games at Dee Stadium. The Tech teams back in those days weren't very good, but every now and then we would beat somebody important, like the University of Michigan or University of Minnesota. Our coach, Amo Bessoni, was a very colorful guy. He was always yelling something from the bench. At one of these games the Tech Pep Band did something that made Tech Hockey history. During the second period break, they arranged for the announcer to say: "Will everyone please stand for the Copper Country National Anthem." All the local fans looked at one another, as nobody had ever heard of the "Copper Country National Anthem". Neither had we. However, everyone stood up and then, the band played "The Blue Skirt Waltz", a song that was played locally, much to the consternation of Tech Students, particularly those from down-state. The result was a huge ovation by the fans and the Huskies came from behind to win the hockey game. Thus, a tradition was born that continues to this day. Ironically, the whole thing had been initiated by the band as a major put-down of polkas and other accordion music that was played so much on the local radio stations back in those days.

During my junior year, I took Organic Chemistry, where I did a special project on a new subject called chromatography. What I did was to repeat the classic experiment by the Russian biochemist Mikhail Tswett, in which chlorophylls and other plant pigments were dissolved in petroleum ether and separated on a column of powdered sugar. The result was a series of bands that he called a chromatogram and the technique he called chromatography. I became quite interested with the technique and was later to do research on various aspects of it over the years.

Off and on during these years, I would receive a letter or note from Pat Mann and drop a note to her. On one occasion, I sent her a picture. When we did get together, while I was visiting in Arlington, they were always rather platonic affairs. We just seemed to enjoy each other's company and would sit outside her house and talk for considerable periods. On these rare occasions, I understand that her mom would show some concern.

At the end of my junior year, I rode a train on my return to Neptune Beach for the summer. On this train, there happened to be a good-looking blond, named Irene. She was a little more mature than I, but I became quite taken with her. The song "Good Night Irene" was bouncing around my head all the time that I talked to her. So, when I got off the train in Jacksonville, I took the address where she was planning to visit in Miami Beach, but in the end, did nothing about it.

I had hoped to get a job in the Jacksonville area, perhaps at the Jacksonville Power Plant where I had worked before. To my disappointment, that job was no longer available, even to an "experienced" chemist like me. Perhaps it was a union thing. Also, my mentor was no longer employed there. I tried a few other places, such as the turpentine mill, but nothing transpired. About this time, my Uncle Francis and Aunt Flo invited me to come to New Orleans to perhaps get a job at the A & P Store that he managed. So, I packed my things and headed for N.O. It was great to see my Aunt Flo again; she was my favorite aunt on my father's side of the family. They had a room for me in their apartment, off Broad St., not far from Canal St. For the first few days, they said, "Why don't you just hang around for a while and not rush into a job". Later, Francis said, I don't think that you really want to work in my store, as I really don't think you should associate with that kind of people. After a week or so, they had convinced me that they needed me to hang around the apartment, help clean up and maybe get dinner ready on occasion (that's where I learned to fry chicken). So, I spent most of my time reading the huge number of paperbacks Flo and Frank had accumulated. Since many of these were about doctors and hospitals, I developed a whole new set of interests. It also turned out that Flo had to have a hysterectomy, which brought me into the hospital environment, as I spent considerable time visiting her and helping take care of her when she returned home. My experience there also taught me more about the earthy side of life. At the end of the working day, they each sat down on the couch and had a beer or "two". And on occasion, we would go across the street to the Harvest Moon, a great bar that sold frozen schooners of Regal Beer, the best beer I'd ever tasted. The result of this experience was that I ended up with a whole new vision of what I wanted to do with my life. Somehow, it had to do with medicine and helping people who were sick. I don't think that I ever seriously considered being a medical doctor, but some kind of chemist that dealt with medical stuff. Gradually it began to dawn on me that this meant Biochemistry!

When I arrived back on campus for my senior year, I began to set the wheels in motion to take a course in biochemistry and also in bacteriology. I wasn't in class more than once or twice when I realized that also in the course were about 50% of the coeds on campus. It turns out that, Biochemistry and Bacteriology were required courses for medical technology, which, at that time, was one of the few majors taken by female students. Up until that time, I hadn't really noticed the coeds, although we did have one in Chemistry. Perhaps my summer with Aunt Flo had stirred these earthier interests as well. The instructor of the med-tech courses was Dr. San Clemente, who turned out to be an absolutely great teacher. I found that much of the med-tech social activity was centered on the Medical Club. So, it didn't take me long to sign up. We had outings about once a month, doing such things as going to the beach, snowshoeing, hiking, etc. Dr. San Clemente was the faculty advisor. By the end of the year, I was pretty taken with Olive Cornish from Calumet, so I took her to the Senior Ball and the sorority party that followed. Despite the fact that we sat in my borrowed car talking until sunrise, neither of us were sufficiently aggressive to initiate any kind of sexual activity.

With my new-found interest in biochemistry, I began thinking of research in that area. One of the things that piqued my interest was industrial fermentation, as I had written a report on that subject for bacteriology. This was a new area at that time and dealt with catalyzing the formation of chemicals by using microorganisms. One process that caught my eye was the making of citric acid by the action of black bread mold (Aspergillus niger) on corn syrup. At that time, they were doing it in open pans. I thought there ought to be a better way than that. So, I took my ideas to Dr. San Clemente and he said, 'let's see what we can do". Well, this is another project that I didn't get very far, but the thought was there. As a result, I read in the *Chemical and Engineering News* (*C & E News*) that Commercial Solvents of Terre Haute, IN was looking for a chemist to work on fermentation projects, so I applied for the job. They were sufficiently interested to invite me down for an interview. This turned out to be a dead-end, but I did enjoy seeing an industrial fermentation plant. One of the things they were making was riboflavin (vitamin B2, not B1) and there were 20-foot high pile of this bright fluorescent yellow stuff sitting around waiting to be purified. Subsequently, it turned out that they were interested in my ideas about citric acid, but not about me. I decided that I didn't want to live in Terre Haute Indiana anyway.

During the previous year, I had been elected the president of Phi Lambda Upsilon. I apparently got along OK, until my most important function came up during the winter of my senior year. I was to serve as the Master of ceremonies for the initiation banquet and the day before started to come down with a cold. By the night of the

88

banquet, it was in full swing. I was coughing and sneezing almost on a continuous basis. While I was eating dinner, my nose was running in a steady stream into a handkerchief, which was placed strategically in my lap. I suppose that I got through the introductions somehow, but it had to be awful. Poor Dr. Makens was sitting next to me at the head table. There is no telling how many people were infected that night, as I must have shaken hands with all the initiates plus an untold number of other people.

After hearing the rejection by Industrial Fermentations and it was getting on into the spring of my senior year, I thought it would be a good idea to decide what I'm going to do when I graduate. Hence, I went back to the *C & E News*, where I found two biochemistry graduate assistantships advertised, one at Purdue University, in industrial fermentation, and one at the Medical College of Virginia, in cancer research. I decided to think big and apply for both!

The one that came through first was the one at MCV. The assistantship would start the first of July. Did I want it? Well, that was not my first choice, as I really wanted to go into industrial fermentation. I waited a week or so, and no word came from Purdue. Finally, I got a call from Dr. Clayton, at MCV, asking if I wanted the position there, or not? He had to know by the end of the week. So, I waited until the last day, and having heard nothing from Purdue, I called and accepted the assistantship from MCV. It was the following

Monday that I got the letter from Purdue saying that I was accepted, did I want to come? Thus, by only a few days, was my life altered forever! It is hard to conceive of what a different life it might have been. Clearly nothing in the following chapters would have transpired.

My folks came up to Houghton for my graduation and then I drove back with them to Florida for a couple of weeks, until it was time for me to start my new life at the Medical College of Virginia in Richmond. It did look like I was going to go into the medical area after all.

CHAPTER 5

PATRICIA WELBURN MANN

Before we go any further with this story about me, I think we should find out a little bit more about Pat, the other main character in this drama. Patricia was born in Washington, DC on May 8, 1930. Her mother was Mary McLouth Welburn, the daughter of one of most prominent doctors in Arlington county, Virginia. Dr. Williamson Crothers Welburn had originally come from Nashville, TN, where he had received his BA and MD degrees at Vanderbilt University. He moved from there to New York City where he did his internship and later met and married Miss Mary Lavinia King. The couple moved to the Oklahoma Indian Territory, because of health issues. It was here that Pat's mother was born. The doctor would later regain his health and the family moved to Virginia, where the King family was living and subsequently settled in the small community of Ballston. Here, the doctor opened his office in their home and Mrs. Welburn opened the first drugstore of Arlington Co and she was the postmaster of the first Ballston post office. It was also here, in the nearby community of Clarendon, that they joined St. George's Episcopal Church and met my grandparents, Bert and Elizabeth Pitkin.

It was in Ballston that Pat's mother grew up and ultimately met my mother and aunt, Frances and Jane Pitkin, in the Girl's Friendly group at church. These girls became close friends and as a result participated in each other's marriages, and when their first children were born, Jane became a God parent to both me and Pat.

Pat's mother, Mary-Mac, married Miles Mann, an architect, who was working on the construction of the Norwich Academy, in Norwich, Connecticut. It was here that Pat (called Patty at that time) lived in a house on the banks of the Thames River, opposite from the New London Submarine Base. Mary-Mac, Patty and her sister, Margo would often return to Virginia to vacation with her mother's parents and stay at their home in Ballston. It was during these times that Mary-Mac would visit with the Pitkin sisters, and Patty would come to know me, Sonny Spain. Several Kodak pictures were taken to commemorate these early visits. The adults would laughingly consider an unlikely liaison in the far distant future, but in some minds, a "Master Plan" began taking shape. These pictures were taken in the garden of the Welburn home and some were taken at the Welburn beach cottage, in Harold Harbor, on Chesapeake Bay near Annapolis, MD. I still remember being attracted to this pretty brunet girl, called Patty.

Pat was in the 3rd grade when the "The Great New England Hurricane" struck Long Island in September 1938 and went across the Long Island Sound almost directly into the mouth of Thames River, where Pat's family was living. Patty was attending school when this surprise hurricane hit Norwich, so after the other kids were turned over to their parents by the teacher, she led Patty home by crawling behind the hedges to her house. They arrived to find the rest of the family hiding in the basement. The house was relatively undamaged, but their boat and boathouse had been swept away by the tidal surge. The memory of this traumatic experience was to last the rest of Pat's life.

It was only a couple of years later that Patty's family split up and her mother and father were divorced, with her mother gaining custody of the two girls. These three moved in permanently with Mary-Mac's parents, at the family home in Ballston (Arlington). They remained here until the Hecht Co purchased the Doctor's property so that they could construct a major department store at the intersection of Glebe Rd and Wilson Blvd. At this point, the Doctor built a new home and office further out on Glebe Rd, near the Washington Golf and Country Club. It was here that the doctor and his extended family would reside, while Pat, as she would now call herself, completed elementary and high school. Since both her mother and grandmother had shown a talent for art and she had strong interest in pursuing this subject as well, Pat attended Woodrow Wilson High School in Washington, DC. This involved a 20 mile daily bus trip down Glebe Rd and Lee Highway to Rosslyn, VA, then a walk across Key Bridge to Georgetown, MD, six blocks up the hill, by Georgetown University, where the high school was located. The commute seemed pretty extreme, but apparently, she enjoyed it as she chose to attend there four years.

On graduating from High School, Pat became focused on Interior Design and attended the Parson's School of Design in New York City, NY. Initially, she lived at the Three Arts Club and got to know many other women in the visual and preforming arts who were attending school in New York. The second year she was there, she was elected secretary treasurer of the Three Arts Club student organization. The following year, she would share an apartment with several other women. During summer vacations, she went out with her old friends from Arlington, including Henry Buck who was attending VMI. We also enjoyed each other's company when the opportunity arose.

After graduating from Parson's, Pat's grandmother offered to send her for a term of graduate studies at Parson's European branch program. Consequently, Pat and her roommate, Ethel Hennessey, departed from New York on the ocean liner S.S. United States for Le Havre, France. Their first stop was in Paris where they rented a pension. Pat told stories of not being very effective speaking with the French. After struggling to speak in French or ask questions, the French would often recommend that she speak English. Pat felt that the French (during the period after WWII) were impatient towards Americans speaking French.

Their academic program involved attending several museums including the Louvre and producing drawings of the furniture and design elements. After their stay in Paris, they went to Italy via Germany where they visited Berchtesgaden. Berchtesgaden was a famous mountain top liar of Adolf Hitler's, that once captured by the allied forces, was being used as a recreational center for the American troops. While there, the two traveling girls were embarrassed and caught off guard when they discovered they were unable to pay for their lunch, as it was being managed by the US army, the only currency that one could use was US Army script. Using their feminine wiles and beauty they easily found two American soldiers who offered to buy them lunch. From here, they traveled forward into Italy.

Their first stop was romantic Venice, where they met two handsome and very friendly Gondoliers. They had heard that Italian guys often wanted to find American girls to marry so that they could immigrate to the United States. They became suspicious that these romantic Italians might have other intentions in mind. So, they enjoyed their company for a while and then realized the smartest thing might be to not get too involved. While in Italy they also visited Florence and Rome. Pat really enjoyed Italy, the people, the language and felt very welcomed there. Pat and Ethel left with many fond memories. They continued to tour museums and draw pictures of traditional furniture arrangements, many of which we still have. When the class work was completed, they booked their return on the famous French ship called the Normandy. During the return voyage between France and New York they were staying in a fairly inexpensive stateroom. Other passengers in their fare category included an Irish family. There was a really bad storm, during which, Pat remembered an old woman saying the rosary almost the whole trip home.

Pat returned to New York City and shared a flat with roommates. She was now ready to begin her career in Interior Design. Her first job was in a shop on Long Island, where her responsibilities included keeping track of finances. She commuted each morning and evening with the maids who were also traveling to Long Island to serve the well-to-do Long Island residents. Most everyone else was, of course, commuting into the city for the day and back to the island at night. She worked there for about 6 months, enjoyed getting to work on some interesting projects, but the future was to hold many more interesting projects in both interiors and finance.

CHAPTER 6

MARRIAGE AND MCV

(1951-1953)

I arrived at the Richmond Train Station at about 5:00 in the morning on about the 30th of June. I was carrying all my school clothes, plus a guitar and needed to find a place to live. It was a big train station, a slightly smaller version of Washington's Union Station or New York's Grand Central Station. Since I was about the only person there, every sound I made echoed off the vaulted ceiling. There wasn't much that I could do at that hour, so I decided to sit on one of the huge wooden benches and wait for the rest of the world to arise. After a while, the sun came up, so I checked my bags and decided to see what Richmond looked like. Well, it turned out that unlike most train or bus stations, this one was in the midst of a reasonably nice section of town. about a block to the east of the station was Monument Avenue, on which many of Richmond's old mansions were built. I wandered around a bit, admiring the beauty of my newfound home, and enjoying the smell of boxwood hedges. I said to myself, "Man,

I'm back in Dixie and my old home state of Virginia." Then, low and behold, I discovered that one of the mansions that I had been admiring had a sign on the door saying, "Room for Rent". I checked my watch and found that it was getting near 7:00 and the lights were on at the first floor. I went up to the door and found that they indeed had a room on the third floor and that two meals per day were provided. It turned out that I had to share the room with another guy, who was a chemical engineer working for DuPont. This appeared to be just exactly what I was looking for, so I paid the lady my first week's rent and rushed back to the train station to pick up my bags.

When I returned, I discovered that it was indeed a mansion, with a large dining room off to the right side and a wide staircase that led upstairs. Our room had plenty of space and looked out on a large balcony that was really part of the second-floor roof. The balcony looked down onto the park-like side street off Monument Avenue. Across the street was another brick mansion that I later discovered had been bought in England, dismantled brick by brick and reconstructed on the present site? You don't get much classier than that. After putting my clothes away, I wandered around town a bit and went to see what I could of the Medical College of Virginia[2] where I was going to begin my research toward the MS degree in biochemistry on July 5th. It was a neat town and not so big that you couldn't walk downtown from where I lived, although I think that I took the bus most of the time.

As it approached dinnertime, I returned to my rooming house and met my roommate. He was a real clean-cut guy who had graduated from Rutgers about a year earlier. Like me, he was quite glad to find a roommate who had so much in common. When we

---

[2] The Medical College of Virginia merged with Richmond Professional Institute to form the Virginia Commonwealth University about a decade following my graduation.

went down to dinner, I discovered that we were sharing a four-person table with two very attractive young ladies; one from Petersburg and the other from Farmville. I fell for the dark-haired gal called Margaret-Ann right away. She was a doll, with a southern accent that you could cut with a knife. Both had jobs as secretaries and talked a mile a minute, about this, that, and the other. Except for a few polite questions, they didn't seem to show much interest in either of us. They both seemed to have boyfriends associated with their work and we were just a couple of Yankee boys fresh out of college. So, for most of the time, I just enjoyed sitting there listening to them talk to one another. For the most part, the food was great. We had fresh hot homemade rolls every night! Man did I love that. The food was, of course, southern style. It is hard to see how I could have found any better place to live than this. What fortuitous luck. I laugh and wonder to myself; how did I get so lucky?

On my tours around, I found that Richmond is a very historic place, being the capitol of the state of Virginia and having served as the capitol of the Confederate States of America. In fact, the same building that served as the capitol of the Confederacy presently serves as the capitol of the state. All of this is in a beautiful park, which turned out to be only a block away from MCV. In fact, on my trips from my office to the MCV library, I was to pass right by the Jefferson Davis' home, which is called the White House of the Confederacy.

All of this is within a block from the main commercial portion of Richmond, where the large hotels and department stores are located.

On the fifth of July, I showed up at the clinic building where the Biochemistry Department was located. I found the office of Dr. Charles C. Clayton, a PhD Biochemist from the University of Wisconsin. He was the man for whom I was to work and after showing me around the department, he began to describe the research we would be doing. The goal of the research was to find out how a particular azo-dye called "butter yellow" caused liver cancer when fed to rats. His hypothesis was that it had something to do with certain liver cells called Von Kupfer Cells which are phagocytic towards any particular material, meaning that they engulf particulate matter like lymphocytes do. What Dr. Clayton wanted to do was to inject powdered iron into the rat, assuming that this particulate material would be gobbled up by the Von Kupffer cells. Later, we would attempt to wash these cells out of the liver and collect them with a magnet. If we could develop this technique, we could do the same thing with rats being fed butter yellow and see if the dye was accumulating in the Von Kupffer cells. As with any project, the first step is to read all the background research, so he gave me a bunch of papers and a desk to use for my work. We diddled around on this project for a number of weeks. A side issue was to find a way to analyze for the butter yellow, and this was more in my bailiwick. Shortly, I had a method that would analyze the dye spectrophotometrically, based on the fact that the dye was bright red in acid solution. Another thing that we began to work on was the injection of particulate materials into rats through the vein of the tail. We began also making rat diet and feeding rat diet containing the azo-dye. A separate experiment was to see if we could block the uptake of azo-dye by an inert particulate material. I had not worked with rats before, so there were several new things that I needed to learn about that: how to handle rats, how to make rat diet, how to inject rats, how to kill (sacrifice) rats, how to prepare and stain microscopic sections, etc. In other words, I learned a lot over the first months. One of the things I learned about rats is that they don't like someone to bang the cage when entering. I was bit several times before I learned to simply reach my hand in and pick one up. An interesting thing about all my rat bites was that they never once became infected. I really think that someone should examine their saliva to see if there isn't an antibiotic of some sort in it. But that was outside my research area.

When the fall semester began, Dr. Clayton and I were joined by a second graduate student, named Henry King, who was from Rutgers University in New Jersey. His project was to see if copper had any effect on the production of liver cancer in rats by azo-dye. Jack Klingman, from Buffalo, New York, joined another research group led by Dr. Abbott. All three of us were working toward a Master of Science degree in Biochemistry and took the yearlong courses in Medical Biochemistry and also in Medical Physiology.

These were taken with about 100 first year medical students, hence were not designed to be easy courses. We were expected to get a grade of B or better. Henry King was a fantastic student because he had a photographic memory. For example, when we were reviewing an exam we had just taken, for any particular question, remarkably he would say things such as: "Yes. That's covered near the bottom of page 393 in our textbook." To be able to remember this sort of thing blew my mind, as it was totally foreign to the way that I prepared for exams. So, the three of us enjoyed going to class together and going across the street to the Skull and Bones Restaurant for a hot dog. Henry had a way of shaking his hot dog down into the bun that I remember and emulate every time I eat one.

My social life was slowly coming alive. Since we didn't get Sunday breakfast, a group of us would go around the corner to a restaurant that had great waffles. As they cost about a dollar each, we usually only ordered one, but we sure did savor it. Often, a group of us guys would go for some sort of trip on a Sunday afternoon. Once we went to Petersburg to see the Crater Battlefield Monument. This was a battle where the Northern troops, with the help of Pennsylvania coal minors, dug a tunnel under the Southern fortifications and filled it with gun- powder. The result was an enormous explosion that killed many troops from both sides. Although it had little effect on the outcome of the war, it remains an amazing place to visit. Another Saturday, we had a party down on the second floor of the rooming house and I took my guitar down to play in the hopes of impressing the fair Margaret-Ann. It didn't seem to have much impact, but we all had a good time. Another time I took the guitar to a party that was located in an apartment further down towards town. Apparently, I did a rather impressive rendition of a song called "Mississippi", as the song caused a cute girl from that area to give me a come-hither glance. I was pretty interested, and I was about to walk her home, when one of the more-motherly gals from our rooming house said, "You don't want to do that. She's not the kind of girl for you." So, I went home with the rooming house gang like a good boy.

An interesting thing that we were allowed to do at MCV was to attend the weekly Clinical-Pathological Conference (CPC) that was open to all graduate students. This was designed mainly for the graduate students in medicine as well as the medical staff, but we somehow were included, if we were to wear our Department Lab coats. Everybody was wearing their distinctive lab-coat or scrubs, each with their own color. So, the three of us got all dressed up in our cleanest white lab-coat with the Biochemistry Department logo on the pocket. The conference was preceded by a standup luncheon clustered around a cart delivered from the hospital kitchen. Sometimes they would have sandwiches, but other times, we had shrimp or oysters on the half shell. Wow! Was that great! That was where I learned to really enjoy oysters. After the luncheon, we proceeded to the large lecture room and CPC would begin. One of the chief clinicians would present a case of a person who had been treated for some time, but who had died without apparent reason. Then, the clinician would give his best shot at explaining the case. Then came the star of the program; Dr. George Zur Williams, Chief Pathologist at MCV. He would proceed to tear down the whole hypothesis upon which the treatment had been based. It was great fun and was also instructive in that often the clinical findings were based on biochemical evidence that we understood.

When I got off for Christmas break, I decided to save some money and go up to Arlington to be with Gramma and Jane, as, it was only a couple of hours by train. After a day or so there, Aunt Jane told me that she had heard that Pat Mann was home for Christmas and that I should call her to see if she would like to go out. This I did and so we went to a movie at the Buckingham Theater. After driving her home, we sat in the driveway for an hour or so continuing the platonic conversation we had enjoyed on other occasions.

Another evening, we went out to a nightclub in Washington that I believe she had been to before. That evening she asked if I would like to attend the New Year's Eve Party at the Washington Golf and Country Club with her. I didn't really know at the time, but this is a really classy place. (Check it out on the internet). I got dressed up the best that I could and went to pick her up in Jane's car. I'm sure all the men were dressed in tuxedoes and women in dresses they had

105

bought for the occasion, but I didn't, and Pat didn't say a thing. We danced and had a really good time. On returning, we sat in the car, and began with our usual platonic conversation. Then, the discussion stopped, and she gave me a kiss that changed the nature of our relationship forever. Despite my humble attire for the evening and the relatively humble prediction for my future, Pat apparently fell in love with me that evening and decided to get me to fall in love with her. She was probably surprised at how little it took. One thing led to another, until it began to get embarrassingly late. Finally, we kissed goodbye and promised to keep in touch with one another, as we were each heading back to our respective jobs.

Well, I couldn't get Pat out of my mind all the way back to Richmond and into the following weeks. We wrote letters and called on the phone for the next several weeks. Then, I felt that I had to see her again. So, I got a bus ticket for Friday evening, packed my bag, and after work went to the Greyhound Station and boarded the bus for New York City. This was a rather long tedious drive up through Washington, Baltimore, Philadelphia, etc. etc., until finally we arrived at the bus station in New York. Pat must have met me and showed me the way to her apartment. She was sharing a really nice place with three other girls, but the roommates were away for the weekend. We walked around her neighborhood and saw some of the sights of New York City including the Museum of Modern Art and Carnegie Hall, which was right outside her back window. That night, she made me dinner, which I believe was the fried ham steak and sweet potatoes with pineapple salad that we still have on occasion. We of course did a lot of necking and watching TV. I spent the night sleeping on the couch. Before I knew it, I was back on the bus, heading for Richmond. But, I had hardly left town and I was already thinking of when I might come back again. Consequently, I went to New York several times during the winter term and we began talking about maybe getting married. Apparently, I did do some studying and research during the workweek, as I got good grades in both Biochemistry and Physiology.

During the spring break, I went up to Arlington to visit my gramma and was able to get together with Pat several times. Somewhere along the way my gramma donated her engagement ring so that I could give it to Pat and thus start making serious plans about getting married, perhaps in the fall of that year. Through it all, Gramma and Jane had helped in any way they could. Of course, they were simply playing their role in the "Master Plan" that had been started so many years before.

The details of all this are a bit hazy in my mind, but I went back to Richmond with renewed resolve to get my degree wrapped up as soon as possible and began thinking about how I would finance the whole marriage thing. Since one of my big expenses was living in the mansion on Monument Ave, I began looking for a place where I could live more cheaply. I hated to think of leaving those great dinner rolls, but something had to go.

As with other aspects of my life, I had the good luck of running into someone who asked if I wanted to live in a vacant medical fraternity house during the summer. Without doing much talking, investigating, etc., I found myself moving into this vacant house with piles of paper, bedding, etc. lying around. I picked out a room on the second floor that was not too grungy and moved my stuff in. How I managed to leave my clothing, etc., but most importantly a Gibson guitar, in this house that had no lock on the door and only occasionally someone else coming by, I don't know. However, it was inexpensive, as I never did find anyone to pay rent to.

In retrospect, it was a pretty amazing situation – I think that they were mainly looking for a house sitter, but I don't remember this coming up. Of course, I had to get my meals at one of the local restaurants, as I didn't want to push my luck too far concerning kitchen privileges. All told, I was able to save a significant portion of my research stipend during the summer. Pat was also in the money-saving mode and had moved home for the summer to get a job at Woodward and Lothrop, a big department store in Washington, DC. I assume she took the bus into the city and back each day. I'm sure that I made many trips during the summer to visit my grandmother, but it is all pretty much a blur. As the beginning of school year approached, Pat

108

and I found an apartment that was going to fit our requirements, as I needed to move my stuff over there before the guys came back to the fraternity. To say the least, it was an amazing summer.

In the fall, my coursework was limited to only one or two graduate courses in biochemistry, so I had the time to think more about the upcoming event on October 3. Finally, during the week before the marriage, I moved back to my gramma's house so I could be handy in case any decisions were needed on my part (generally, they weren't), but Pat and I got together on a fairly frequent basis. By that time, she had quit her job in Washington to work on the preparations for the wedding.

Our wedding was held at St Mary's Episcopal Church in Arlington and the reception was held at the Washington Golf and Country Club on Glebe Road, where Pat's Grandparents were members. This is one of the classiest country clubs in America as it is known for all of the Presidents who have been members (Roosevelt, Taft, Coolidge, Harding, Wilson).

I had invited several people I had gotten to know at both Michigan Tech and MCV. My roommate at Tech, Paul Uitti, was my best man, Dave Uitti, Henry King, Jack Klingman, and his girlfriend Gerta. Pat of course had many friends she had invited because she had grown up in Arlington. In addition, there were many people that we

109

didn't know because the reception was also serving as the 50th anniversary party of her grandparents, Dr., and Mrs. Welburn. Everything at the reception went off wonderfully and went by in a flash. Fortunately, lots of pictures were taken so that we have been able to relive the memories.

After the reception, Pat and I were whisked away to THE famous Willard Hotel in downtown Washington D.C., near the Whitehouse. The following day we strolled around town and recovered from the wedding. That evening we boarded the historic Old Bay Line Steamship that went down the Chesapeake Bay to Old Point Comfort Hotel near the mouth of the bay, arriving at about 5:30 the following morning. Of course, we failed to wake up in time, so found ourselves on the dock in a partially dressed condition, well after all the other passengers had been transported to the hotel.

Hence, we had to walk up the long dock and climb the stairs at the end, carrying our bags. We checked in and immediately headed back to bed. Later in the day when we came down to the lobby, we discovered that the excitement for the day was a cat show, which we enjoyed, as both of us liked cats. Later, we visited Fort Monroe and the historic prison where Jefferson Davis had been held. The following day, we took the train up to Richmond where we settled into our apartment.

Our apartment turned out to be not too bad, plenty warm in the winter, but also pretty warm in the summer. We didn't have any cross ventilation, so I would often end up waving a big piece of cardboard out the open window to try to get some air circulating when it was hot. Pat cooked some very good dinners. Pat's grandfather came down for Thanksgiving Dinner and we cooked our first turkey in aluminum foil, and it was just great! That turned out to be a tradition for many, many years. Every now and then we would go out for dinner. I especially remember the Chinese dinners that we had. The restaurant that we went to specialized in Cantonese style, that was much milder than what we eat now, but it had delicious vegetables.

I continued to get the research assistantship pay and Pat started working at Thalhimers Department Store, in the decorating department, so we were making out reasonably well. Since we had no car, we often walked back and forth to town, or took the bus if in a hurry. This had the added advantage that we didn't have to worry about where to park the car, or pay for the gas, insurance, and we were really healthy.

My research was coming along as well as one would expect. I had developed a good analytical procedure for the azo-dye that we were feeding the rats and could do this on a routine basis. I had learned to prepare microscopic sections of rat livers and stain the sections for microscopic examination. I was doing this not only for my own project, but for Henry's project as well. I learned to take care of the rats without getting bitten, make injections into their tail vein, as well as intraperitoneally without upsetting the rats too much. I even learned to anesthetize the animals with ether and operate on the liver, without killing them, which also means that you must know how to give them artificial respiration, as this is a constant problem when working with ether. I also learned to kill the rats to take liver samples for microscopic inspection. But the research on the Von Kupffer cells was not as successful as Dr. Clayton had hoped. The cells were just not easily dislodged from the liver and the blockage of the cells did not show a significant reduction of rat liver tumors as hoped. On the other hand, I was able to show that the reduction in tumors from copper was explained by the direct effect of copper on azo-dye in the diet before getting into the rat. That is often the nature of research.

It was later during the winter term that Jack Klingman married his girlfriend, Gerta, who was getting a master's degree in pharmacology from MCV. She had been taking many of the same courses as we had. Gerta was an interesting gal, partly because she had come from Germany, but also because she had a funny sense of humor. On Valentine's Day, she gave Jack a Valentine that consisted of small box that contained a complete kit of heart medicines, a small syringe, and a live mouse. I believe that Pat and I were present at the party where this was presented and also served as witnesses at their wedding.

As I got into the last term at MCV, I began to wonder about what I was going to do next. If I was just wondering, poor Pat must have been going out of her mind! My discussions with Dr. Clayton and others indicated that the master's degree in biochemistry was not going to be worth much by itself. The Klingmans were going on to Duke University to work on their PhD's. Henry King was applying to the medical school at MCV, which apparently was his original intent. In retrospect, it was strange we had no plan for what I was going to do after leaving MVC and had never considered going forward for a PhD. Fortunately, Dr. Clayton had a friend at Stanford University who had also gone to the University of Wisconsin and was doing a similar kind of research with azo-dye and rats. A lightbulb went off in my head and I began thinking that I might want to continue my research towards a PhD.

When I mentioned my plans to Pat, she indicated that she was hoping that I would get a job so we would be able to start a family. However, she finally saw the wisdom of my idea. So, I began to make a few applications for research support: one to Dr. Clark Griffin at Stanford in California and the other to be a specialist in endocrinology at Emory University in Atlanta. It turned out that I had positive response from both of these applications, so it seemed like I was back in the same quandary that I had before coming to MCV. Which school should I choose? I decided to discuss this with Dr. Abbott and see what he suggested. He laughed and said, "Spain, if you don't know enough

113

to decide between Emory and Stanford, you don't deserve to go." Apparently, I hadn't realized, but this sort of brought me to my senses and I began to get really serious about my application to Stanford, which I discovered was one of the top graduate schools in the country, especially in the field of chemistry.

In retrospect, my decision to go to MTU was a good decision because my acceptance at Stanford may have been based on the fact that my two Advisors were University of Wisconsin graduates. I believe they were familiar with MTU because the Hockey Teams were rivals and were familiar with the reputation of MTU to produce serious and hard-working students. With Dr. Clayton's and Dr. Griffin's help, I had no trouble getting accepted at Stanford.

Pat and Jim ~ October 3rd, 1952

This time, I was wearing a tuxedo

CHAPTER 7

STANFORD

(1953-1956)

Fortunately, my folks had given us $1000 to use in case (in hopes?) we had a baby during our first year of marriage. So, we had a nest egg with which to buy a car. Unlike all married couples in recent times, we had had no car up until that time. We went out to see what we could buy and ended up purchasing a gray 1949 Ford Fairlane, so that we could drive to California. Thus, we packed up our limited belongings and headed off. I believe we first went to Arlington to say goodbye to our two families there and then drove down to Florida to spend a week or so at Neptune Beach with my folks. Then, we headed northwest, as we wanted to stop in to visit my Aunt Flo and Uncle Francis in Kansas City. Next, we headed west to the Rocky Mountain National Park, as I wanted to see it again and Pat had never seen it. After spending the night in Estes Park, we headed up onto Long Ridge Trail, and got out to enjoy the view at the top. We both had splitting headaches from the 11,000 feet altitude and could hardly wait to get back down in the valley. From there we headed west toward Utah and across to Nevada and into California. This was the fall and it seemed awfully dry to us. Finally, we got into Palo Alto, and I can remember how disappointed I was at first seeing the Stanford campus because everything was so dry and dusty.

Palo Alto is located about 30 miles south of San Francisco. The campus was built on a farm that once belonged to Leland Stanford who had been the president of the Union Pacific Railroad and was at one-time the Governor of California. His son Leland Stanford, Jr. died of smallpox at the age of 18, so he and his wife decided to build a university in his name. It is actually called Leland Stanford Junior University. Gov. Stanford died even before the main construction was completed, but Mrs. Stanford stayed close to the development of the university right up to her very death. On his behalf, they built many of the buildings that are still there, including a beautiful church that is the centerpiece of the main quadrangle (the Quad) that surrounds a beautiful Spanish courtyard. Because of the smells that Mrs. Stanford assumed might emanate from the Chemistry building, it was built well off to one side of the Quad, but of a similar architecture. The nickname for the university to this day is "The Farm". This campus is on the western side of El Camino Real, the main road that connects San Francisco to Monterey which is some 60 miles further south and was the original capitol of California.

On the day that we arrived, we checked into the department, met my new boss, Clark Griffin, and he put us in the hands of Charlie (Scotty) Robertson and his wife. They offered to help us find some

118

housing. It turned out that they weren't much help, as they were living in Stanford Village, where veterans were given first priority. After looking around there, we decided that we didn't want to live there anyway, as it was an old temporary army hospital from WWII. We ended up in a new apartment in Atherton, across the street from a classy steak restaurant and behind a decorator's studio that was built all around a huge live oak tree.

We soon got to know the only other couple in the apartment, whose names were Joyce and Jerry Aparton. I think that we met them when they happened to look into our dining room window and saw that we were eating our supper off of a pull-down ironing board, one of the few pieces of "furniture" the apartment provided. They were nice enough to loan us a table until we could find something of our own. During the time we were in California, we were to become very close friends with the Apartons and in fact we still correspond with Joyce.

The town of Atherton was a very high-class suburb of San Francisco, through which the commuter train ran and on which a major portion of the population commuted daily to the city. People were often amazed that we lived in such a classy place, but actually our apartment was quite inexpensive due to its proximity to the restaurant. It turned out the restaurant was not a bad neighbor, as every evening we got to enjoy the smell of barbecuing steaks. This was a new experience for us, as back east few people cooked steaks that way until into the '60s. We became so interested in that way of cooking that Jerry and I bought enough bricks to rig up a simple barbecue in the space across the parking lot from our apartment. Here, we barbequed steaks on a regular basis. Thus, we were introduced to the California lifestyle.

There were four graduate students working under Dr. Griffin. These were: Charlie Robertson, an MD who didn't much like clinical practice, so was working toward his Ph.D.; Marge O'Neil, a sexy blond from LA, who was working toward a master's degree; Howard Hoffman, a Reformed Jew, also from LA, who was working toward a Ph.D. and me. The Chemistry Department was in an old sandstone building that had survived the 1906 earthquake, despite the fact that the San Andreas Fault ran quite close to Stanford and caused considerable damage to the campus otherwise. Howard and I occupied an office/lab on the first floor. Our animal room was in the attic. My graduate assistantship was partly for research and partly for teaching in the medical school biochemistry lab, which was taught in the same building. Initially, the research was concerned with finding out why rats without pituitary glands did not get azo-dye liver cancer. Since the pituitary is responsible for producing several hormones, such as adrenal cortical stimulating hormone (ACTH), and growth hormone (GH) and lactating hormone (LH), we wanted to know what was required for cancer production. To explain this, the rats lacking the pituitary were fed the azo-dye, then one of us would inject ACTH, another GH, another LH, etc. The hope was that one of these

120

hormones would restore the liver cancer formation. Our job was to feed the rats the diet that contained azo-dye and inject them daily with one of these hormones. I don't remember that any of them had a marked effect. My suspicion was that the poor little rats without any pituitary just didn't eat enough of the diet to get sufficient azo-dye to cause the cancer. Despite the lack of good results, we did get a paper out of the project.

Jim at Stanford

After the first term, I began research of my own design and thus had little more interest in pituitary research. Howard was carrying on a project that was supported by the Tobacco Research Foundation. It consisted of feeding rats the azo-dye while at the same time making them live in a cage into which cigarette smoke was being pumped. This had an elaborate wheel with holes on the outside for holding a couple of packs of cigarettes. The wheel moved around to a lighter, which started the cigarette, so that bellows could pump the smoke into the rat cage. It was a smelly job, "but somebody had to do it". Near the end of the term, Howard killed the rats and examined their livers. It did appear that the ones with cigarette smoke were much less influenced by the dye, that is, the livers were relatively smooth compared to the ones that had received the dye and no smoke. He reported this to the boss and took off for Christmas break in LA. While he was down there, he was amazed to read in the paper an article that said that some unnamed researcher at Stanford had shown that cigarette smoke had reversed the effects of cancer. He was anxious to get back to find out more about this and see who this unnamed researcher was. Well, it turned out that it was Dr. Griffin, who had leaked this information to the newspaper because his project was being considered for renewal of support by the Tobacco Foundation. Again, I felt quite sure that the difference between the two groups of rats was in the different amount of diet (hence azo-dye) eaten, as the smoked rats were about as sickly as one could imagine.

Pat was fortunate to find a decorating position in Menlo Park, an upscale village between Atherton and Palo Alto. She basically walked in and introduced herself to the owner, Edna Johnson, an experienced decorator who was quite aware of Parsons School of Design, from which Pat had graduated. So, they hit it off from the beginning. Initially, she took care of the shop while Edna went off on appointments, but later Pat was allowed to accept decorating appointments herself. There were some big housing developments going on in the town of Mountain View, south of Palo Alto, so the decorating business was pretty good at that time. Over the three years that she worked there, we got to know Edna quite well and were invited to her home on a number of occasions. Edna had some very interesting friends, many of them from San Francisco, where she had previously run her business. What with Pat's salary and my assistantship, we were able to live pretty well. Although Pat never told me so, I think this must have been a tremendous experience for her due to the growth that was taking place at that time, as this was the center of what was to become Silicon Valley.

My classes during the first term at Stanford turned out to be a wakeup call. My big class was in organic chemistry from Carl Noller, who was the author of one of the top texts in the field. His mode of lecturing was to come into class and say, "Today, I want to show you ten ways to make alcohols." He would then proceed to write ten reactions on the blackboard. All of the other grad students were writing like mad in their notebooks. I was sitting there trying to draw generalities from what he was giving us, much as I had previously done in lectures. The following day he would come in with eight ways to form double bonds between carbon atoms, etc. So, it went until midterm exam time came and I studied for the exam by reading his book and thinking back to the lectures. When he handed out the exam, question number 1 was, "Write 10 ways to make alcohols." Question number 2 was, "Write 8 ways to form double bonds between two carbons." It went that way through the whole exam! I could remember a few of these reactions, but not all that he had given. As a consequence, I ended up getting an F on my first exam. Wow! This was a great way to start graduate studies at Stanford, where I had to maintain a B average. So, I scrambled and in the end of the course, I was able to eke out a D. I think that one can see that all I needed was two A's to cover that D and keep my B average. From that point on, I learned how to take notes, which I had never done up to that point. At the end of my courses at Stanford, I had filled about ten steno pads. You might think that since I already had a master's degree, there was little need to take courses for a Ph.D. That was not the case since my MS was in Biochemistry and my Ph.D. was to be in Chemistry. My first hurdle was in the Qualifying Exams, which were to be in each of the four major fields of chemistry: organic, inorganic, physical, and analytical. These exams were to be given at the end of the spring term. I have little remembrance of the exams, so I must have done alright. However, another reason for taking as many courses as possible was to prepare for the personal oral exams that were given by each member of the faculty in his office. This came at the end of the second year, so there was plenty of time to prepare.

At that time, the Stanford Medical School was located in San Francisco, but the first-year courses were taught on campus (in Palo Alto). Just a few years after I graduated, Stanford sold (or leased) a big chunk of land just north of the campus for a huge shopping mall. This gave them the money to build a whole new medical school on campus. This contained a new biochemistry department, so that biochemistry faculty that had been in the chemistry department moved over there.

Getting back to the story, During the second term I had my first chance to teach, albeit strictly in a one-on-one basis, as it was the laboratory for medical biochemistry. I enjoyed teaching, what little that I had. Which was nice as it encouraged me to ultimately head in that direction. As I said earlier, Dr. Griffin gave me the freedom to develop some research projects on my own and I became interested in looking at some of the early biochemical changes that occurred in the rat during the development of azo-dye liver cancer.

Perhaps before I go any further, I should explain that the ultimate way to determine if the rat has liver cancer is to sacrifice the rat, usually by chopping off its head, letting it bleed out and take samples of liver that would be placed in formaldehyde. Later, thin sections were taken, stained, and examined under the microscope. This is basically the same procedure that is done when a pathologist performs an autopsy or biopsy. Microscopic examination of this type is the only true verification of cancer. In the rat liver, one of the characteristics is an involvement of the bile ducts and grossly the liver has the knobby appearance of cirrhosis. So, one of the obvious changes to look for would be some component of bile. Therefore, my first study was to look for changes in bile pigments. These are the yellow compounds that cause a person to have jaundice. So, I spent the entire term studying the various bile pigments and learning how to analyze for them. It was a new area for me, and I had a lot of fun isolating them from feces and urine and then using colorimetry and fluorimetry (measurement of fluorescence) to distinguish one from another. Once I had gotten the analytical methods squared away, I was ready to start my study. What I was looking for was some significant changes in the bile pigment picture during the course of cancer development in the rat. And, to correlate bile pigment changes with pathological changes occurring in the rat liver. Since I was going to be following the microscopic changes in the liver, I needed to set up a lab where I could carry out the sectioning and staining of the rat liver slices. They found such a place for me on the third floor of the chemistry building near the photo lab and down the hall from the rat lab. Dr. Griffin either had, or purchased, a nice binocular microscope to examine the specimens produced. I had learned this histological technique while I was at the Medical College of Virginia. After a lot of work correlating the concentrations of various bile pigments from both the feces and urine of the rats with the histology, we did have some significant correlations and had enough data for a paper on the subject. However, it wasn't very exciting, certainly not the answer to cancer. But that's the way it goes.

Fortunately, Dr Griffin, had perceived how my research was going and recommended I explore the subject of histochemistry. He urged me to see a professor of histology in the Anatomy department. The result was that I took a course from him in which we met on a one-to-one basis for the next term, studying from a book on

126

histochemistry. Histochemistry is the technique where one carries out chemical reactions right on the slice of tissue. The suggestion that Dr. Griffin provided led to my first major pioneering adventure using the field of histochemistry to research azo-dye carcinogenesis. That led to the research I worked on for the remaining time at Stanford.

I also took many other courses to bring me up to speed in chemistry, and physics, including nuclear chemistry, biochemical genetics and advanced organic. However, despite Stanford's expertise in computer science, artificial intelligence, and cryptology, all of which would be of great interest to me down the road, I had no interest or use for these offerings at that time.

Things took a strange twist at the end of my first year, as two very important things happened. One was that Dr. Griffin, my advisor, was appointed Head of the Department of Biochemistry at M.D. Anderson Hospital and Tumor Institute in Houston, Texas, which of course meant that he was leaving Stanford. Initially, this looked very bad, as it seemed that three of us no longer had a research advisor at Stanford. Thankfully, he made an agreement with the department and the university to let us stay under his direction and he would continue to advise us, returning to give us our oral exams at the end of the year. We were assigned a laboratory, space in the animal room and my space to work on my histochemical research. So, it began to appear that this might not have been as bad as it seemed at first. The other important thing was that I received a fellowship from the DuPont

Company to carry on research with a stipend of $3000, with no strings attached. Apparently, Dr. Griffin was able to talk the Fellowship Committee into giving me this, based on my research results and my above-average academic achievement. Now, $3000 may not sound like much, but it was more than anything I had made before and with Pat's salary, it gave us a budget of about $5000 per year. This would be equivalent to about $50,000 per year in today's money, so we could make some changes in our lifestyle. It was not realized until some years later that this stipend must have also included many thousands of dollars in graduate tuition.

Menlo Park Apartment

One of the first things that we did was to move into a beautiful little California-style apartment in Menlo Park. It was a one-story ranch with shake-roof that looked out on a patio with porch and hanging plants. It had two bedrooms, a large living room-dining room, fireplace and one bath. It was to be quite a number of years before we had anything to equal this. We went back to visit about thirty years later and it still looked just as good to us. I don't remember who found this apartment first, but the Apartons also moved into an adjacent apartment. So, we already had friends and we quickly got to know others. We also had some money with which we could buy a new pair of end tables, lamps, and a black coffee table. It was not far from Pat's place of work, so that most of the time I was able to drive to school. We were beginning to live the high life.

The Palo Alto area, at the time that we were there, was an absolutely glorious place to live. In the United States, it came as close as any to be called the "Land of Eternal Springtime". That is, it never got too hot in the summer and it never got too cold in the winter. The towns along El Camino Real were on a peninsula with San Francisco Bay on the eastside and the Pacific Ocean on the west. But, unlike San Francisco, where it is often cold, the Palo Alto area is protected by the coastal mountain range. So, often we would see the clouds of fog breaking over the mountains like a massive wave that would dissipate as soon as it came down into our valley, while we continued to enjoy beautiful sunshine. There was some rain in the winter, but even this was pretty infrequent. The hills were covered with peach

129

and plum orchards that were beautiful in the spring. However, even while we were there these began to disappear as people moved into the area and the developers began building homes up on the hills. It's easy to understand why this area became highly developed and is now known as the famous Silicon Valley.

We took numerous trips on the weekend. For example, it was about an hour's drive over to the ocean. The small winding roads would first go through small horse ranches or vast open fields of the Stanford property, every now and then crossing the small streams that came down from the mountains. Frequently there were the large homes of the well-to-do that were beginning to build there. Gradually you would begin to work your way up into the mountains, where there were a few remaining stands of redwood trees. Then you would go over the top and the temperature would begin to drop. As you worked your way back downhill it looked more and more desolate, with only a few ranches here and there. Finally, you got to the ocean where there were very few trees and no homes to speak of. Usually, we took a quick look at the shore, perhaps driving along the coast road to the next route back to the valley, then up the hill again and back to the warmer, sunnier side beyond. If we had brought a lunch, we often ate it in the car. Another trip that we took was to go north of the Golden Gate Bridge and up along the coast to see the really neat towns in the wine country. This was quite a drive, so we would spend the night at one of the quaint little motels. This was a part of the country where several movies had been made.

We went on some nice trips with the Apartons. Several times we went up to San Francisco, sometimes to just wander around like tourists, other times we went to a nightclub to see a band playing. Once we went to see Louis Armstrong and his band. On another time we went to see the Firehouse Five Plus Two, a Dixieland Band that was a favorite of my Dad's. Another time we walked across the Golden Gate Bridge and back. That was a brisk outing as I remember. Pat and I took a couple of trips alone, mainly to go to a Japanese restaurant, where we took off our shoes and sat on the floor while we would eat sukiyaki that was made right at the table by our waitress. She would kneel down beside us and fire up an electric frying pan, to which she added raw strips of beef, spinach, onions, mushrooms, and soy sauce. It was delicious and we went back a couple of times.

Jerry was a great sports fan, so one time we went to the Cow Palace in South San Francisco to see University of San Francisco play basketball. This was quite spectacular, as Bill Russell was their star and they went on to become national champions for that year and the next. We also took trips down to Monterey, about 85 miles to the south. On our way we passed great fields of artichokes at Castroville and Seaside, where my Aunt Nora was living at the time with her daughter Leota, whose husband was in the service. Our main objective was a particular restaurant on Cannery Row that Jerry had found during one of his business trips. It had great steaks and salads. Of course, we spent the day driving around the Monterey Peninsula, looking at the seals along the shore and going on Seventeen Mile

Drive that went right through Pebble Beach golf course and past beautiful homes. Even then, you had to pay a fee to drive through. We also walked around the old town of Monterey, which was the original capital of California, going back to when it was part of Mexico. There are also a couple of very old missions that we toured. Pat and I went down there at least once by ourselves, going to Carmel, driving down the shore towards Big Sur, etc. We made several shorter trips down in the direction of Santa Cruz. I particularly loved to go through the redwood forests that are found in that area. I remember one place where the hippies had sort of taken over a big campground. So, there were all kinds of weird houses and meeting buildings. It must have been some kind of commune, built back in the woods. We went there a couple of times.

When Pat's mother came out to visit us for a week or so, we took a major tour down to San Jose and across the Central Valley to the Sierra Nevada Mountains and the Yosemite National Park. I remember driving into the main park, where you could look up to several beautiful falls dropping into the valley and El Capitan the huge block of granite that is so familiar in pictures of Yosemite. But, most of all, I can remember the suffocating heat on the valley floor that was further enhanced by all the parking lots. I was happy to drive back out of the park. From there, we drove north to the highway out of Sacramento to Reno, across the Sierra Nevada at Donner Pass. This was the same road that we had struggled up a year earlier when coming into California. It seemed easier going the other way. We spent some time touring around Reno. Then, we went south to Carson City and back up the hills to Virginia City, where Mark Twain had spent his cub reporter days at the local paper. After a full day, we spent the night at the town of Lee Vining in a motel on the shores of a salt lake called Mono Lake.

The following morning, we took one of the most hair-raising drives of our lives. The road is called the Tioga Pass road into the backside of Yosemite. The initial part of the drive was to gain altitude by going up a number of switchbacks that left poor Mary-Mac grabbing onto the car on one side of the back seat or the other. Finally, we made it to the top of the hill from which point we began to drive east along a two-lane dirt road with the stream valley a thousand or more feet below. Fortunately, this shear drop-off was on the far side of the road, but for one who is somewhat afraid of heights, it was a real test of my nerves. Finally, we made it to the woods beyond and began driving along with trees on either side. But my day was not over.

As we moved higher and higher and the day began to get warmer and warmer, the car sputtered to a stop. What had happened that was causing this? I tried to start it, but about all it would do was sputter a little, but there seemed to be nothing wrong with the battery. Was I out of gas? If we were, we were in tough shape since I hadn't seen even a house in the past hour or so and I sure didn't want to walk back along that cliff. However, the gas gage showed about half a tank.

Then a car came up behind us, paused beside us and said through the open window, "Whatcha' got, vapor lock?" I said, "I don't know?" They said, "That's probably it" and drove on. With that, we had a short discussion to try to figure out what vapor lock was. This encounter was repeated several times, with cars both coming and going uphill. On hearing our response, each drove on and no one offered a possible solution. Gradually, we concluded that this was something that was so common and so benign that no one considered it worth more than a passing nod. Eventually, we sat there long enough that the car cooled off and I was able to get it started. We managed to get to the top of the hill before it happened again, and we were on our way. The remainder of our trip back to Menlo Park was fortunately uneventful.

Through that year, Pat continued working, as did I. I completed my course of study on histochemistry and began applying the techniques to the investigation of early pre-cancerous changes in the rat liver. It wasn't long and I discovered that certain cells of the liver showed a total absence of glycogen after a couple of weeks of azo-dye treatment. The early observations were followed by repetitions of the experiment with samples being taken at shorter and shorter time intervals. These were accompanied by gross analysis of the liver for glycogen to see if histochemical changes were confirmed by more conventional analytical methods. There were slight changes, but it became obvious that the key thing was that certain cells were affected while others weren't. Why? To answer that question, I needed to learn a whole lot more about the microanatomy of the liver. It turned out that the cells affected were those that were closest to the little branches of the bile duct, from which bile is formed. This led to the investigation of other liver damaging agents, like carbon tetrachloride, to see if there was a commonality of action on the liver glycogen of cells surrounding the branches of the bile ducts. One day, while I was in the midst of these microscopic studies, my microscope suddenly disappeared! Did somebody come into my lab and steal it? What happened? I began asking around and looking in other people's labs, and low and behold, I found it in the office of a new biochemistry instructor who had been hired to replace Dr. Griffin. It turned out that he had been going around collecting various items of equipment that had belonged to our old boss. I forget exactly how I got it back, but I guess the department head asked him to back off on equipment that the three of us were using until the end of our final year. So, I was able to complete my research on a project that was clearly worthy of publication, hence thesis material. During the final months, I began wrapping it up, getting my thesis written, taking my final exams, and getting ready for my orals

In the meantime, something exciting was happening on the home front. Somewhere along the line, we had decided that it was about time to start thinking about a family. I was about done going to school and so things were not so tight from a financial standpoint. at least, not at that moment. So, suddenly, we found ourselves pregnant and the little bundle of joy was to arrive in September. Actually, we could have timed it a little better, since I was still writing my thesis at that time, but it all worked out. Pat had a good doctor and the quality of the hospital was as good as one could expect, being staffed largely by Stanford graduates. So, in September, Pat gave birth to a 9-pound bouncing baby boy, who was named James Williamson, Willie for short. We had the usual settling in period for new parents. But, eventually, he began to sleep through the night. I am sure Pat could fill several pages about this pregnancy and birth, partially because she wasn't getting much help from me because of the other things that I had on my mind. But from my point of view it was a breeze, well almost.

I had no problems with the final classes that I was taking. But somewhere in there, I had to take an exam in both German and French, the two languages that I had selected to meet the requirements of the Ph.D. These were taken in the offices of the professors assigned to make the test. Each was preceded by a period of study and consisted of translating a selection of scientific writing from the published material. About all I can say is that I passed.

Then, there were the individual oral exams that were given by each faculty member in the department. Some would say, "Did you take any courses from me?" If I said "No" and they were not in an area related to biochemistry, they would just sign the sheet and let me go. Others might ask me to describe my research in a few words and sign. But some gave me a serious exam. Dr. Hutchinson, an author

136

of a text in nuclear chemistry, asked me to sit on a stool next to his desk and grilled me for an hour. At the end of the time, he told me that I was not prepared and sent me off to come back again in a few days. So, I studied everything that I could think of and went back. Then, he said; "I think you must know it by now." and signed my sheet.

Dr. Mosher, later a famous author in asymmetric synthesis, asked me some questions about asymmetric synthesis in biochemistry. This was followed by a really great discussion between the two of us, in which I told him my interpretation of the Ogsden Concept that explains how asymmetric synthesis must occur from a mathematical standpoint. This was such an interesting discussion that he remembered it many years later when I ran into him at a meeting. So, went the individual oral exams, some good, one or two, not so good. But they took time to prepare for and several weeks were consumed.

The next major project was to produce the "final" form of the thesis that could be presented to the thesis committee. This had to be coordinated with the preparations by my two buddies, who were trying to complete their theses at about the same time, so that Dr. Griffin could chair all three thesis exams at about the same time, thus making only one trip from Texas. Fortunately, things seemed to be working out to accomplish that. This meant that we were all three madly trying to complete writing, so that the drafts could be put in the hands of a typist. All my work was being done on the portable typewriter I had been carrying around since my sophomore year at Michigan Tech. However, I was totally unable to produce the final document, as my output had numerous erasures and misspellings. So, there was a lot of running around delivering sections to be typed, editing, getting pages retyped, etc. But, finally the form to be delivered to the committee members was ready and passed along to them. Dr. Griffin was involved in early versions, but he rarely made any major changes. So, as with the last year, he had pretty much left it up to me. When the final day for the defense of thesis came, I was very confident, and it was a piece of cake. I had most of the answers to questions that were raised, and we just had a nice friendly discussion. However, after it was over, there were several questions raised about specific points in the thesis, so that there were significant sections that needed to be retyped So, on the day that we were planning to move out of our apartment, I was still making a few corrections. This was a hectic ending to the entire thesis project. But it was completed and in the hands of the bookbinder before we left the campus.

You may be wondering, where we were headed? Well, somewhere in the midst of all the preparations for the completing the degree, Pat must have raised this question too. So far, I had made no attempt to get a job, or to even consider what I might do with the vast knowledge I had accumulated. I sure didn't have any time to devote to a major job search, so we did the easiest thing, I called Dr. Griffin to see if there was a position, I could take at M.D. Anderson until I could find something more permanent. This was not a new thing, as three ex-Griffin students were working there already. Scotty Robinson, Marge O'Neill, and Darrell Ward were all there. Darrell was a top-notch person who had gotten his Ph.D. at Stanford and had done post-doctoral work with a Nobel Prize-winning biochemist at Cornell University, for several years. So, he was building quite a reputation and was carrying on research of a similar nature at M.D. Anderson. Thus, Clark said that there was room for me there and it would give me an opportunity to wrap up any loose ends of my research and get some publications written up. All of which made a lot of sense. We were due to move out of the apartment at the end of the month and we were anxious to begin the next segment of our life, so we packed up and headed off for Houston, Texas.

CHAPTER 8

MD ANDERSON

(1955-1956)

Commencement ceremonies and the actual awarding of the Ph.D. degree were not due to take place for a couple of months. But all the requirements for the degree had been met, so we decided to commence with the next stage of our life anyway. I had arranged for a post-doctoral position at University of Texas, MD Anderson Hospital and Tumor Institute in Houston. Thus, we packed up our old Ford and U-Haul trailer, and prepared to leave Menlo Park with our six-week-old baby, Willie. Our trip took us down into the Central Valley and over the Tehachapi Pass, across the desert to Needles, on the border of Arizona. Our trip was uneventful as it can be when traveling with a six-week-old baby. The one thing that I remember was that once we were driving on the long straight roads of New Mexico, when I realized that I had the gas pedal all the way to the floor and the car was hardly moving. I thought there must be something wrong with our car, or was there something wrong with the gas? I was really beginning to worry about this problem, since we were miles from help of any kind. After about half an hour, the road made a 90-degree turn and the car suddenly sped up to about 80 mph! I pulled over to the side of the road to see what was going on and found that there was about a twenty mile per hour wind, which in one direction was blowing our trailer backwards and in the other direction, forwards. I couldn't believe how much difference it made. So, after a couple of more days, we made it into Houston with no further problems.

Houston is a modern city that is only about 50 miles from the coast. Sometime in the not too distant past, this was turned into a seaport city, by the dredging of the Houston Ship Canal. As you are also probably aware, it is the financial center of the oil industry in the United States. For this reason, there are lots of skyscrapers and lots of money. This fact led to the development of one of the largest medical centers in the US. Clustered together are among other things, Baylor Medical College, Baptist Hospital, Methodist Hospital, Children's Hospital, and many other institutions, spread around a park-like campus of about 100 acres on the south side of town. Included in this complex, is the University of Texas M. D. Anderson Hospital and Tumor Institute, where I was going to work. At that time, it was just beginning to build its reputation, but by 2005, it was second only to Sloan-Kettering Hospital, in New York City, for cancer research and treatment. I had no knowledge of all this at the time we arrived in town, so needless to say, we were somewhat impressed when we got our first look at M. D. Anderson. It was a pink marble building with different colored drapes in each window, giving it a beautiful modern appearance, unlike anything I had ever seen. Wow! This was where I was going to work?

Clark Griffin was, at the time, serving as Head of the Department of Biochemistry. He had brought along Charlie Robertson, who had his Ph.D. from Stanford, and Marge O'Neill, who had her MS and was now working on her Ph.D. from the Department of Biochemistry at Baylor Medical School, where Griffin held a professorship. Also, from Stanford was Darrell Ward, who had spent several years' post-doctoral research with Vincent du Vigneaud, a Nobel Prize winner at Cornell Medical School. I was to share an office with Robertson until they could find a more permanent location. With the help of somebody at MDA, we were able to find a nice two-bedroom apartment that faced out on to Bray's Bayou that ran down between streets on either side. The bayou was little more than a 30-foot-deep drainage ditch with some water at the bottom. It looked as though anything could be living in it either in the water or along the steep sides. In fact, the same bayou ran through the back yard of Houston's Mayor, and once while we were in town, he reported a six-foot alligator climbing out on to his lawn. However, we enjoyed the apartment and were able to invite my mother and brother George to spend Christmas with us. This turned out to be fun, except that we had to run the air conditioner all the time, a problem we had never before encountered.

My initial responsibilities at MD Anderson consisted mainly of writing up most of the work that I had carried on at Stanford under Dr. Griffin's aegis. During this process, I copied all the research papers that I thought I might need in the future. At this time, there was no such thing as a Xerox machine, so the papers had to be laboriously copied by a photographic process that involved liquid developer and produced an unattractive copy. To make copies of material to be passed out during a meeting, one either used the Mimeograph machine or a Hectograph. In either case, the process was time consuming and the resulting product was unattractive. It was to be several years before I would enjoy the simplicity and elegance of the Xerox machine. Despite these difficulties, I was able to turn out a couple of papers and one monograph, dealing with the work completed at Stanford. In addition, I was invited to give a paper at the symposium that was headed up by Darrell Ward, who was becoming a good friend and mentor.

At some time during the first couple of months at MDA, Scotty Robertson came down with a severe case of hepatitis and was confined to the hospital for several months. Since he was working on a Pathology Specialty to go with his MD degree, it was thought that working in the autopsy room had led to the disease. The good news was that I was able to take over his laboratory space and make use of his two lab technicians. This was good, as I had run across a few things that I wanted to either repeat or extend the research I had been doing. The bad news was that I had responsibility for his two technicians. Scotty was such a nice guy that he had run a fairly "loose ship", as far as the technicians were concerned, whereas, I had been used to starting work at 8 o'clock and getting right down to work. So, I would line up an experiment I wanted to do and get there ready to go. The two Texas gals working for Scotty would get there at eight, but then make coffee, and settle down to discuss the previous evening's activities until about nine. Then, I would have to explain to them what the plans for the day were, which led to further discussion, etc. We really wouldn't get going until 9:30 and then before you knew it, it was time for a coffee break. They wouldn't get back from that 'til about 10:30. Then at about 11:45, they needed to start getting ready for lunch, etc. As I was just filling in for Scotty, there really wasn't much that I could do, besides, I rather enjoyed listening to their Texas accents. Scotty eventually recovered and ultimately, he ended up as the camp physician for the Climax Molybdenum Corporation, on top of a mountain in Climax, CO. A few years later, he and his wife moved to Casper, WY, where he spent the rest of his life as a family physician.

Sometime during that summer, we went over to visit my folks, who were living in Altamonte Springs, FL. It was during this time that I had the opportunity to spend some time with my Dad. At the time, he owned a car wash in downtown Orlando, FL. This was not the best deal that he ever made, because shortly after the purchase, they built I-4 as an elevated freeway right at the end of his street. This significantly reduced the traffic that passed by his front door. Besides, he had to manage a bunch of workers with all the social problems of the world. This meant that he had to get some side businesses just to keep the company going. One of these was the shipping of cars back to the northern states, mostly for baseball players who traveled with their teams each spring and fall. Of course, this was a job that my dad really loved because it put him in contact with all the pro ballplayers. While I was visiting, I had time to help him with some of the car pickups in order to drive the car back to Orlando. During one of these trips, I told him that I was beginning to think of going into the teaching profession. This stunned him, as I guess he had visualized my going into research, perhaps for a pharmaceutical company or something. His response was something like "my gosh son, don't you know that teaching is one of the most poorly paid professions there is!" I guess I explained that I would be teaching in a college somewhere and that the salary was not really that low. This exchange must have made a big impression, as I remember exactly where it took place on the road driving to Lakeland, where the Detroit Tigers have their training camp. Over the years I have thought of this many times, wondering what he would have thought concerning the different salaries I would receive during the next 50 years of my career.

For a variety of reasons, Houston was not our favorite city. For one thing, it is on the coastal plain with very little scenery no matter what direction you drive. We did take several trips to Galveston, where we could go swimming on the beach. And we did take a tour of the battleship *Texas* that is permanently moored on the ship canal about halfway to Galveston. But the climate is hot and humid over a large portion of the year, so outdoor activities are limited. We didn't have many social activities, partly because we had a young baby to take care of. Also, because of the climate and that we faced onto Bray's Bayou, I came down with a very serious sinus infection like I had never had before. And, for one reason or another, we really never had any close friends all the time we were there, partly, because most of my colleagues at work lived on the other side of town. Even though there may have been opportunities for me at MDA, we were ready to look elsewhere. At the time we had exactly zero thoughts or opportunities to go anyplace where I might have a position in a chemistry department and it would take months to explore. Then a very interesting thing occurred!

Sometime near the beginning of September, I received a postcard from Michigan Tech asking me if I was attending the ACS meeting at Atlantic City. If not, it asked, "what are you doing?" I replied that I was looking for a job in academia. Surprisingly enough, the response to this card was a call from Dr. Makens, asking me if I would be interested in an assistant professorship in chemistry, starting on September 25. The salary would be less than I was presently making, but the cost of living in Houghton was considerably less than either Palo Alto or Houston. So, I accepted the position and finished up the various projects I was doing at MD Anderson. Shortly, we were heading north toward Michigan. I have always felt that I must

147

be one of the very few people whose job application was on a postcard.

A few years after we left Houston, the American Cancer Society awarded Dr. Griffin a Lifetime Research Award to continue his work there at MD Anderson. Shortly after that, Darrell Ward was appointed Head of the Department of Biochemistry, where he was to serve for 21 years. In the previous years he had completed the task of unraveling the structure of Luteinizing Hormone, a peptide responsible for stimulating ovulation and conception during pregnancy. For this work, he received a prestigious award from the Endocrine Society of America. Recently, the MD Anderson Cancer Center has been named the number one cancer research hospital in the United States. Considering the positive occurrences in Houston, you might wonder if we made the right decision in moving to Michigan Tech. However, we have always been satisfied that we did.

CHAPTER 9

COPPER COUNTRY

When I decided to enroll at Michigan Tech, I didn't realize that I was going to one of the most interesting places in the country and one that I would be connected with for well over half a century. This is because Tech is located in a region of the US called the Copper Country. It got this name because of the range of hills about 100 miles long that contain "native copper", a form of copper that requires no chemical smelting to retrieve it from the ore. Even from pre-historic times, natives and explorers were able to find pieces of copper metal simply lying around on the ground. One piece, near the town of Ontonagon weighed almost a ton[3] and raised such a stir, as to start a copper rush to the area about ten years prior to the gold rush in California. Because of the remoteness of the region, most people were only able to arrive by taking boats from Lake Huron, up the St. Mary's river to Sault Ste. Marie, from there by boat across Lake Superior to Copper Harbor or Eagle Harbor on the Keweenaw Peninsula. The

---

[3] A portion of this (called Paul's Rock) is on display outside of the old Smithsonian Building in Washington, DC.

Keeweenaw Peninsula is the finger-like projection of land that extends into Lake Superior and is almost synonymous with the Copper Country, because of the range of copper containing hills that runs down its spine. It is sufficiently large that it makes this area easily identifiable even on a world globe. Despite the easy access of the copper, it took several years for the early miners to find the best sources of the ore and figure out how best to separate the chunks of copper from the rock. Most of these early sites were in large holes that had previously been mined by prehistoric people. The mining by modern people really got going about the time of the Civil War, so that the Copper Country was able to provide the major source of copper and brass to the war effort, particularly for cannon barrels.

The initial source of supply for building mines and extracting ore was Copper Harbor because the Keweenaw Waterway was not open for ships. But, as the major activity began moving down the peninsula, closer to a town called Red Jacket and the twin towns of Houghton and Hancock, it was obvious that a waterway was needed to provide access to this area. The existing Portage Lake required some dredging at each end to remove some major sand dunes that separated it from Lake Superior. When the resulting canal(s) were completed, Houghton became the center of commerce and finance for the entire area. Calumet became the main center for mining and Lake Linden, on the shore of Torch Lake, just down the hill from Calumet, became the center for ore extraction. At the peak of the mining activity, these four cities had a combined population of about 100,000 people and acquired some of the most modern conveniences of any cities in the country. Houghton had some of the first phone lines in the US, connecting the hockey stadium with the hotel up the street, so that scores could be relayed to fans sitting in the bar. This town also had an active stock exchange that was still in existence when we moved there in 1956. Calumet had some of the first concrete streets in the state and an opera house that brought in some of the country's most illustrious stars. It was here that professional hockey was born in North America and one of the local teams won the first International Hockey Tournament (with the help of some imported Canadian players) right there in Houghton.

One final feature of the area that further contributes to its uniqueness is the climate. Because it is surrounded on three sides by water, the Keweenaw Peninsula has a climate that is dominated by Lake Superior, the largest freshwater lake in the world. The lake serves as a major heat sink, causing spring and fall to come later and be longer than that of the surrounding landmasses. During most of the summer, the lake stores heat, as the breezes blow across it, causing the resulting air to be cooled and during the winter, it releases heat and helps to moderate at least the early portions of the winter. Summer breezes are also dried by the fact the surface temperature of the lake is below dew point causing water to be removed from the air and the lake to have a negative evaporation rate well into the month of August. In the winter however, the heat is released from the lake largely by evaporation so that it releases a large amount of water into the air. This causes fall rains and snow showers in the form of "lake effect snow". This results as the winds rise up over the hills of the Keweenaw, it cools and triggers the release of snow. These Keweenaw snows are some of the deepest in the Eastern US, sometimes reaching as much as 300 inches per year. One year while we lived there, we had a measurable quantity of snowfall every day for 60 days. You can imagine that with all this weather that it becomes the major topic of conversation, both at home and away. Put these things together: geography, history, and climate, and you have what is one of the most unique places in the United States.

Part of the history of the Copper Country relates to interaction between the workers and the companies. Because of the nature of the mines in this area, many of the initial workers were from England, primarily Cornwall, where there are many mines of a similar type. Thus, most of the "mine captains" were Cornish, while most of the laborers were from whatever country people happened to be immigrating from at the time. These included Italian, Finnish, Swedes, Irish and Croatian. The work in the mine was very hard and during the peak periods of mining, workers were dying on the average of one a day. These deaths were recorded in the Mine Inspectors Journal as "Finn killed in Osceola #13, 12th level, due to rock fall", "Italian died of heat exhaustion, level #15 Quincy #3", etc. So, there was little regard for the individual by either the Mine Inspector or the mining companies. However, most of the mine companies operated in a very paternalistic fashion, each building a company town in the vicinity of the mine. The most powerful of these was the Calumet and Hecla Mining Co that was financed in Boston, MA. Their mining town, called Red Jacket, later to become Calumet, was the most elaborate, providing in addition to houses, the steam to heat the houses, fire protection, police, an opera house, a club for the upper level staff and a guest hotel for visiting officials from Boston. The club that C&H owned was called the Miscowaubik Club, the name being Indian for red metal. Initially, membership was limited to C&H employees, but gradually opened up to various professionals in Calumet and later Houghton. When we joined, there were a significant number of people who were members from the "South end", as Houghton and Hancock were called. After a few years, I was elected to the Board of Governors and it was during this time that the Miscowaubik Club was sold by C&H to the members, as they were devolving themselves of ownership of all properties and operations other than the mine. Even the latter was being shut down as a result of bad economics and the strike of 1963. This was tough on everybody in Calumet, as they could no longer count on the free heat, free fire safety, etc. that the company had been providing. The Miscowaubik Club had to buy a furnace, among other things, at the same time it was losing members, etc. It managed to survive this period, but it wasn't easy, and it continues to struggle to this day.

However, I'm getting ahead of myself, as the strike of 1963 was simply the last of a series of strikes that ended the relationship between the C&H and its employees. Ironically, the problems started as a result of the introduction of technology to "make it easier for the miners". The technology in this case was the power drill that replaced the two-man hand drilling, where one person holds the drill-bit while the partner pounds on it with a sledgehammer. The difficulty was that one-man drill could now do the work of two men and so a significant number of people had to be laid off. This occurred at about 1911 or 1912, which is about the same time that the mining unions were being formed. They organized in the Copper Country and went on strike in early 1913. By Christmas 1913, they had been on strike for the better part of the year, the companies had brought in the strikebreakers and things began to get ugly. But Christmas was coming, and a group of the miners got together to have a Christmas party for their kids at a building called the Italian Hall. Unfortunately, the building was poorly designed, with the steep stairway rising directly behind the entry doors. After the party had been going on for quite a while, somebody yelled "Fire!" The resulting panic caused everyone to rush down the stairs and left about 70 people, mostly kids, crushed in the stairwell. There was <u>no</u> fire. The result was a national tragedy during the Christmas of 1913, called the "Italian Hall Disaster". There was some talk that the entry doors opened in, but this was <u>not</u> true, as Pat and I talked to a man who, with a Catholic Priest, had opened the doors outward and helped remove the wall of bodies. The strikers blamed the company people – the company people blamed the strikers. The town was split by the resulting controversy, which <u>continues until today</u>, over 90 years later. The building was finally torn down in the

154

1990s, only the doorstep remains as a memorial to the strife between the companies and the unions.

As I said above, the early transportation into the Copper Country was by boat and thus was only available for about 9 months of the year. Even then the trip was often hazardous, because storms come up quickly on Lake Superior and the shores are rocky except for a few scattered beaches. Hence, there were many wrecks, even up to the recent past. For example, the Edmond Fitzgerald went down as recently as 1980 and a coast guard ship went down more recently than that. To help prevent this, there are several beautiful lighthouses on the Keweenaw Peninsula, a particularly good example being right in the town of Eagle Harbor. Since the early settlers were icebound for several months during the winter, one of the first things they worked on was a road to Green Bay, about 175 miles distant. The existing Indian trail was gradually improved to become what was called the Military Road that went south from Houghton. Even this was of limited value and as late as 1948, there were stretches of US-41 south of Baraga that were still unpaved. US-41 is a major route that starts at Biscayne Boulevard in Miami, heads west as Tamiami Trail, then north to parallel I-75. Eventually, it heads North to form a major route through downtown Chicago, then continues through Milwaukee, Green Bay and becomes the main route into the Copper Country, finally passes through Houghton, Calumet and Copper Harbor, terminating at the tip of the Keweenaw Peninsula. However, even before the roads were fully paved a railroad was brought in to supply the Copper Country. This later became part of the Milwaukee Railroad system. The main passenger line, called the Copper Country Limited, left the Milwaukee station in Chicago at about 6:00 pm and got into Houghton at 9:00 am the next day, finally terminating in Calumet. It was the main mode of transportation until about 1960. It was about that time that the Houghton County Memorial Airport was built. Since some of the early Canadian flights flew over the Keweenaw on the way east and west, a portion of the funding for the airport came from Canada, to provide a place for emergency landings[4]. This is memorialized in the airport initials, CMX. The first commercial flights out of Houghton were in the 1920's, but eventually, they were bringing in the DC-9 jets that were quite comfortable. Our flights went mainly to Green Bay and from there to Chicago. Now that federal support of airlines has been limited, all we have are a limited number of flights to O'Hare on small jet planes.

It is safe to say, that the Copper Country is a unique place, so it is not surprising that the people who live there are unique as well. I didn't start to appreciate this until I returned as a member of the Michigan Tech faculty. But first, let me tell you a little about the school. When I arrived as a student, it was called the Michigan

---

[4] At that time, the country north of Lake Superior was total wilderness, containing few towns or roads to provide for emergency landings.

College of Mining and Technology, having been started in 1885 as the Michigan College of Mines. For a period, it was carried on in a single sandstone building called Hubbell Hall. This was located at the end of what came to be called College Avenue. Along this avenue were many of the large homes of Houghton's well-to-do residents. As the college grew, it added science and engineering departments, particularly those related to the extraction of minerals from the ground, such as geology, chemistry, metallurgy, mechanical and civil engineering. As time went on, buildings were added and the student population grew, although in a modest way, as the school was located about 550 miles from the population centers of the state. And, more importantly, it was about 500 miles away from Lansing, the state capitol, and the source of funding. When the state funds were short, there was often talk of closing what was known by some as "Houghton Tech". However, it weathered all the storms and survived until the period following WWII, when enrollment received a major spurt from returning veterans with support from the GI Bill of Rights that provided free college education for every veteran. It was about this time that I arrived on campus after one year at Tulane. At that time there were mostly a group of older buildings. About ten years later, political support was greatly strengthened by a couple of legislators from the Upper Peninsula and the campus began a building program that continues until today. Thus, Michigan Tech now has a modern campus rivaling any in the state of Michigan and is called Michigan Technological University.

When I chose Michigan tech from its catalog because it had pictures of skiing and ice skating, I didn't realize that I was going to such a hotbed of sports activity. I was later to find out that Houghton was the original home of professional hockey in North America. In about 1900, an entrepreneur named James R. Dee had been talked into starting a professional hockey club by a local dentist , named Doc Watson , who knew several Canadian hockey players who were out of work and we're willing to come to the United States to form a hockey team. This was later joined by teams in Calumet, Mich., Sault Ste. Marie Mich., Sault Ste., Marie, Ont. and Pittsburgh, Penn. The Portage Lake team of 1904 turned out to be winner of the 1st international hockey tournament, held in Houghton. Professional hockey soon expanded 1st to Canada, later across the United States and the world.

A few years later, college hockey was started as a division 1 sport by Michigan Tech, which carries it on to this day. At about the same time that Pat and I arrived in Houghton to be on the Michigan Tech faculty, John MacInnes arrived to become the hockey coach. He had been born in Toronto, Ont., gone to the University of Michigan, where he was a goaltender for several successful years. He had a few years of experience coaching junior hockey in the Ann Arbor area. After coming to Michigan Tech, he quickly developed one of the strongest teams in college hockey and became recognized as one of the best coaches in NCAA college hockey. His teams won the national championship in 1962, 1965 and in 1975 and league champion seven times. He was NCAA Coach of the Year twice and League Coach of the Year five times and finally received the Legend of College Hockey Award in 1999. Pat and I had the good fortune to know John and Jerry, his wife, for all of this period. One of John's great characteristics was that his team always appeared at a visiting hockey tournament as clean shaven, sports jacket wearing young men. Unfortunately. John died young at age 57.

Another local sports hero was Herman "Winks" Gundlach" who had graduated from Houghton High School and gone to Worcester Academy in Massachusetts, then to Harvard University where he had become the captain of the Harvard Football team in about 1930 and was selected a member of the first team nationally. He went on to play in the NFL for the Boston Redskins. On his return to Houghton he went into the family business, where he directed the construction of most of the buildings at Michigan Technological University. I got to know him after I joined the Houghton Rotary Club where we sat at the "old timers" table. Once, when I was out on the golf course, I admired his gold braided golf hat and was surprised on returning home to have a visit from his assistant with a copy of his hat which he had sent me. For some people, you have to be careful with what you say.

Another sports figure that we came to know was Clarence "Clancy" Kalmer. He was born in Milwaukee but grew up in St. Ignace, Mich., which is on the north-side of the Straits of Mackinaw.

It was here that he began his long-distance swimming career, by swimming across the straits and back. He also swam from St. Ignace over to Mackinaw Island. Clancy came to Michigan Tech about 1962 and helped start the Michigan Tech Skydiving Club, making an historic decent from 10,000 feet into Lake Superior. After getting his engineering degree, he helped build the Mackinaw Bridge. While at Michigan tech, Clancy began to see the Keweenaw Waterway as a challenge to his swimming ability. So, after 2 previous tries, he swam the twenty-five-mile waterway, in 38 hours. He was accompanied by his good friend Dick Madison and his brother, in a rowboat. It was the end of this trip that is described in the chapter on the *Pat-Sea*. He also swam under the Golden Gate Bridge from San Francisco to Marin County and later returned to swim an "Escape from Alcatraz". He finally got into the Guinness Book of World Records by playing 126 holes of golf in one 24-hour period. He was a true Copper Country Sports Hero.

A Person that everyone knows, is a kid named George Gipp who was born in 1895 in a town right next to Calumet. He went to Calumet High School and then went on to Notre Dame University, where he was discovered by coach Knute Rockne, who recruited him for football (although he had never played organized football before). Gipp played every position in football, but his specialties were quarterback, halfback, and punter. In 1918, 1919 and 1920, he set records in all these positions, some of which still remain to this day at Notre Dame. Unfortunately, he broke curfew one night, got locked out of his   dorm and caught pneumonia, from which he never recovered.   However, he is said to have told Knute Rockne "Win one for the "Gipper".   Since Ronald Reagan had played George Gipp in the movie *Knute Rockne: All American*, he claimed the line as his own when running for president as a Republican and the rest is history, although, I believe he was actually a Democrat at the time the movie was made!

The Copper Country has many more sports heroes.   I read about them practically every Sunday in the Daily Mining Gazette. Some have gained fame by going on to the Olympics after starting their skiing careers at Mount Ripley and receiving training by my neighbor, Fred Lonsdorf.   One of these, Nonie Foley, an 18 year old from Houghton, was considered by Sports Illustrated to be the top US Women Skier while training to go to international races in Austria. Another, Chuck Ferries, was pictured on the cover of Sports Illustrated in 1963 as the best male skier in the US.   It is amazing that two people who grew up in Houghton, just down the street from Michigan Tech and got there early training at Mount Ripley from the same teacher that I did, could have been, at one time or another, considered by Sports Illustrated to be the top male and top female skiers in the United States.

What we discovered, when we moved to Houghton, was that many extraordinary people lived in the copper country.   I think this happened because most of them were either pioneers in one way or another or they came from families of pioneers who went way back.

It happened that approximately 100 years before Pat and I came to Houghton, her great-grandfather had gone to Ontonagon to teach school. He didn't last long, and we were not sure we would either. But the pioneer spirit was there. Anyone who lasts through 200 to 300 inches of snow during the winter has to have it. They call it Sisu (Finnish for "Guts"). This, and other features of the Copper Country make the people different.

When we first arrived, our neighbors across the street were Pete and Joe Romig and their three daughters. Pete was a really neat lady from near Madison, Wisconsin, who became one of Pat's best friends and Joe was an instructor of law who was one of the most enjoyable people to discuss almost anything with. Whatever the topic, politics, religion, you name it, Joe could find interesting and thoughtful things to bring up about both sides. He had grown up in China, the son of a Presbyterian missionary, so had an interesting youth in its own right. Joe ultimately moved into the administration, where he became secretary of the board of control and for a time, the academic Vice President of the University. Although we were not aware of it at the time, the large house where the Romigs lived had originally been the home of the Gundlach family. At the time we lived there, Tech faculty lived on all four corners of our street. Directly across the street was the family of Gill Boyd, the famous metallurgy professor who had been the bane of the mechanical engineering students, back when Dave Uitti was in school. I never got to know him, but his red-haired son was our paper-boy, who could always be counted on to provide all kinds of sports statistics when he collected for the papers. So, it was an interesting neighborhood, but after a couple of years we moved to Ruby St., which is one half-block back from College Ave., near the college. When we moved, the Romigs moved to a house only half a block from ours. This is where they remained for the rest of their lives.

At the time, we moved to East Houghton, many of the large houses were in the process of being bought up either by fraternities or student apartments. However, one of the few remaining residences was right across Ruby St, but faced onto College Ave. This was owned by Dr. Simon Levin, who had been the Chief Medical Officer for Calumet and Hecla Copper Co, based in the company hospital in Lake Linden. In his later years he had been carrying on his medical profession out of the St. Joseph's Hospital in Hancock. I think we got to know him through his daughter Marion Hoyt, who was working as secretary in the Geology Department. I knew her from there and also from membership in the Miscowaubik Club. As we got to know her better, we began asking if she wanted a ride to the club for various affairs and also to the Michigan Tech hockey games, particularly when it was snowy. It turned out that Marion's husband was killed in WWII, so she had joined the WACS, leaving her baby daughter, Mary, to live with her grandparents, the Levins. Even after the war, Marion continued to work, either in the Detroit area or at Tech, leaving Mary to grow up with the Levins, "Grammy and Boppy", until she later attended the University of Michigan majoring in Geology. By the time we moved into the neighborhood, Mary had gone off to Canada and was working on various mining exploration jobs, where she met and later married a Welch man, Hugh Clayton. Hugh was a geophysicist who specialized in aerial exploration of minerals. Ultimately, they were married during a Christmas vacation in Houghton, and Pat and I stood up for them at the wedding that was held in the Miscowaubik Club. After the reception, we helped them leave on their honeymoon, boarding the Copper Country Limited at the Calumet Station about midnight, for the trip to Chicago.

For most of our years in the Copper Country, we lived in Houghton, but after our retirement from Michigan Tech, we moved to a cottage in Chassell. This was a town about seven miles south of Houghton on US41. It was located near the mouth of the Sturgeon River, a large stream that drained the sandy plains south of Copper Country, where great stands of White Pine once grew. These trees were harvested toward the end of the 19th century and shipped south to Chicago and other centers of major building construction. So, in its hey-day, Chassell was a major lumbering center. Logging was done mainly during the winter when the swamps were frozen, and it was easier to get back into the woods. Then, in the spring when the Sturgeon River was high, the logs were floated down the stream and across Chassell Bay to the sawmill, where they would be cut up for shipment south. By the time we moved to Chassell, the white pine trees were all but gone and the town had cleaned up most of the remnants of the lumbering industry. If there is any local industry, it would be focused around the sale of antiques. Most people are either retired or working at Michigan Tech. However, by chance, our cottage was built on property that was originally the farm of John Chassell, the man for whom the town was named. The large property next door was that of Worchester, the original lumbering baron, now owned by the Sigma Rho fraternity. In the intervening years, our property had been owned by the town of Chassell and was used as the boat ramp. So, it was nice to have become a small part of the history of the Copper Country.

CHAPTER 10

THE NEW PROFESSOR

(1956-1962)

As you recall, there was not a formal application or interview for the position at Michigan Tech, although there was some justification in my appointment as the man who was offering the position was R. F. Makens. He was the leader of the chemistry section of the department, and one of my old advisors, who knew me as an undergraduate research assistant, President of Phi Lambda Upsilon honorary chemistry fraternity and honor graduate in chemistry. It also helped that I had gotten my Ph.D. from Stanford, one of the most prestigious universities in the country. However, he did go out on a limb for me since he had not seen me for about five years and I'm sure there was some dissention about his decision from the other chemistry faculty members. In any case, I was hired to the position of Assistant Professor of Chemistry starting in the fall of 1956.

Pat and I, of course, discussed some of the ramifications that the job entailed, but definitely not in the detail that we should have taken. Pat trusted my decision, but it was based on my experience while attending the school as a student. Thus, I had not been thinking of it as a faculty member, having a wife and family, living, and working in the community. As a result, I had never thought to consider such things as the type and quality of the housing available, the quality of the schools, quality of the shopping district, things that we just took for granted in Palo Alto and Houston, things we would have discussed, had we visited the campus as all modern faculty applicants do before accepting a job. Had I known what we were in for, I would have done more research and we probably would have not moved to Houghton.

About the middle of September, we packed up the car and the three of us headed north to Houghton. The furniture was to be shipped by truck the following week. As we headed north, the weather got colder and colder. So, when we got to Ashland, Wisconsin, we had to do some shopping for heavier clothes, particularly for little Willy. Pat began to wonder about the wisdom of moving to the North Country. This wondering became more serious as we drove through Painesdale, Trimountain, and South Range, the towns south of Houghton that in those days had little paint on the outside and looked like little more than "ghost towns". Finally, we arrived in Houghton, and it was little better, as the power plant at the west-end of town was coal-fired, so that many years of soot accumulation coated the outside of buildings and homes, most of which were over 50 years of age. To make things

168

worse, snow flurries began to fly! We decided that the first thing we needed to do was to get the newspaper and check the ads for apartments. We had previously decided to hold out for something really nice, with an all gas kitchen, etc. The paper was not due out for an hour, so we cooled our heels in the Restaurant that was about the only place to go. It was a typical restaurant of the early 1900's. When the paper finally came out, we discovered that there were no apartments for rent. When we broached the question with the Houghton real estate agent across the street, he laughed and said, "We haven't had an apartment rental for over a year." We now began to wonder if the department head had really been kidding when he joked: "We haven't had anybody sleeping in tents, yet." The situation was so discouraging, what with the snow, the general appearance of the place and the housing situation that Pat began to cry and I wasn't very far from it.

That same afternoon, we went to the Dean of student's office to see if they had a list of vacant housing, which fortunately they did. And, wonder of wonders, there were two apartments available in the area: one in West Houghton and one in the nearby town of Dollar Bay. The latter was a totally impossible place over the Dollar Bay Post Office, with major cracks under the doors that separated the apartment from the adjoining one. The apartment in Houghton was not bad, especially considering the alternative. The problem was that it would not be available for six weeks and we had furniture coming in the next day or so. And, we were not even sure that we could have it, as the landlady seemed somewhat skeptical. Later that evening we gave her a call and she asked what church we went to. Apparently, our religious preference was acceptable because she said that we could have the apartment. We have always been suspicious that it was little Willy's smiling face and blue eyes that did it. So, we stayed for about six weeks in one of the vacant cabins at the otherwise closed Travel Rest Motel, across from the old Houghton Beach. When our furniture arrived, having made a slight detour to Houghton Lake, 350 miles away in Lower Michigan, we stored it in the garage that went with the apartment. It was a rather dreary time, but we made it.

The apartment was located on the corner of Houghton Avenue and West 2nd Street. It was on the second floor of an old house, in which the kitchen was a converted hallway and the living room had been a front bedroom. The bathroom was very classy, with a purple marble platform under the toilet that had two footmarks to guide men when they were urinating. The bathtub was of the old style with claws holding balls. The toilet tank was above the toilet, with a pull chain for flushing. The wallpaper was characterized by a large flower print in almost every room. All this didn't quite match up with the housing that we had planned while driving up to Houghton.

Pat, Jim, and Willie's first home in the Copper country was a small apartment upstairs in this house in West Houghton.

One of the nice things about the apartment was that it came with a built-in babysitter, as Gladys Johns, our landlady, loved kids and she became particularly fond of little Willy. Gladys was a large lady, so that she had plenty of lap to hold kids on. She turned out to be the sextant for the Christian Science Church that was located next to her house. She lived with her father, who was the actual owner of both her home and our apartment. So, whenever we wanted to go out, or Pat needed to go to the store, Gladys was happy to come over from next door and help out. Pat was pregnant when we arrived in Houghton, so this was a definite help. After, daughter, Caryn, was born, it was convenient to have her come over when we wanted to get away for the evening.

My initial teaching assignment was certainly designed to get me off to a running start, as I had a couple general chemistry recitations and general chemistry labs in addition to one organic chemistry lab. Recitations were classes of about 20-25 students who were able to ask questions of the instructor about either their homework assignment, or the latest lecture. Each general chemistry student took three lectures, one recitation and a three-hour lab each week. The recitation was also the place where students would take a 10-minute quiz each week. It was during these recitations, that a young instructor really found out how little chemistry he knew, because, if you can't explain it, you don't know it. So, to put it simply, I was scrambling to keep up. I think that on Wednesdays I had an 8:00 am recitation, a general chemistry lab from 9-12, and a four-hour organic lab in the afternoon. Wow, those were the days when college teachers made their pay because there were few graduate students to carry out this kind of instruction.

The man who was directing the general chemistry course at that time was Roy Heath. Another recitation instructor was Mike Berry, who had come to Michigan Tech the year previous to me. Of course, I survived this baptism under fire and even had time for other things. Since it became clear that I needed practice in public speaking,

I joined the Toastmasters Club and participated in their meetings for about a year. I also joined the Michigan Tech Little Theatre and had speaking parts in several plays, including the lead in Arthur Miller's *The Crucible*. From these activities, my speaking ability began to improve, and my time no longer allowed for these extracurricular activities.

As you know from previous chapters, my main research during my graduate career was in the area of chemical carcinogenesis. However, I decided that Michigan Tech was not the most appropriate place to continue this, as there was not even a biology department, let alone a medical school. So, I decided that the more appropriate research for Michigan Tech would be in the area of pulp and paper mill waste utilization. For the first term on campus, what little time I had for research was spent on looking up what had been carried on in that area. After a couple of months of library work, I decided to go to the Institute of Wood Research, on campus and see what potential for support was available in that area. I went to see the director and told him what I was proposing to study. After listening to my story for about 30 minutes, he sort of laughed and said that there really wasn't anything left to be done in that field, as there wasn't a problem with paper mill waste that he knew of. So, I left with my papers and plans, and he went back to making paper clip chains, or whatever. What a jerk! Since that time, there have been untold millions of dollars spent on the problem of pulp and paper mill waste disposal and utilization, and it isn't totally solved yet. Anyway, I decided that without support, I would spend my efforts in another area.

I also did some library research during that first year. An interesting thing occurred there. One day, I walked back into the stacks as I had been accustomed to doing at any other library during my graduate studies. However, in this one case, the head of the library, Madelyn Gibson, came up to me and said, "Young man! Undergraduate students are not allowed to enter the stacks without a special pass!" I explained to her that I was Doctor Spain and that I was an Assistant Professor of Chemistry. This was an embarrassing situation for both of us, but a source of laughter, when we were at a dinner together some years later. From this incident, you might surmise that I was pretty young looking, which was true. It was also part of my problem in handling recitations. I heard later that Roy Heath was not too happy with my performance in general chemistry and tried to have Dr. Makens "let me go". It is likely that he was comparing me with Mike Berry, who was already an experienced teacher when he came to Tech and one of the smartest guys I had ever known. He had gotten his Ph.D. at Harvard University and was later to be the coach of Michigan Tech's College Bowl team. I would be the first to admit that my first year as a teacher was a learning process for me.

I think that it was not until the following year that I was able to get my biochemistry course started. Initially, this had only about a dozen chemistry majors sign up, perhaps for one or two quarters. Also, during the first year, I had proposed a senior course in "phase distribution techniques". This would have included chromatography and countercurrent distribution but would have been a very specialized course. So, Dr. Makens talked me into modifying this and developing it into an "Instrumental Analysis" course, I accepted the challenge and started putting together a lab with the equipment available in the department. Previously, the only thing approaching instrumental analysis was a course in spectroscopy that Bart Parks had taught and that I had taken as a student. About that time, we received a grant that provided an infrared recording spectrophotometer and an ultraviolet spectrophotometer, which became important components of the course. We also had electrical measurement apparatus that could be put together in a variety of ways. Many of my pieces of homemade equipment taught students more about what makes an instrument work than any of the glitzy stuff that they work with today. Altogether, this was not a bad course and ultimately became a required component of the chemistry curriculum, as it still is today. At about that time, Dr. Makens was developing a master's degree program in Nuclear Engineering. So, another course he talked me into teaching was in the area of radiation measurement. I had never taken such a course, but like many courses that I have taught since, I accepted the challenge. Hey, it's all in the books - If you can read, you can learn.

So, the first time through, the students and I were learning together. Basically, that is what I had to do with the Instrumental Analysis course as well. They were only beginning to write the books for either of these courses. In essence, I was providing the role model to the student, demonstrating that one should be able to learn on his or her own, the ultimate objective of any college course. It wasn't long and I became recognized as the go-to-guy whenever a special course needed to be taught. A couple of times, I taught a one or two quarter physical chemistry course and eventually, I was given responsibility for the two-quarter course in organic chemistry. As a result, my responsibilities in general chemistry became less and less.

During the first year or two I think that Pat was kept busy with her two babies and thus did not have much of a chance to worry about the possibility of leaving. Right from the first week we were at Houghton, Pat went to the beautiful Trinity Episcopal Church, where we met Mike and Betty Berry who were also Episcopalians and with them soon became involved in the upcoming Centennial celebration of Houghton and the church. Both Mike and I were scheduled to play roles in the church pageant. I can remember returning from our summer vacation with tears of joy on first seeing the Quincy Mine and the Copper Country, such a difference from the year before.

About the second year I was at Tech, Roy Heath was elected the President of the Faculty Association and he came to me and said,

"Spain, how about taking the job of Social Chairman?" Amazingly, I took the job. It was probably one of the best things that I did in those early years, as it put Pat and me in contact with almost all the faculty on campus. The big social event of the year was the progressive dinner. Here the faculty members and wives formed into groups and each group went to three different homes during the course of the dinner, ending up at the Union Building for dessert. So, what we had to do was to put the groups together and send out invitations across the campus, asking questions, such as: which course do you want to be responsible for? And, do you want non-alcoholic cocktails? Then, we had to sort the responders into compatible groups. This I did initially with the help of Roy Heath, as I only knew a few faculty members. Then I had to contact the people to let them know which group they were in. Finally, I had to respond to all the phone calls that occurred as a result of our decisions. The result was that after doing this for a year or two, Pat and I knew most of the active people on campus and they knew us. These were fun times. Pat and I usually selected cocktails as the course and worked with some other couple who provided the hors d'oeuvres. Typically, we had frozen daiquiris made with frozen limeade and rum. They were so good, that you had to watch carefully that you didn't drink too many. In fact, it was not unusual for somebody to get wiped out before getting to the main course and once it was me. The progressive dinner was typically towards the end of the fall quarter, when the snow really hits Houghton. So, cars were often floundering around in a couple of feet of snow and people were helping each other get out of a ditch. It was always a fun time. Roy Heath was a well-liked person, so he was president about three years, and I was social chairman for a like amount of time.

After two years in the apartment, we bought a house over on Ruby Street in East Houghton. This we purchased on a land contract from a ROTC couple who had gotten it on a tax sale and fixed it up during their tour of duty at Michigan Tech. It was only a block or two from Tech, so I could walk to work, and Pat could have the car for most of the time. It was a two-story house with four bedrooms on the second floor, a big dining room, kitchen, and a double living room on the first floor. It was at least 35 years old, with broad plank white pine flooring throughout. This was beautiful except that the pine had dried out and left large cracks between the planks. Ladies with high heels had to be careful that their heels didn't get stuck in the cracks. The previous owners had installed an oil furnace in the basement under the kitchen, but the only entry was through an outside door that opened upward. This was because they had covered up the previous cellar stairs to remodel the kitchen. These things and others, such as poor wiring, only became evident with time. We did find a trove of antiques when we visited the attic. For example, I discovered an old Gibson tenor banjo. We also found a stereopticon viewer and numerous slides, as well as a magic lantern with many slides. Of course, there was a great number of books that belonged to the original owners of the house. Unfortunately, we gave some of these things away and have been kicking ourselves ever since. We enjoyed this house for several years, doing various things to improve the appearance of the outside and correcting some of the problems on the inside. This is the house where we had our second daughter, Lisa. So, we have fond memories of our kids growing up there. I'm sure that they also have some memories of this house, such as raising a chicken from a baby chick and finally giving it away to a neighbor who had a farm. We still have many good friends from that neighborhood.

We did have problems with the house, however, mainly because of the outside door to the basement. A couple of times the oil jet in the furnace would get clogged, once in the middle of the night. Of course, I had to get dressed, go outside and shovel off the door and break away the ice in order to get into the basement. Then I still had to take apart the front of the furnace to get into the place where the jet was. Of course, this had happened before; otherwise I wouldn't have learned how to solve the problem from the furnace man. One time a fuse blew in the evening when Pat was having a meeting of church ladies. and the minister. I think that he shoveled the cellar door open while the ladies all sat in the dark.

One of the things that we did was to put in a brick patio near the back door. The bricks were obtained from the Kerredge Theater in Hancock that had burned down the previous winter. It was the location of most of the stage shows during my undergraduate years. So, we thought that it would be great to preserve the bricks as relics and thus hauled a couple of hundred back to the house in the trunk of our car. It was a lot of work cleaning them off and getting them ready to make the patio. The result was not too bad, and we now had a place to set up some outdoor furniture.

Since Pat had access to the car during much of this time, she began going to afternoon bridge parties with some of the community ladies who she had met. She had learned to play bridge from her grandfather, having had to substitute in some of his doctor foursomes as a high school senior. Many of these women became future clients of Pat when they became aware of her expertise in Interior Design

When we moved into the Ruby Street house, Pat decided that we knew enough people that we should have a Christmas party. I think we had about 50 people who were invited to the parties even in the first year. We made a "secret family punch" that was very simple, consisting of one bottle blended whiskey, one bottle of seltzer water, a cup of lemon juice, a splash of maple syrup and a few drops of red dye. Despite its simplicity, everyone seemed to like it. I can remember only once when a Scotsman, Norm MacLaine, said that he would rather have a glass of Scotch and water, which I gave to him. (I think Sue had the punch.) We had these parties for several years in a row and they became so popular that one year it was even crashed by one of our acquaintances and his girlfriend, who hadn't been invited. I, of course, asked them in and they had a good time, as they have thanked us on numerous occasions. We laughed about this for all the years I worked at Tech.

One year, our sedate Aunt Jane was visiting for the holidays and attended one of our parties. She got along very well with all of our friends. As the party was breaking up about 1:00 am, almost everybody was gone except Jane and Marion, our friend from across the street. The Romigs walking home looked back to see Jane in the kitchen window, tipping up the bowl of punch to drain the last few drops, a great memory of our wonderful Aunt Jane

I think Pat began attending the faculty women's club meetings right from the very beginning and therefore made a considerable number of friends, which must have been enhanced by her activities, helping me during the progressive dinners. For whatever reason, she soon became the Assistant President of the Faculty Women's Club. in very short period of time. Somewhere there is a picture of Pat serving as the President, during the annual Faculty Club meeting during which, she was pregnant with our second daughter, Mary Alisa. It is clear that she was off to a pretty good start.

In my second year at Tech, I was still rummaging around looking for an interesting research project, when, during one of my general chemistry labs, some ammonium sulfide, used in the qualitative analysis of metal ions, spilled on a paper towel and was mixing with one of the test mixtures of ions. It had resulted in a couple of colored bands, not unlike that which one sees in an agate. This gave me the idea to put the ammonium sulfide reagent in agar gel and pour the mixture of ions on top. Low and behold, it produced an interesting series of bands. Because these bands were based on the precipitation equilibrium, I called the technique Precipitation Chromatography.

I have since considered this as one of my first encounters with the special type of perusal in which I was unconsciously searching for a novel research idea to work on. In this case I recognized the similarity of the banding from my previous experience with chromatography, some five years earlier. Thus, I was perusing for something interesting while carrying on my other job-related activities.

A review of the literature showed that the only technique of a similar nature had been done in Japan and Russia. The more I studied it the more involved I got and shortly, I had enough results and pictures to publish a paper in the *Analytical Chemistry* journal. I also showed the results to the head of the Geology Department and he was sufficiently interested to assign a geology graduate student to work with me on economic applications through the following summer.

That fall we wrote up a paper and submitted it to *Economic Geology* journal, where it was immediately accepted.

The following year, I began to work with filter paper as the medium rather than agar gel. I saturated the paper with zinc sulfide to provide the sulfide ions. The test solution was then run onto the center of the paper from a capillary tube. As the precipitation occurred, it formed concentric circles on the paper, with the most soluble precipitate on the outside. This procedure allowed one to obtain not only qualitative analysis, but also semi-quantitative analysis because the size of the circle was directly proportional to concentration of ions.

I decided to present a paper on this at the upcoming ACS meeting in Chicago. Since it had been billed as "Precipitation Chromatography", it attracted a number of chromatography people, including the most famous chromatography researcher at the time. My paper happened to be at the end of the session, so I invited people to hang around to see it demonstrated. Several people, including the chromatography specialist, came up on the stage, and I set my demonstration materials on the top of a grand piano. Amazingly enough for a demonstration like that, it actually worked, and I received some kind words from all that attended. A year or so later, one of these researchers from Japan, who was traveling the country was interested enough in my work to fly up to Houghton to visit with me about the techniques I had used. It is amazing how much one can achieve from a simple observation of nature.

These papers would probably have been the last from me, except that a bright young lady who had just graduated from the Chemistry Department named Adele Liimatta came into my office and expressed interest in carrying on research with me. I told her that I really didn't have any money to pay her at that time and she said "that doesn't matter because I am receiving a scholarship to work on my master's degree, as I was the valedictorian of the Michigan Tech senior class." I congratulated her for her success and suggested that she might want to continue with the research in the precipitation chromatography area and gave her a copy of the paper I'd just written. She returned later expressing interest in the topic and I gave her some additional suggestions. That's about all I remember of our interaction. I'm sure I must have helped her some along the way but, I was so busy, it couldn't have been much. Later that year she returned with enough experimental results that we were easily able to write another paper for the *Analytical Chemistry* journal.

Shortly after I got involved in the instruction of instrumental analysis, I became interested in gas chromatography (GC). This is a technique where one separates volatile compounds by passing them through a tube of adsorbent that causes some to stick tighter than others. Some of the first work on GC was done by Phillips Petroleum chemists in separating the hydrocarbons of petroleum. After some preliminary work with glass tubes, I built a gas chromatograph using coiled copper tubing that I placed in a drying oven to maintain a constant temperature. The sensor at the end of the tube was a "glow plug" from a model airplane engine. This produced an electrical output that I recorded with a surplus circular chart recorder that I had gotten from the chemical engineering group. (ironically, this was not unlike the recorders I had worked with back at the Jacksonville Power Plant almost 20 years earlier) The flow-gas that I used to run through the tube was hydrogen. Amazingly enough it worked, and I was able to get clearly defined records showing the separation of the test mixtures such as gasoline. The chart recorder made an impressive clicking sound as each component exited the tube. I was so excited to have put together this important new chemical technique that I decided to give a campus-wide seminar and tell everybody about it. Of course, the highpoint of my seminar was to be a demonstration. When I was getting it set up, I decided that I really should use helium rather than hydrogen for safety purposes. So, I brought in a tank of helium to use in my demonstration. A fair number of people showed up at 4:15 for my seminar, including some department heads and the Dean of Faculty, Frank Kerekes. I talked a bit longer than planned, so my demonstration didn't get going until about ten minutes to five. I started it off with the gas setting the same as before and so I would know when the material would reach the sensor. When the time

185

arrived, I announced that: "We should start hearing the recorder begin it's clicking any moment now." This was followed by dead silence. Then I made the announcement again and only dead silence followed. After a few more minutes a few people started dribbling out, some saying: "Good talk, Jim", etc. I couldn't figure out why it wasn't working. Finally, at about 5:10, with only a few friends still clustered about, it started to click and proceeded to do its thing. Only then, did it hit me. I had been tripped up by something that we teach all freshman chemistry students. Hydrogen diffuses at least twice as fast as helium, so at the same pressure, it is going to take more than twice as long for helium to move through the copper tube full of adsorbent. I made several more gas chromatographs after this and students in the organic lab used one of my final models for at least ten years after I left the department.

Another project that I worked on was an attempt to make a separation of optical isomers by using an adsorbent with L-tyrosine covalently attached. The general idea was that when a mixture of D and L isomers of a compound were passed through the column containing that adsorbent, that either the D or L form would stick more tightly to the adsorbent and thus cause a separation of stereoisomers. Now, this is not just an idle exercise, as usually when drugs are synthesized the result is a mixture of D and L isomers, where only one of the two forms is biologically active. Also, it is often true that the

186

other isomer is toxic! So, there is great need to have a tool such as I was attempting to design. Unfortunately, at the time I was not aware of the full ramifications and was doing it just to see if it could be done. Hence, after a few tries, I gave up and went off to another project. Had I stuck with that project, maybe I could have made a great contribution to the pharmaceutical industry, because today, the separation of optical isomers is still a major area of research.

Since I was not smart enough to get funding for any of the areas of research that I had played around with, I finally concluded that if I was going to do funded work, I needed to go back to cancer research. So, I began using interlibrary loan and whatever means possible to get myself back into the chemical carcinogenesis business where I had a reputation. I had been still working on a few papers that were left over from earlier work, so I was not totally "dead in the water". After a couple of months, I had submitted a couple of proposals. I left no stones unturned. I even submitted a proposal to the Copper Country Section of the American Cancer Society. Although it wasn't really my field and had no intention of doing any research in it, I gave several talks on the effects of smoking on lung cancer. In other words, I put myself back into the "cancer research business" full time. Some months later, I received grants from both the American Cancer Society and National Institutes of Health. The Chemistry Department fixed up the end of the old inorganic lab for my research and I began to accumulate the equipment that I needed.

Shortly after receiving word of the funding, I heard from the public relations department at Tech asking if they could come get some pictures, as they were writing an article on the new grant we had received. As I remember, the photographer wanted to meet me at the lab at about 7:30 the following morning. I said OK. I dragged myself down to the lab and when the guy got there, he said, "Now, I don't like to take anything posed, so I just want you to do what you would normally be doing at this time of day." I felt like telling him that I'd normally be finishing my breakfast. Anyway, we managed to get some "un-posed" pictures and I got back to doing what I would normally be doing. It always irked me that the University Relations people were only interested in writing articles about grants that had been awarded to the university. You never saw them when the actual research was giving results. For example, they were never interested about the precipitation chromatography work I had done, or the work on gas chromatography. This was true also when we began generating some results from the cancer research. I always felt that such a policy had the effect of making the public think that research is simply a bottomless pit into which you pour money and no results are ever forthcoming.

During my fifth year, we got a new head for the Department of Chemistry and Chemical Engineering. Ed Williams was a Chemical Engineer who came from Pennsylvania State University, where he had taught and co-authored a text on industrial stoichiometry. He turned out to be a spark plug that was able to rally the department in a way that hadn't happened to that point. Some other faculty began carrying on research and participating in development more than previously and a group of us began going to the gym to play paddleball together. The high point of that year was a group trip downstate to recruit graduate students. The participants in the trip were Ed Williams and three chemists, including myself. We stopped in at several small schools such as Albion and Kalamazoo College to meet with potential students. The result of this recruitment is lost to antiquity, but the hockey games that we "happened" to attend are not. Prior to our trip downstate, Michigan Tech had its best hockey record ever during the previous months. The final games of the season, between Tech and the University of Michigan, were to determine the winner of the Western Collegiate Hockey Association. Our schedule just happened to put us in Ann Arbor for those two games. It was a thrilling time, as Michigan Tech won both games, despite the efforts of superstar Red Berenson on the UofM team. We went back to Houghton on Sunday, highly elated from the success of our trip and Tech went on from there to easily win the NCAA championship in Boston.

During the years of my cancer research, I had two graduate students and two undergraduate students working with me. My first graduate student was working on rats who were eating radioactively labeled azo-dye. The objective was to find the location of the dye in

189

the liver by using a technique called autoradiography. In this technique, you place photographic film over sections of the liver, while in a darkroom. Since the radioactivity would darken the film, it would occur only where the dye was located. The results were quite tricky, in that they required that the student understand clearly what were the microanatomical structures of the liver, as well as applying statistical analysis to the counts that were made. Since I was not totally confident in the results that had been obtained and did not have the time to repeat them, I withdrew the paper that I had planned to give at the Cancer Society meetings

The other graduate student was working on a technique that involves replacing the typical sacrificing method of cutting the head off of the rat, by injecting an isotonic formaldehyde solution into the rat peritoneum. I thought this actually was less traumatic then the process of cutting the animal's head off. The purpose of this novel technique was to leave the blood in the liver to provide a means for clearly showing the complex pattern of liver circulation. He produced some beautiful results, but for some reason, disappeared before completing his thesis. Even to this day, I wish this work had in some way or the other been published.

My undergraduates at that time were Mike McCarthy and Jack Rowe who were looking at the possibilities of using electron microscopy to explore rat livers during chemical carcinogenesis. They carried on quite well without much help from me, as I was mostly busy with the early stages of running the Department of Biological Sciences. We had received an electron microscope as part of the equipment for the new building and it was being maintained along with the other electron microscopes being used at Michigan Tech in the Metallurgy Department.

As I have indicated earlier, our social life has been largely determined by Pat's leadership. Most of it was outside of the university group. One reason was that she began playing bridge with a group of women who were wives of the up-and-coming business-people of the area. One of the ladies in her bridge group was Loret Ruppe, the wife of Phil Ruppe, the Republican congressman representing the Upper Peninsula of Michigan   Years later, she became Director of the Peace Corps under President Ronald Regan. However, the most significant thing that I believe grew from this friendship was Pat's introduction to Phil's aunt, Katherine Bosch, who was one of the main heirs to the Bosch Brewery and perhaps the most socially connected women in the Copper Country. It also turned out Ms. Bosch was an alumnus of the Parsons School of Design and had taken some of the same coursework as Pat. Because of their common interests, she welcomed Pat with open arms and a gave us access to the social community that went well beyond any based on my qualifications alone. As a result, Pat was asked to do several decorating jobs for the Ruppe family. I think this may have also been a factor in our joining the Miscowaubik Club, an exclusive social club in Calumet that was originally started by the Calumet and Hecla Mining Company to entertain company officials and guests. Pat also learned that on occasion, they would have lobster dinners and had oysters on the half-shell at Christmas time. Since this fare is a favorite for both Pat and me, we decided to join. This brought us into contact with other people who were "movers and shakers" of the Copper Country. On one occasion, our son Will had a lesson in billiards from the CEO of the Detroit and Northern Savings and Loan Company.

On another occasion, we were invited to a large dinner with the Ruppe family. I believe now this may have been due to Pat's close relationship to Katherine Busch. As far as I can remember, we were the only couple who were not in some way related! Phil Ruppe and the rest of the family were staunch Republicans and so was Pat, as she had served as an election inspector in the local elections. So, I was the lone Democrat at the table. A funny thing happened as a result.

The election was coming up shortly and McGovern was running for President. Because of my southern background, I was strategically seated next to Phil Ruppe's sister-in-law from Texas. As part of the conversation, she "Innocently" asked who I would be voting for. I thoughtlessly said that I would probably be voting for McGovern. Then, she said at the top of her voice, in her thick Texas accent, **"You gonna' vote for that Mc Governor person?"** For what seemed like a few minutes, you could hear a pin drop, but then the conversation went on to other topics. For me, it was an embarrassing occasion; however, we have continued to be good friends with the Ruppes. Several times, Pat even dropped in to see them when they were living in Bethesda, when she was visiting her mother or sister in nearby Arlington.

Pat also volunteered on the Vestry of the Trinity Episcopal Church and served as treasurer for many years. After being active in the Vestry for several years, she was voted by the Parrish to be their representative to the Bishop Council and became the first woman representative for the Bishop of the Diocese of Northern Michigan. Later she built on her experience as church treasurer, took a few accounting classes at Michigan Tech, and became the Manager of UP Tax Service a position she would hold until we moved to South Carolina.

At work, my research continued to develop. One day, I was called over to the office of Dean Frank Kerekes and offered the position of Director of the Freshman Chemistry program. A few years earlier, I might have been interested in this advancement, but now after spending all the time building up my research program, I just couldn't see abandoning it. Cancer research and general chemistry were just not compatible in my mind and directing the freshman chemistry program was definitely a full-time job. So, I had to say thanks, but no thanks. Shortly after that, Mike Berry was appointed as the director and went on to become a general chemistry lecturer who was well-liked by most of the students and extremely well-liked by a few, who continued to visit him on a regular basis until he died at age 80. Part of this was due to his excellence as a lecturer and his involvement as the coach of the MTU College Bowl team for several years since he had a special attraction for very gifted students. Mike and I remained good friends for the rest of his life. One of Mike's most admiring student friends continues to communicate with me by e-mail. As you will see in the next chapter, my decision not to accept the freshman chemistry directorship turned out to be the correct one for both Mike Berry and for me, as shortly after this, I became involved with a much larger adventure.

The family was growing in the Ruby Street house: Pat, Lisa, Jim, Willie, and Caryn with our dog, Bop

CHAPTER 11

FISH STORIES

I've never really been much of a fisherman, but there have been a few times when I have enjoyed fishing and at least one period of my life when I was even a bit obsessed with it. I guess that the problem with fishing is that it requires patience and that has not always been my strong quality. When Pat and I would go fishing in the *Pat-Sea*, we would find a place that seemed like it should be good, and we would fish a while. She would be perfectly happy to stay at that spot, but before too long, I was ready to try a new place. So, we would go roaring off to find a better spot. When we found a likely location, we would throw our lines in the water again and Pat would just get comfortable, when I would decide that there just weren't any fish there. Every now and then she would catch something, so we would work that area pretty well. But generally, we never caught enough to make a meal out of it, so we would wish we had thrown the first fish back. Obviously, she is the better fisherman. I like fishing when there are a lot of results from a little effort. For example, I like to catch my fish by hand.

When we first moved to Houghton, an eight-inch fish called the smelt would run in the rivers every spring at a certain time. So, people would gather along the banks of streams at about ten o'clock at night, with lights and bonfires and scoop the smelt out of the water with wire smelt nets on the end of long poles. Often, people who lived along the streams would have smelt dipping parties, where you could try your hand at the sport. These were great fun because they would bring frying pans, flour for dipping, and cooking oil, so that the fish were hardly out of the water and people were cooking and eating them. They would be eaten much like an ear of corn, holding the head and tail, you would bite gingerly so as not to burn your tongue or eat the backbone. They were delicious. It was nothing for one to eat a dozen or so during the evening and still be able to eat a few more. When the festivities were done, you would often leave with a bucket of smelt to take home. Unfortunately, one good meal of smelt was about all you wanted for the year. So, often the smelt ended up as fertilizer for your yard. One year, I guess we had not been invited to any smelting party, so I decided to see if I could catch any during the day. I went to Coles Creek, out on the Canal Road, and wandered down along the shore. At first, I couldn't see anything in the creek to speak of, but the bottom was covered with some dark stuff. Then, I realized that the dark stuff was actually fish backs that were undulating gently with the flow of the stream. In other words, it was solid smelt. I found a grassy place where I could lie down along the creek and stick my arm into a deep spot. I grabbed and came out with a handful of squirming smelt all sticking out between my fingers like a bunch of eels. These I deposited into my bucket. I was able to hold on to these fish because they were males that have a fairly rough, scaly skin, compared to females that arrive later in the season and are quite slick, with essentially no scales. I dipped my hand into the stream several times until I had about half-filled my bucket and had plenty for dinner. This was a once in a lifetime thrill, as shortly after that year, the smelt runs became less and less and are now only rarely seen in our area.

Several years in a row we had the good fortune to be invited to spend a few days at the Isle Royale National Park station on Mott Island. It was during our first trip to Isle Royale that we had the best Lake Trout fishing that I ever experienced. A group of us men got in the *Pat-Sea* for the short trip to Middle Island, near the entrance to Rock Harbor, where we could troll in the channel on each side of the island, using light spinning gear. Here, the water was very clear and only about 30 feet deep. The result was that you could actually see the big Lake Trout, lying on the bottom. One might say that it was almost like "shooting fish in a barrel." We would troll around the island, then as we went over the trout, we could predict about when they would hit. Bam! Maybe even two people would have one on at the same time. I would stop the boat and we would reel them in. Here, the water was shallow enough that the fish were still plenty feisty as you brought them into the net. We went around and round, finely bringing in a couple of 24" fish for each person. Later, I brought Pat and a few other people for a second trip and she was able to get one or two really nice Lake Trout, as well. Unfortunately, there was only one day like this. The next day only a few fish were taken and subsequent trips we never had such good fishing again. One only has a few opportunities in life. It is great if you are there when it happens.

I saw another similar situation once when I was fishing with Pat's grandfather. He had a group of doctor friends who regularly went to Solomon's Island in Maryland, not far from Washington, DC and I was fortunate to be invited to go along once. We loaded up a bunch of food and drinks and took off early in the morning. They had arranged a charter boat that went out from the Patuxent River, a tributary of Chesapeake Bay. We fished all morning without much success, so we were happy to have some lunch and a beer. As the afternoon wore on, most people were dozing away in their deck chairs. Then the captain said, "I think we have something over there." So, I began looking in the direction he had indicated. Off on the horizon, we could see, several charter boats, perhaps as many as ten, moving in the same direction we were going. As we got closer, we could see a cloud of gulls also converging on the same area. The captain's mate began to help us rig our fishing tackle for something they called "blue fish". All the boats slowed down and began to weave in and out across a line of scud that separated river water from bay water, and we were instructed to get the lines in the water. Then commenced one of the most exciting fishing experiences I've ever had. No sooner were the lines in the water, then we had a fish on and were reeling it in. Boats were weaving in and out, with engines barely turning over, almost within touching distance. Everybody was laughing and carrying on, as they pulled in fish, all to the sound of sea gulls calling as they swooped in to see what they could get. This melee went on for maybe fifteen minutes and then suddenly it stopped. The fish were gone and soon the boats slowly drifted away and began looking for other opportunities. The gulls also began slowly flying off in all directions. And we were left with the golden sun slowly sinking in the sky, but I had experienced another once in a lifetime experience.

One time before we got married, Pat's grandfather came down to Florida while we were visiting at Neptune Beach and he suggested that we go out on one of the public fishing boats that left from the mouth of the St John's River. So, we met him at the dock with our bag of lunch and boarded the boat. He set himself up in a comfortable place close to the stern, but the young lovers took their tackle and the bucket of squid we were using for bait and headed for the bow. I guess the best fishing was about 20 miles out, near the Golf Stream. When we finally got on site, we began baiting our hooks and fishing along with the rest of the people. It didn't take long, and we noticed that there was a slight swell that caused the bow of the boat to rise up and down and when this was combined with bending over to pick up the slimy squid from the bucket, it had an untoward effect on both the head and the stomach! At that point I told Pat that I had to get the heck out of there, or I was going to be sick. I guess she wasn't feeling too well either, so we grabbed our stuff and made for the stern of the boat. When we got back to where her granddad was sitting, we found him smoking a cigar and drinking a beer, just enjoying himself. I don't remember fishing at all on that trip, just the great feeling of getting away from the bow of that boat.

My friend Bob Papworth owned a farm that had a trout stream running along one edge called the Pilgrim River. Bob had been brought up in an area of Lower Michigan that had lots of hunting and fishing, so that he had many outings with his father to teach him the lore of the woods. Hence, when he found out that I had none of these opportunities while growing up, I think he decided that perhaps he should be my mentor, at least in the fly-fishing area. I guess the first time he took me out, he loaned me some of his homemade flies and a fly-casting pole and we went out on to the stream that ran by his farm. After a few tries, I had the hang of it, although this was not a very wide stream and one had to be very careful not to get the line hung up in the overhanging trees. Despite the inconvenience of constantly having to untangle the line from the trees and frequently replacing the hook on the line, I began to get the fly-fishing bug. The main attraction is that one can see the fish rising for little bugs on the surface of the stream, so you know just where you should put the fly. Typically, this is done by facing up-stream, so that you try to cast the leader with the fly at the end and allow it to drift down just over the place where the fish had just broached to take a fly. The problem is that when you see the fish rising, your excitement builds, as you cast the fly back and forth letting out line from the pole. Unfortunately, about the time you are ready to make your final cast, the line often gets caught in a tree and what's left goes flapping on the surface of the water, scaring the fish. To say the least, it is a rather challenging sport.

From the above, you might wonder if I actually managed to catch anything during my initial outings with Bob. I think that I must have, but nothing of any great consequence. My instructor had explained that if I got a bite, I should give the line a good yank to set the hook and then pull in the line through the fingers of the hand that was holding the rod, while keeping the line taught and the end of the rod raised. In most of my early catches, when I gave the line a yank on feeling the bite, the fish was so small that it came flying back, straight into my face, or over my shoulder. I was usually on my own, as Bob was off somewhere fishing either up-stream or down-stream, so there was little on-the-spot instruction. However, I slowly learned on my own, I suppose pretty much as he had. The best time for fishing as you may know is just after dusk, so we continued until it was almost dark. Then one of my most memorable experiences took place. I was casting back and forth, letting out line trying to reach a spot that was now barely visible because of the darkness. When, all of a sudden, my line took off in all directions, in a totally unexpected fashion. It was not a tree and it was not a fish, because it was somewhere up in the air. Suddenly, I realized that my fly had been caught by a bat and he was trying to make off with it. I sure didn't want to deal with a bat in what was now almost pitch darkness, so I waited for it to get in a tree then yanked the line free from the hook. I decided that was definitely enough for my first lesson, so I climbed out of the stream and set about finding Bob. I think that he was not too far away, probably watching my struggles while he enjoyed a cigar. This was not to be the only time that my greenhorn travails were to provide amusement for my mentor.

Another time in the afternoon, we went off to find the beaver ponds out west of Houghton. He brought some beer and a cigar for himself and we drove off on the old logging trails for almost a half-hour. When we got out, he described the lay of the land and explained that I should go around the other side of this rather large pond and we would meet at the beaver dam at the far end. So, I took off with my wading boots on, carrying my fly rod and a box of flies. The day was warm, and so it didn't take long to get quite hot and sweaty, because of the boots. When I got near the dam, I realized that there was deep grass extending right up to the water's edge, with no apparent trail to follow. So, as I waded through the grass, I fell into a deep ditch, which was made worse because of the stuff in my hands. Of course, the ditch had water in the bottom, so it took me several minutes of work to climb out. No sooner did I get out of the first ditch and I had fallen into another. I learned later that beavers make canals back and forth between their dam and the source of their food and structural material, usually aspen. So, I spent over an hour floundering around trying to get to the head of the dam, where I was to meet Bob. When this was finally accomplished, there he was drinking a bottle of beer, sitting with his line in the water. He had apparently followed a trail from the car right up to the dam. Since he had not had very much luck, he concluded that somebody had already fished out the pond and we might as well head home.

One evening about a year later, Bob asked me if I wanted to go fly-fishing on the North Branch of the Otter River. This was a little bit larger stream than the Pilgrim, so I was anxious to give it a try. When we got down there, he described what he would like to do. He was going to drive in on the farm road that intersected the river. Here, he would let me off to fish up-stream, then he would go back to the main road and would drive one mile up-stream to the next farm road, where he would fish down-stream. Presumably, we would meet somewhere in the middle. This sounded like a good idea to me, forgetting that one-mile as the crow flies, can be many miles on a river, given all the meanders it can make. So, I got out with my stuff and did some fishing right near the bridge where there was a nice big whirlpool. After a half, an hour or so, I decided that I better start working my way up stream. When I got above the bridge, the stream began to narrow, and it was much more difficult to fish. Pretty soon, what with tying on flies, untangling my line, etc., the time began to slip by. When I made the next turn in the river, I found that Tag Alder was growing almost to the center of the stream. Tag Alder is a miserable bush that grows about 10 ft. high and is very difficult to get through. So, I began a struggle just to move upriver. I began looking for a path on one side of the river or the other. What there was, was not much, so with gathering darkness, the remainder of the journey was a total struggle. After almost two hours slogging through swamps and Tag Alder patches, not unlike that encountered in the movie *African Queen*, I finally came out into an opening in pitch darkness. And there, visible only as a silhouette against the sky, was Bob's car and on further squinting, the red glow of Bob's cigar. Yes, there he was enjoying the beautiful evening sitting on the side of the river with a bottle of beer. I was wringing wet from perspiration, still carrying my fly rod and what was left of my flies. The time must have been well past eleven and I was ready to go home.

Fly-fishing is more of a solitary sport, so, much of my fishing was done largely on my own. Thus, I looked around for a nice trout stream and came across one way back in the woods west of Atlantic Mine. It required driving on a dirt road, which was only barely passable most of the time. Several miles back in, it opened into a clearing called Obenhof, that had once been a logging camp. Quite near there, was a railroad trestle on the line that connected Houghton to the Red Ridge Mill on the shore of Lake Superior. Under the trestle, ran the Salmon Trout River, which drained into the pond at Red Ridge

Dam, the provider of water for the stamp mill. I could park my car at the edge of the gorge and climb down to the river. I fished at this site many times and may have even caught a few keeper fish there. I remember one time; I became so involved that I fished until it was almost dark. I think that I may not have noticed until I heard something crashing through the woods behind me. "Wow" I said, "I think I better get out of here". All I could think of was that this was black bear country and some of them could get fairly big. So, I went splashing back down the stream, and up the bank next to the trestle to the car. I threw down the fly rod on the roof of the car, so that I could take off my waders and chuck them in the back. Then, I searched around for my keys and quickly drove off. I think that it must have been a mile or so down the road that I remembered the fly rod. Obviously, it wasn't still going to be on the roof. I considered my chances of finding it and just kept on going, deciding that I deserved what happened as punishment for losing my cool. Never again have I put stuff on the roof of my car.

Most of this time, I was tying my own flies. The reason for this is obvious to anyone who has purchased such things in a store. When you combine the price of a purchased fly, with the number that are lost in trees or on rocks, the sport would be just too expensive for a young college professor. So, early on, I bought an inexpensive fly-tying kit. This contained a cheap fly-tying vise and enough bird feathers, thread, etc. to last me for most of my career. Later on, Pat

205

gave me a professional style fly-tying vise, as my cheap one was barely satisfactory. For the most part, I was tying floating flies, as they are easier to fish with, since they are on the surface where you can see them. The basis for these is that they have lots of hairy stuff sticking out, making them ride on the surface tension of the water. Real professionals try to make their flies "match the hatch", that is, to make each fly look like one of the real insects that would be hatching out on the surface of the stream during certain times of the year. The most famous of these is probably the May Fly that hatches from a larva that spends most of its life growing on the surface of the rocks in the stream. However, my flies were what you might call "generic flies". They would be tied as follows: place a hook about ¾ in long in the vice with the bottom sticking out to the left. Then, take a piece of gray feather and lay it along the hook so that about ¼ in would be sticking out to the left. Next, wrap it on with thread, building up the body as you go, then wind on a feather from the hackle of a chicken, so that the barbs stick out at 90 degrees all the way around; finally tie this off to form a head. Of course, there is much more to it that one learns with practice, but this should give you the general idea. Fortunately, Bob Papworth had given me an illustrated fly-tying book with step-by-step instructions and numerous examples of typical flies, used on all the great fly-fishing streams around the country (none of which I used). The fly was then dipped into a paraffin solution to give it a hydrophobic surface that would keep it from sinking. Then repeat this several times over, as you need plenty of flies for one reason or another. One of these I will discuss next.

When you are on the stream, sooner or later you are going to catch a fish and no matter how big or little the critter is, the fly goes into the fish's mouth. At that point, it comes in contact with the most hydrophilic saliva that one can imagine and comes back to you like it has been dropped into a bottle of detergent. At that point, you try to clean it off by sloshing it around in the stream 'til most of the saliva is washed off, then try to re-coat it with paraffin to make it float again, but no matter how you try, it's probably done for the day. So, being a chemist, I began looking for something to make flies from that would retain its hydrophobic nature. This was all going on when I was at the peak of my obsession, due in large part to a geology graduate student who was working with me for the summer (probably about 1958). He was a real fly fisherman, who spent most of his evenings on a stream somewhere and had great stories to tell. So, while he was doing his masters research under my direction, I was spending way too much time testing all kinds of synthetic fibers to try to find something that could survive fish saliva. To make a long story short, I was unable to find anything that had both the shape and hydrophobic nature to use for making flies. But I had a lot of fun talking about fly-fishing and testing the various products that I put together. I finally decided that the best fly was made by the old tried and true method with perhaps various kinds of solutions to take to the stream for washing off the masticated fly.

The one time that I actually did make a fly that matched the hatch was when I tried to mimic the flying wood ant. The wood ant is a black ant that at a certain time of the year goes off on its mating flight. During this time, thousands of ants fly off to find a mate. When they land about the first thing they do is to shed their large wings. Since these are big fat shiny black ants, I thought that the trout ought to like them. So, I made up some flies using electrician's tape and a nice black hackle to provide the legs. These were sort of semi-dry flies. About that time, the wood ants had just started their mating flight, I took some of my specimens off to the stream to test them out. Low and behold, they turned out to be very effective, as I caught two or three keeper fish. So, I decided I should make several more the next day and come back to the stream again. However, the next day my "ant" fly was not nearly as effective, apparently the hatch was off, or the fish had gotten tired of eating ants. My early success was never quite the same again and so I guess it was just a good memory like many other fish stories.

My fly-fishing adventures came to an end shortly after I joined the Biological Sciences department. It occurred after we instituted a fisheries biology course and purchased a fish shocker to teach the students how to make stream surveys. So, although it was not my responsibility, I went out one afternoon when they were going to carry out a fish population survey on the upper portion of the Pilgrim River. In this process, you go out and shock as many fish as you can in about 100 yd. of stream, capture the fish with a large net and clip their fins so that they can be recognized, then carefully put the fish back into the stream. A couple of days later, you come out again and shock the same stretch of stream. This time you count the total number captured and the number of those fish that have clipped fins. Finally, you put the fish back and calculate the total number of fish in the 100 yd.-stretch. I forget what the total was, but it was several thousand. Of course, most of these were small, but there were some nice trout, rainbow, brown and brook, some around one-foot long. At any rate, I said to myself "I'm going back there and get some of those fish". So, a few nights later I was back with my fly-fishing rod and some of my trusty flies. To make a long story short, I was only able to catch a few little six-inch fish, if that. And, I finally had to accept the fact that my failure at fishing was not because there weren't any fish there, but simply because I wasn't a good fisherman. But I told you that right at the beginning of this chapter didn't I, so I guess it shouldn't be much of a surprise.

Our summers spent in Chassell were full of fishing. We had what might be considered the ideal place to *watch* people fish, since we bought a summer home right on Chassell Bay, about seven miles south of our old home in Houghton. Consequently, we had people almost constantly trolling back and forth in what might be termed our back yard, usually only about 30 yards offshore. Since our window on the lake side was about ten feet wide and full height, we could sit in our living room, in complete comfort while people in small outboards would putt-putt back and forth from sunrise to sunset. When they got a bite, we could enjoy it almost as much as they did, meanwhile continuing with our other activities. We tried fishing one year, purchasing a license for about $60 and buying a small plastic boat with electric motor for about $1100. But it was a little tipsy for the two of us, so we didn't get out very much and I think that we didn't get any more fish than we did from our living room. One year I dreamed about getting another boat like the *Pat-Sea,* which we could pull into the mouth of our little stream, but I later lost interest when I thought of all the work involved, so we continued with our fish watching.

Sometimes something really exciting happens. One year, we had the Professional Walleye Tournament taking place right out front. This means that about 50 Walleye Pros from all around the Central US came to Houghton to fish in the Keweenaw Waterway, which includes Chassell Bay, Torch Lake, Houghton Canal, and adjacent waters. Because of the facilities provided, they usually put their $50K-$80K rigs into the water at the Chassell Marina, which was within walking distance from our house. So, it is great fun to see them head out in the morning and return in the afternoon. It is also fun to

210

see them go screaming by the house with their 150hp engines spraying water out behind as they try to beat someone else to the best fishing holes. The last time they came, they weighed their fish at the park, which was less than a block away. So, during the summers we spent in our home in Chassell, we still enjoyed fishing. It's just that we were not actively doing it anymore. It was sort of like a parade. It was fun to be in one, but you can also have fun watching.

Some years later I realized that fishing is just another application of the word perusing! Because, if you are a fisherman that consistently catches fish, you are not really sure exactly what kind of fish you're going to get. The people who fish out of Chassell Bay have the possibility of catching a Sturgeon that is up to six feet long and needs to be thrown back, or smaller fish such as panfish which may be too small to keep, or medium size northern pike or walleye that they may want to take home for dinner. It's the luck of the draw and the major source of the excitement of fishing.

This analogy between fishing and research is part of the reason for including this chapter and hopefully is useful in understanding the meaning of the word perusing. The fishermen of Chassell Bay are perusing the waterway to discover what fish species it might contain. My life might be viewed as one long fishing expedition in which I was perusing science to find the interesting and exciting areas for further study.

CHAPTER 12

ADVENTURES OF THE *PAT-SEA*

(1966-1984)

I had always liked boats. As I have previously explained, I made a little sailboat in our basement back when I was in junior high school. So, it was to be expected as soon as we had a few dollars that could be spent on such things that we would get a boat. Since sail boats were not very practical for a family with three little tykes, we were looking for a power boat. We lived in an ideal spot for boating. Houghton is located on the Keweenaw Waterway which spans the Keweenaw Peninsula, located in roughly the middle of Lake Superior, the largest freshwater lake in the world. The waterway consists of Portage Lake, a hundred square mile body of water with extensions north and south that are connected by short canals to Lake Superior. There were several marinas, as this area is ideal for docking of pleasure boats sailing on the big lake, especially those in transit from Sault Ste Marie on the east and Duluth on the west.

So, Pat and I, began to look around for a power boat costing about a thousand dollars. Of course, shopping for a boat is like shopping for a car - once you get the itch, it is hard to stop until that itch has been scratched. Well, I don't remember how many boats we looked at, but if it is anything like cars, probably not many! What I do remember is that we went to the garage of John Smith in Hancock and there she was! Love at first sight. A beautiful tri-hull built by the Evinrude Corporation. It had a red stripe down the side, four red and white seats, a 91 HP outboard engine, rugged wind screen, flat deck - ideal for children, all mounted on a rugged red trailer, and called the Evinrude Sweet 16, for only about $2000. Well, this was about twice what we had planned to pay, but it came with a boathouse down on the lake, that we could rent for at least a year. I guess we went off saying "Let us think it over". But I think that Pat was as taken as I, so it wasn't long before we were back again to take a second look. We found out what a canvas top would cost, then started writing out a check.

Well, it did turn out to be a beautiful boat. So beautiful in fact that Evinrude was only able to make that model for a year or two, until all the other boat builders forced them to stop building it "or they wouldn't buy Evinrude Outboards anymore!" It turned out to be very convenient to have it sitting in the boathouse ready to go, anytime that we got the urge. Unfortunately, we were able to keep the boathouse deal for only a couple of years, but we enjoyed it while we had it. During that time, we toured all around the Keweenaw. This includes about 10 miles on either side of our Hancock boathouse, with additional extensions into Torch Lake and Chassell Bay. Initially, the engine would get us up to about 30 mph, during which we were really skimming across the surface of the water. It took about six gallons of gas to go to Lake Superior and back. The name *Pat-Sea*, of course, was primarily for the mother of the family, but also for the slapping sound it made as we skipped across the water. This was a spontaneous decision we never regretted. Another example of being lucky by choice, the boat was used for family fun, fishing at Isle Royal, later for research and camping along Lake Superior.

Reading the above paragraph would lead you to believe that it wouldn't take long to see the whole waterway and then things would start to get a little boring. But that is not the nature of boats, at least boats in the hands of a novice like I was, so that it was almost a given that something rather exciting was going to happen on almost every trip. Probably one of the first outings of this type resulted from my having become overconfident about bringing the boat into the boathouse. I thought that with a boat this powerful, one should be able to stop it on a dime, so to speak, by throwing it into reverse, and gunning the engine. Of course, this was most fun when bringing it into the boathouse. So, instead of bringing it in at about two mph and gradually slowing to a stop, I would head it into the slot at about 5-7 mph, throw it into reverse and stop right at the end of the slot. Well this worked fine for a couple of times, until once the engine died on my reverse maneuver and we were left with a 2000 lb. boat coasting into the slot at about 5 mph! Pat and I and the kids were left grabbing for pilings as they went rushing by. Well, it just barely stopped before slamming into the dock. So, except for some scraped arms and diminished confidence by the captain (and the crew), everyone was OK.

During that period, there was a great lakes cruise ship called the *South American* that docked at Houghton several times during the summer. We had often enjoyed taking the kids down to see it dock. Usually the high school band would come out to play and spread a big blanket to collect money that was thrown from the deck of the ship. Also, an Indian from Baraga would come up with his feather bonnet and have his wife sell trinkets to one and all. The weird people from the ship would come off to wander around town and look at the weird people in town. It was one of our summer treats. After we got the boat, we joined with several other small craft to go out to "Big Portage", the wide spot in the waterway, to welcome the ship and wave at the passengers. One of the treats this provided was to run the boat over the bow wave. Usually this resulted in rather mild excitement. However, on one occasion, I had mistakenly maneuvered our boat into the angle formed by the bow waves when the ship made a 90-degree turn at the top of Portage Lake. At that point, the two bow waves, one coming from one direction and one from the other, combined by constructive interference to make a humungous wave, about eight feet high. Well, there was nothing I could do, but to go straight into it. Fortunately, our top was up, and our little boat went straight through while the wave crashed down across the top. Unfortunately, our son, Will had his head hanging out the side window and took it full in the face. Other than getting soaking wet, there was no harm. We sat there stunned for several minutes watching the South American move on down the lake, trying to figure out the physics of what had happened to cause such a huge wave.

This was still during the time when instructors wore suits and ties and even taught class on Saturday. So, one Saturday morning in 1965, I was down at my office working in my charcoal gray woolen suit, when Pat called and said: "Clancy Kalmer has gotten to the north end of the canal and is about to complete the swim." Clancy was a Tech alumnus who had made several attempts to swim the entire 20-mile length of the Keweenaw Waterway on previous summers. This was particularly difficult since the cold water of Lake Superior tended to pour into the north entry during most of the summer months. Anyway, this was quite an occurrence, so it would be great to see. She said, "I'll pick you up as we drive by Tech". Of course, it would be even better to witness this occasion from our boat. So, without changing clothes or anything, I hopped into the boat and we went roaring off to the upper entry. We arrived just as he was swimming across the area between the two arms of the breakwater. But, as we approached, someone with a loudspeaker said: "All you boats get back. We don't want him to get any exhaust fumes." So, we headed off toward the beach on the west side of the sea wall, not realizing that the wind was blowing strongly in that direction. Before I knew it, we were in the breakers coming in on the beach. Well, since I had cut the engine, there didn't seem to be anything to do but jump into the water to hold the boat off the beach. Since our son, Will, assumed this was a command to abandon ship, he jumped in as well. So, there I was in my gray suit and jacket, holding the boat off and trying to hang on to Will. Eventually, we got Will back into the boat, then with the help of volunteers from the beach, Pat got the boat started and into neutral, while I climbed aboard. Finally, we got out into the open water and headed back to Hancock with our tail between our legs and some very wet clothes to show for the experience. The evening paper reported that Clancy did complete the swim, and fortunately no pictures showed our boat floundering around in the waves nearby. Years later Clancy was visiting the Bluffs where we were living, and he had a good laugh from this story.

One of our favorite trips was out the south entry of the waterway into Keweenaw Bay of Lake Superior. Here the water was gin-clear, so that you could see the bottom 30 or more feet below. Sometimes we would take a picnic to the beach north of the sea wall. Sometimes we would go a few miles further north to the sandstone cliffs, which were cupped in spots that caused a wonderful echo when you yelled or blew the boat horn. Once we took my mother up there for a picnic and thought that we would wade in the lake a bit before lunch. We only got a foot or two offshore when we were attacked by the aching cold of the water. We quickly decided that this wasn't fun at all... So, we found a nice sunny spot to dry off and have our lunch. Then, just before we got back into the boat to leave, we decided to try wading again, since I had noticed that the wind had switched from offshore to onshore. It was amazing the difference a few minutes had made, as the temperature of the lake water had gone up 30 degrees or more. So, we stayed around for a while to pick up the flat sandstone skipping rocks that abound in that area, some of which have perfectly round white polka dots with a red background. From an historic standpoint this is the source of Jacobsville Sandstone that was used for much building construction around the Midwest during the late 1900s.

Another area that I liked to go was the gull rookery in Torch Lake. I always got a thrill as the herring gulls would swoop and dive when trying to drive people away from their babies. This was never such a thrill for the female members of the crew since the diving was often accompanied by dive-bombing. But the boat was easy to clean off and it always made for a memorable trip.

When the kids began to grow up, we could do things that involved them in a more effective manner. Once when Will was in high school, we got together a crew of his friends with the goal of circumnavigating the Keweenaw Peninsula, or what is sometimes called "Copper Island". The entire trip is well over 100 miles and would take several fuel-stops to maintain our three 6-gallon tanks. The crew consisted of Will, Power Han, Steve French, and me. We put the boat in at the Hancock Marina and headed out the lower entry for the trip up the east side of the peninsula. With a few hollers and horn blows at the echo cliffs, we moved up the shore past the Gay Smokestack and after an hour or so, around the point into beautiful Bay de Gris. The first order of business was to go into the Lac La Belle marina to fill up on fuel. After that, the kids did some trolling for fish out in Bay de Gris and caught a nice salmon. We thought this would be great for dinner, so we ran a stringer through its mouth and hung it behind the boat. Everyone was ready to catch some more, but to no avail. After about a half hour of trolling I thought we had better move on up to Keystone Bay and find a campsite. So off we went and only later realized that the stringer had been yanked out of the fish's mouth and our dinner was long gone. We got to Keystone Bay in plenty of time, so we pulled the boat up on the beach and went exploring. Just around the end of the bay, we found a wonderful agate beach. Because the sun was shining from the west it made the agates glow in an amazing way, unlike any agate beach we had seen before. Since they were so easy to find, we collected a large bottle of them before quitting for dinner. We had a good night there eating our hot dogs and sleeping in the boat. I'm sure that the mosquitoes buzzed, and the bears growled, but I don't remember, so it must have been alright. The next morning, we had a brief breakfast and headed on towards Keweenaw Point. It was a beautiful trip as this is a totally uninhabited area once you get north of Bay de Gris. We pulled into Copper Harbor Marina at about 10:00 and filled the tanks again and arrived back at the Hancock Marina at about 3:00 pm, having experienced no further excitement, but having completely circumnavigated the Keweenaw Peninsula.

I think that it was later in the fall of that same year that we took a trip back to Keystone Bay, probably to look for more agates. As I remember, we were going along at a pretty good clip, when the engine

221

stopped, clunk, just like it had locked up or something. Wow! What had happened? Certainly, we had not run out of gas or anything like that. We tried the starter and it wouldn't even turn over. We got out the starter rope and tried to pull on that. It would not move. Apparently, the engine had seized up in some way. The only explanation was that one of the tanks had not gotten the lubricating oil that it needed, or that the oil had not been mixed properly with the gas. In any case, here we were several miles up in this uninhabited area, well after Labor Day when there were no boats to be seen. There was nothing to do but start paddling back. The nearest thing was Smith's Fishery probably a good mile or two down the shore. But paddling was all we had, so we took turns, me for a while, Will for a while, Pat for a while, etc. Finally, when we were almost to the Smith's Fishery dock, a small boat saw our predicament and came over to give us a tow. After what seemed like an hour, they were able to get us to the beach at the entry of Lac La Belle. However, that was as far as our helpers wanted to go, so we thanked them profusely and began to wonder, what now? The car and trailer were still several miles away at the Lac la Belle Marina. So, I caught a ride back to the marina and in fifteen minutes or so, had the trailer backed onto the Bay de Gris beach. With the help of people who were camping there, we put down boards and got the trailer in to where the boat could be hauled on to it. Again, with the help of many people, pushing, moving boards, etc., we were able to get our trailered-boat back on good solid asphalt. What a workout that afternoon turned out to be. We didn't know whether the engine could be fixed or not. So, some months later we took the boat to Jack Stevenson's Garage. Amazingly, there was no permanent damage and Jack was able to get it going again, although that had been the last trip for the year.

During that period, we were good friends with Hugh Beattie, the superintendent of Isle Royale National Park, an island park about 45 miles across Lake Superior, with headquarters in Houghton. On one occasion we were invited along with several other friends to come as a guest to stay in the superintendent's lodge on Mott Island, the location of houses and dormitories for park personnel. We were going to be carried to the island on the *Ranger III*, the 140' ship used for park visitors. We were also invited to bring our boat on board, all at no charge. So, we cleaned up the *Pat-Sea* and got her ready for the trip. The boat was hoisted on board the *Ranger III* with a large crane and tied into one of the cradles that they use for such boats. The trip takes about 5 hours to get to Mott Island, which is the first stop before letting the paying customers off at Rock Harbor. So, when we arrived, all the passengers were lining the rails watching the activity as our boat was lowered into the water and I moved aboard to take it away from the dock. I was busy getting the engine started when I noticed that the water was beginning to come up around my feet. What the heck? Then I realized that we had forgotten to put the petcock back into the drain hole after we washed the boat! Well, the water was so clear that it was sloshing around pretty good by the time I got the boat going and up to the planing speed, so that the water could siphon out. After it was all gone, I quickly put back the petcock and went back to the dock to pick up Pat. For some reason, she had decided to walk with the other people to the lodge. All the other passengers had enjoyed a good laugh about my fine seamanship.

We made a couple of trips to stay with the Beatties, then, after he was transferred, we made several trips to Isle Royale with the kids. Once, we stayed in the Rock Harbor area in a cabin and another year we stayed in the Adirondack shelters, which has a roof and back with screens on the other three sides. On our final trip the wind began to blow really hard towards the end, so we stayed in the campground close to the dock where the *Ranger* came in. At this same campground we met a family of three, a father, son, and grandson, who had come all the way from Ontonagon in a boat smaller than ours. They had been waiting several days to start back because of the wind. The wind whistling through the screens was so loud that it was hard to sleep. All night I had to keep getting up to check the boat to make sure that it was still moored properly. So, the following night we spent in the hotel. When we returned on the *Ranger*, the little boat with the three from Ontonagon followed closely in the relatively calm water behind the big ship. I think that was our last trip to Isle Royale.

Our good luck fishing at Isle Royale made us think that there ought to be some place around the Keweenaw where we could get that kind of lake trout fishing, at least some time of the year. Standard fishing for lake trout is to drag a line at over 100 feet deep and then when you snag one, haul it up from the bottom. When it gets to the surface it has little or no life left in it to make it fun. So, we tried trolling in Eagle Harbor, in Copper Harbor, in the North Entry, in the South Entry. Every now and then we might catch a fish of some sort, but nothing really interesting. Pat was the most eager fisherman, but I didn't have much patience for it. If it wasn't there after a few passes, I was ready to move on to somewhere else. Trying to use our 91 hp engine for trolling was not the best thing either. At the slow speeds it would often choke to a stop. We could have saved ourselves so much grief and a lot of paddling, if we had just gone into the store and bought an electric trolling motor. Eventually we did just that and kicked ourselves for not doing it many years earlier.

When our daughter Lisa got a little older, Pat and I took her and her friend Martie on a camping trip to Keystone Bay, near the tip of the peninsula. Since my last trip to that site, I had obtained about 200 ft. of polyethylene line with which to secure the boat on the beach. So, when we arrived at Keystone Bay, we selected a nice stretch of shore and I headed the boat in for mooring. After running the boat well up onto the beach, I attached the line to each side of the stern and then stretched the other end of the line well down the beach in either direction to tie to trees. After the boat was firmly attached, we removed the seats onto the beach to put around the campfire. The girls had decided to put their tent up the beach a ways, while we were going to sleep on a mattress that we had brought in the bow of the boat, with the top and sides all closed up to keep out the bugs. While we were eating our dinner, we noted some clouds and lightning far off to the south and a slight breeze beginning to blow from that direction. When it got dark, the girls headed to their tent and we got in the boat and buttoned up the windows for the night. After about an hour of slapping mosquitoes, I think that I might have gotten a little sleep, when I noticed that the waves were pounding harder and harder against the stern. Then, I noticed that after each wave, there was a dripping of water from somewhere. So, I got up, with the flashlight and found that water was filling the engine well and pouring into the boat through the holes for the control cables. So, I got up and jammed some boat bumpers into the cable holes. After this, I crawled back into bed and lay there listening to the surf crash into the stern of the boat. I could feel the boat inch up further onto the beach with each crashing wave. Then, even though my lines were designed to keep the boat on the beach that was no longer the problem. Now I began to wonder if I would be able to get the 2000 lbs. of boat off the beach in the morning. After worrying about this for almost an hour, I suddenly realized I needed to begin working on shoveling out a channel to release the boat from the clutches of the sand. So, up I got and began gathering my tools for the project. There was sufficient light from the moon and the gathering storm to the south. So, I lined up the three gas cans to direct the waves and began shoveling to assist

226

in the development of a channel under the side of the boat. After an hour or so, it became obvious that my plan was going to work, and the *Pat-Sea* began to work free. By this time the sun was beginning to lighten the sky in the east, but the storm was drawing ever nearer, so I got Pat up to work on breakfast, while I went to raise the girls and untie the lines. As soon as we had something to eat, it became obvious that we needed to get the heck out of there, so I began throwing stuff into the boat in a helter-skelter fashion. I got Pat into the driver's seat and held the boat offshore, while the girls climbed in. Then I pushed it out in the bounding waves, while Pat got the engine started. Finally, I climbed over the side and flopped into one of the loose seats. She gunned the engine and we headed out into the gathering waves, when all of a sudden, the engine sputtered a few times and quit! Oh no, here we were again miles from the nearest habitation, dock or boat and the engine had quit. What were we going to do? Then, I noticed that in my rush to load the boat and get aboard that the gas line from the tank to the engine went right under my chair. After I moved the line and pumped the gas a bit to get the engine supplied it started up with no problem. We headed back to the marina in darkening skies and got the boat back on the trailer. We were only about a mile down the road when the storm hit with all its force, so bad that we had to pull off the road until it had passed. We were so lucky that we had not waited any longer until managing to get off the beach! A memorable boat trip to be sure.

On the north side of the peninsula, we enjoyed several camping trips to the East Sleeping River. This was about 20 miles down the shore of Lake Superior in a westerly direction from the North Entry of the waterway. We had discovered this site with our friends, Bob and Jan Papworth. At that point, the river ran into the lake and formed a spit of land on the lakeside. It provided a safe site for the boat since it was possible to get the boat over the shallows into a large lagoon that had formed behind the spit. We would build our campsite on an older part of the spit. This was up on a hill in an area with lots of blueberries, so we could make blueberry biscuits, pancakes, etc. Unfortunately, Bob and I were never able to catch any fish in the lagoon, despite the fact that he was an experienced fisherman. But we always brought steaks to barbecue and it was a great campsite, where we went several times.

Our final trip to the campsite on the East Sleeping River we made alone since Bob Papworth had died. However, it was such a beautiful place; we had to visit it one more time. We trailered the boat to the little marina near the upper entry of the waterway, went out the breakwaters and headed west along the shore. There was quite a bit of wave action, so it took the better part of two cans of gas to get to our destination. When we got into the lagoon of the East Sleeping River, we unloaded our stuff and were just beginning to relax when we heard two motorcycles approaching along the shore. When they saw us up on the bluff, they circled around a couple of times and began talking. I thought, this has never happened before, suppose these guys get rough. But they got back on their cycles, drove across the beach and then right up the hill through our campground, without saying a word. Actually, it was the only way to go as we had built our camp in the middle of the trail. After we recovered from this minor scare, we looked out to sea and saw about four fishing boats that were coming directly to our campsite. Oh No! Were we going to have a bunch of guys camping here too? They continued coming until a couple of hundred yards offshore when they apparently saw us and circled back to 14-mile point. We had no more excitement and slept fine that night. The following day, we took the boat over to Ontonagon to fill up with gas, fighting waves all the way, as there was a strong wind out of the west. We got back about lunchtime, ate and I went swimming. Pat was concerned that we should get going because of the wind. I finally agreed, so we headed on back toward the Entry. No sooner did we get out from behind 14-mile point, where the campsite was located, and the wind really began to blow, with waves at least 6 ft. high. We were moving right along, but I wanted to go even faster. Suddenly, the boat went down the front of a wave and smack into the next wave, with clear blue water going right over the windscreen. This is one scary thing, as all of a sudden you find most of your belongings floating around in about six inches of water. What I should have done at that point was to put up the top, but I didn't think of it. All I really did was to try to drive slower, so that we would stay on the backside of the waves. But as hard as I would try, my body wanted to get off the lake and so the speed would edge up, little by little and BAM, it happened again, clear blue water coming over the windscreen right into our laps. That was enough to make a believer out of me, so for the rest of the trip, I really kept the throttle back. Finally, we made it into the Entry and back to the trailer. Well, you would think that this would be enough problems for one trip, but it wasn't! As we pulled the trailer out of the water, I noticed that it had a funny feeling and all the way through Hancock and Houghton, it seemed strange, but I was so anxious to get home, that I didn't stop to look at it and Pat wasn't any more interested than I. So, on we went. At the bottom of our hill, I asked if the insurance was paid up and she said yes, so up the hill we went. We turned the corner at the top of the hill and finally came to a stop in front of our house, at which point, KLUMP, the trailer hitch crashed into the street behind the car. The bumper to which the hitch was attached was still intact, but the hitch had been stripped entirely away from the bumper. Apparently, we had driven all the way through Hancock, Houghton, and up the hill, held only by the last sliver of metal that attached the hitch to the bumper. Fred Lonsdorf helped us push the trailer into the garage and there it sat until the next year. In retrospect we were very lucky, however there were several places where I should have taken more responsibility, as captain.

Unfortunately, the kids had grown up and moved away and so did we, thinking that we might never come again. Consequently, the last year or so, we hardly used the boat at all and finally as we were getting ready to sell the house, we put the *Pat-Sea* up for sale. We had hoped to get $1200 for it, but only had a few people respond to our ad and finally decided to sell it for $800 to a young family with a couple of small children. However, as we drive around the Copper Country during our summer vacations, we see it, or one like it, every now and then and think, "Boy, I would give $2000 for that boat in a minute".

Other adventures of the *Pat-Sea* will be described in the chapter on Limnology and Oceanography, where it served as one of research vessels for the MTU Lake Superior Research effort.

CHAPTER 13

DEPARTMENT HEAD

(1962-1968)

For a few years prior to 1962, at least two faculty members had been agitating for a separate Department of Biology at Michigan Tech. The two leaders of this activity were Robert Brown, who had been teaching botany courses in the Forestry Department for almost ten years and Ira Horton, who was responsible for the Medical Technology program, teaching microbiology and comparative anatomy courses in the Chemistry Department for about five years. As with many such proposals, the main deterrent was lack of funds and limited interest by administrators. In 1961, the Forestry Department accreditation was jeopardized by the lack of an "independent biology department". This caused an immediate change in the attitude of both the Forestry Department, led by U.J. Noblet and Gene Hesterburg and the University Administration, which was led at that time of Dr. J. R. Van Pelt, President and Dr. Frank Kerekes, Dean of Faculty. It was decided to form a committee to study the feasibility of setting up such a department. This committee consisted of Robert

Brown and Gene Hesterburg, representing Forestry and Ed Williams and Ira Horton, representing Chemistry. Since there was concern that there might be some conflict between Brown and Horton, I was selected to chair the committee, as I was not expected to join the department, but did have some background in the biological sciences. The committee met a number of times and quickly concluded that we should move ahead as rapidly as possible, as it was clear that the Forestry Department could no longer have responsibility for teaching basic biology courses. Then, it was determined that because of the university mission statement, the goal of the department should be to stress more technological aspects of biology, particularly biophysics and biochemistry, which were just becoming recognized as key elements to the future of biology.

To emphasize this distinction, the new unit was to be designated the Department of Biological Sciences (rather than the Department of Biology). The next order of business was to determine just who would make up the faculty of the new department. It was already clear that Bob Brown, Ira Horton and Ken Kraft, a zoologist teaching in Forestry, would join. The focus of the new department made it clear that I would also join, since I was the only biochemist on campus. The final member selected was Bob Janke, of the Physics Department, who wished to transfer to the department and take a leave of absence to obtain a PhD in biology at U. Colorado. Thus, we had five positions with which to start the department. There was some

234

contention arising from Forestry, as they wanted the new department to operate under their control. However, this subsided when it was pointed out that to meet the accreditation requirements, the new department needed to be totally independent. I subsequently wrote up the committee's recommendations, submitted them for the committee's approval and then submitted them to the Dean of Faculty and the President. These were accepted by the administration and recommendations were submitted to the Board of Control, for their approval, which was obtained at the next regular board meeting.

Apparently, I had done a reasonably good job as chairman of the committee, as I was subsequently appointed Head of the Department of Biological Sciences. Actually, there was more to this decision than indicated here, as I was the only one of the five individuals actively engaged in funded research at the time. MTU history shows this to be a key factor in most administrative appointments. It also did not hurt that I was reasonably well known and liked by both Kerekes and Van Pelt, having visited both of them in their homes and knew them from the church and the Miscowaubik Club. I think also that Ed Williams had recommended me, which meant a lot to both Van Pelt and Kerekes. But, most importantly, I was in the right place, with the right background, at the right time. That's a combination that is almost unbeatable.

Head of the Department of Biological Sciences

As soon as we had approval, the four-department faculty members began working on the curriculum for the BS Degree in Biological Sciences. We were also to be responsible for the BS Degree in Medical Technology, but this was to continue with no immediate change. For the biological sciences degree, we designed a strong program in physical sciences, with one year of general chemistry, two or three quarters of organic chemistry, one year of physics and one year of math through calculus. Amazingly, there was little contention within our faculty about this, as Bob Brown had a chemical engineering undergraduate degree, Ira Horton had worked several years under a curriculum that was strongly influenced by chemistry and Ken Kraft recognized the strength of our arguments. In biology, we planned to require one year in general biology, at least one additional year in either botany or zoology, followed by microbiology, genetics, and biochemistry. Other courses included such things as comparative anatomy, animal physiology, plant physiology, histology, entomology, and ornithology designed mainly to meet the requirements in botany or zoology. When we completed the curriculum design, we were all reasonably satisfied that it was very strong compared to those at other universities. In fact, years later I was amazed to see biology curricula from highly respected schools that were significantly weaker than the one we designed, particularly in the basic science and math area. However, it was obvious that we were going to have to scramble to cover all these classes, but electives could be taught on an alternate year basis and the number of students during the initial years was going to be small.

My personal teaching assignment was, of course, biochemistry, which the first year I continued much as I had been teaching it. I also took responsibility for animal physiology since I had taken the full medical school physiology course while at MCV. Since I had taken biochemical genetics at Stanford, and had the math background needed, I elected to teach genetics. Fortunately, Colorado State U was offering an NSF sponsored faculty institute in genetics, for which I was able to qualify. So, during the summer, I spent three weeks at CSU learning lab techniques and theory that helped me immensely. I also met some nice people and had an opportunity to do some real trout fishing in the Cache le Poudre River, a beautiful stream that ran down from the Rocky Mountains. When I got back home, I began ordering the supplies that we would need and developed a plan for recruitment of a replacement for Bob Janke, who had already left on his one-year leave of absence to begin studies at U. Colorado. It was decided that we needed someone else to teach in the general biology area, as well as more help in botany. Other important jobs during that summer were student recruitment, publicity, finalizing new course approval, etc. There are dozens of little things that a department normally does. Initially, I had no secretary and no assistant, so I was doing it all myself. It sounds like a lot of work, but it was all new to me and I was having a lot of fun planning it out and getting it done.

While I was involved with the problems of getting the Department of Biological Sciences started, Pat had become involved in some of the university's problems. During the course of constructing the new Math-Physics building, President Van Pelt had lost the home that he had been living in. A favorable presidential mansion was selected on the western end of the campus but needed refurbishing by an interior decorator. Pat was chosen to do the job of converting the old Quandt home into the president's mansion. Because of the political nature of this job it turned out to be rather controversial.

238

A year or so later she was hired by the University to make major interior design corrections of the Wadsworth Hall dining room. This was a fairly large job as it entailed updating the furniture and drapes and restructuring the salad bar to ease overcrowding in one of the largest dormitories in the country. The results of the changes were quite remarkable and were appreciated by the students and staff.

The problem of where we were to be located was, of course, a major one. However, Physics and Math were in the process of building a new building, so would shortly be moving out of Hubbell Hall, the original building constructed for Michigan Tech when it was called Michigan College of Mines. This was a substantial building made of Jacobsville Sandstone, so there was talk that we might be able to move there in a year or so. During the fall of 1962, we started with Bob Brown and Ken Kraft still having offices and classrooms in Hubbell School (the old Forestry Building) and Ira Horton and I still having offices in Koenig Hall (the old Chemistry Building). Sometime during the fall, Fred Erbisch, a PhD, botanist-lichenologist from the University of Michigan came to interview for a position. He was a very happy-go-lucky guy, who drove up from Ann Arbor and spent the night at our house. He parked his Volkswagen in front of our house on Ruby St. and the next morning it had somehow been moved up into our yard. It turned out that the students next door had done it as a prank. This didn't bother Fred and everybody in the department seemed to like him, so he was hired to fill Bob Janke's position.

I found that the biggest problem with animal physiology instruction was in putting together the lab. We had essentially no equipment and yet lab experiments are extremely important to this subject. So, I ordered some kymographs for recording data and a few other small items. Fortunately, we received as a gift, some old medical equipment from Dr. Levine, a retired doctor friend and neighbor of ours. This included one of the original EKG machines, as well as some apparatus used for studying basal metabolic rate. It was amazing how much mileage we got out of this equipment. Several years later, after we had obtained modern equipment for physiology, we donated these items to the Houghton County Historical Museum, where they are still on display. Although genetics also posed a problem in preparing for laboratory, it was not nearly as expensive. The major problem there was in learning to take care of fruit flies and getting the skill needed to successfully mate one specific genotype to another. The trick is to know when most the flies are going to hatch out and eliminate all the stray flies from the bottle, so that only virgin flies are available when the lab is to take place. This requires that one prepare your flies at about 6:00 am on the day lab is to take place. If you screw up, either your students don't have any flies to work with or they get flies that have already mated.

We stayed in the Ruby St. house until we heard that the little neighborhood store behind our house was going to be replaced by Jim's Supermarket. This was the signal to us that the neighborhood was about to be taken over by student housing and an increase of traffic. So, we began looking for a new place to live. It turned out that there was an almost new home available east of the college in an area called Royalwood. We liked what we saw there and moved our family in the spring of 1966. The house was a manufactured home built in Wausau, Wisconsin and installed on site over about a two-day period. It was a split-level, with living room, dining room, kitchen, and bathroom on one level and four bedrooms and bathroom on the upper level, over a recreation room, laundry and workshop that opened out into the double garage. The home was all electric and proved to be a quite comfortable, except that the ceiling was also the roof, so there was quite a large leakage of heat that caused ice to build up on the roof. Eventually, we got a double roof and did some work under the eaves that solved that problem. The kids and I had a lot of fun there as the woods began just on the other side of our back yard, so we went on many walks and could cross country ski right from the back yard.

New home in Royalwood addition 1966

During my first year as department head, we had weekly meetings in the third-floor conference room of the union building. This meeting was chaired by President Van Pelt and co-chaired by Frank Kerekes. Thus, it was a college-structure rather than a university-structure. All the real decisions were made by President Van Pelt. About a year after I became department head, Frank Kerekes died and was not replaced. About this time, Ed Williams was appointed Vice President of Development. His role was to deal with the State Legislature and to acquire funds from alumni, foundations, and industry. He would also meet with the Board of Control along with the President and Vice President of Finance. I think that Dr. Van Pelt's initial intention was to groom Ed to take over the presidency, as he was planning to retire within a year. However, when Dr. VanPelt retired, Dr. Raymond Smith was appointed the new president.

A couple of years after becoming department head, four departments of the university were approved for giving the PhD, one of which was Chemistry. After this became official, I had a visit from Jack Holland, who was manager of the clinical chemistry lab at St Mary's Hospital in Duluth. Jack had gotten his MS degree in chemistry from Michigan Tech in 1948 and was several years older than I. He was dropping by to see if he might work towards the Ph.D. in chemistry, by carrying out research under my direction. I told him that I had no immediate source of funding and I really wasn't in the Chemistry Department anymore. However, he was very interested in working towards the PhD and after some thought, I realized that he had all the experience needed to assume the responsibility for the Medical Technology program. I began to investigate the possibility, and it turned out that the Chemistry Department agreed to allow me to serve as Jack's advisor. I quickly got to work on putting a program together for research and funding...No small task! I suggested that Jack study the changes in bile acid concentration during the early stages of azo-dye carcinogenesis. Somehow, we obtained money to purchase a new gas chromatograph needed to detect low concentrations of bile acids and Jack was given the space to carry out the work in the Chemistry Department. We worked out a program of courses needed to bring him back up to speed in chemistry and meet the requirements for the Ph.D., which the Chemistry Department approved. Jack completed all the requirements for the Ph.D. in Chemistry in time to receive his degree at the 1968 commencement. This was a particularly proud time for both of us. About the same time, he was finishing up his work, Ira Horton retired from the department and Jack was appointed to fill his position. Shortly after that, he was made Director of the Medical Technology program. This turned out to be a wise decision, as he became an outstanding director of the program and in 1976 was selected by the students to receive the MTU Teacher of the Year Award. During the years that followed, he directed several research projects and led the growth and development of the Clinical Laboratory Science program at Michigan Tech.

After a year or so in our original locations, Physics and Math moved to their new building and we were able to move into Hubbell Hall. We did this with essentially no reconstruction, using the old Physics Department lab benches, etc. However, it wasn't that bad, as these labs came very close to fitting our needs and I inherited a nice office on the back corner of the building. At the time, I thought I would be happy to stay there for the remainder of my career. However, it was the plan of the administration that we would obtain funds to renovate the building and share it with the Liberal Arts Department. We worked for some time on plans for this reconstruction project, including laboratory equipment needed, etc. Then, one morning, when I just happened to be there at about 6:30, dumping fruit flies in preparation for the genetics lab later that day, when, here came President Ray Smith and Senator Gar Lane, Chairman of the Appropriations Committee for the State Legislature. Since I was handy, Ray asked me to show them around the department, which, of course, I did. After about 30 minutes they left and I collapsed back in my office, thinking what "brownie points" I had just made with the new President. Shortly, we heard that Gar Lane had decided to recommend that the legislature should not spend any more money repairing "Old Hubbell Hall". Instead, they should give Michigan Tech money to build a new Chemistry-Biological Sciences Building. So, from that point on, we trashed our old plans and began working on plans to move into a new building, where we would occupy about one and a third floors.

After we learned that the Tech Board had approved the PhD program for the first four departments in the University, we began talking about a graduate program for the Biological Sciences Department. We knew that we weren't ready for the PhD program yet, but we decided to at least move in that direction, by initiating the degree of Master of Science in Biological Sciences. So, we wrote up a proposal showing our strengths in the area of graduate research and course instruction (All faculty members and proposed faculty members had a PhD). Also included was the proposed plan for the program. This proposal was submitted to the president for presentation to the Board of Control, where it was approved in fall

245

1964. We then set about contacting all recent graduates of either biological sciences or medical technology, telling them about the approval of the program and the research topics available. We received response from about eight graduates and were able to start the program with six students during the fall of 1965.

While we were in Hubbell Hall, Michigan Tech acquired a new Director of Research in a rather fortuitous manner. Dr. Carl Moyer, well known nationally for his treatment of burns with silver nitrate solutions and Head of the Department of Surgery at Barnes Hospital in St. Louis, visited Pres. Ray Smith and said that he would like to move back to the Copper Country (He was from nearby Baraga.). After some discussion, Ray decided to make him the Director of Research, a position that had been vacant since Ray had held it before becoming president. He decided to put Dr. Moyer on the second floor of our building, as we had some interests in common. Initially this made me somewhat apprehensive, as I had previously heard him give a paper and knew him to be rather bombastic. After a few meetings, I found him to be a perfectly engaging person and I would drop by his office on occasion just to chat.

One night, following one of our meetings, I invited him home for dinner. As soon as he got there, he met the kids and with a few words, had them in the palm of his hand. He was a large man with white hair and a big square face. We always thought he must have

246

been part Indian, as Baraga is a center of Indian culture. As he walked around the house, he had something instructional to say about almost everything he saw. When he came to our large picture of a country road from someplace in Europe, he named the specific province in France where they have roads of that type. But the kicker was when Pat began to cook the lake trout in the oven. He said, "No, No, that's not the way you want to cook lake trout! Here, let me show you." Anyone else, she would have thrown out of the kitchen, but Moyer had a way about him that was different. So, he showed us how to wrap up each chunk of fish in aluminum foil and placed it into a frying pan. Then using his huge hands to check to see if it was ready to turn over, he cooked away. And, of course, it was delicious. It was a memorable time for us all. Dr. Moyer was moderately effective as a Research Director, helping a number of people get research going, particularly in our department. Unfortunately, he also became involved with the hospital, where he made some enemies and ultimately was asked to leave. A couple of years later, he built his own clinic down just over the Baraga County line, with the support of some of his friends in Baraga. Unfortunately, he had barely gotten the clinic started before he had a heart attack and died.

We were planning our space in the new Chemistry-Biological Sciences Building, while at the same time, Mike McCarthy, was working with me on cancer research, as an undergraduate assistant. One day he came in my office while I had some rough plans lying on

247

my desk. He got interested in them, asked some questions, and had some good suggestions. Since I was working on something else, I said, go ahead and make some changes, just do it in pencil. After a while, he came back and for the next week or so, we put together the final plans. Unfortunately, the amount of space that we had been allotted in the building was based on the number of students that I had projected using a linear projection of the early enrollment numbers for the department. By the time we moved into the building, the space was already too small for us because of the exponential growth we had experienced. At the same time engineering enrollment was declining and biological and medically-related curricula were booming nationwide. In part, the reason for this was the very controversial book called *Silent Spring*, by Rachel Carson. The irony was that, during the first year of the Bio-Science Department, Ken Kraft had chaired a term-long seminar devoted to review of Ms. Carson's book. It was an excellent seminar, as it provided an early focus for the department. Unfortunately, we (I) had failed to appreciate the implications as they pertained to our department's enrollment projections.

In addition, I had pulled out all the stops when it came to student recruitment. We sent letters to all high schools in the U.P and all recent graduates in either medical technology or chemistry, telling them about the biological sciences program and the pending master's degree program. We also did everything that we could to sell the

248

university recruiters on our program. Another factor that contributed was the development of NSF summer institutes for high school teachers. The most effective person in writing proposals for these institutes was Bob Brown. Another recruitment tool was to have faculty make speeches at high schools. Usually the speaker was me since most faculty members were not available and sometimes, these were dinky little schools, but, if they invited me, I would go. All these things began to pay off as our enrollment began to climb. After a year or so, we added a secretary who was a great help in keeping these activities going.

During the planning of the Chemistry-Biological Sciences Building, we of course had an opportunity to order the equipment for the new laboratories. During this process, an interesting and important thing occurred not only for the department, but also for me and the remainder of my career. A couple of us had noticed a programmable calculator developed by the Olivetti Corporation that not only could be programmed to do various statistical analyses but could be programmed to do almost any repetitive analysis within limits. There was general agreement that such a machine would be useful in many areas of research and that it was the essence of what our department was about. Thus, the first "computer" was ordered despite the relative expense of the item. (1965)

After a couple of years, we received permission to add another permanent faculty position. This time, we sought someone to teach Anatomy and Physiology. One of the applications we received was from Bob Stones who had received his Ph.D. from Purdue University. He turned out to be a nice clean-cut guy, whose research was on circadian rhythms (daily physiological patterns). His research animal was the bat, which was prevalent in the mines locally, so there was no shortage of biological material. We got along fine, so he started the following year. No sooner was he established in his home in Boston Location, that he started a Mormon Church in his living room. Later this church was moved to the house across the street and within not too many years a beautiful new church was built in the Volin Estates area, near our home on Royalwood. I really admired Bob's research, as he employed some really inventive techniques to study bat's temperature control. In particular, he designed a calorimeter, made of two metals in a checkerboard pattern, attached so that it became a series of thermocouples, capable of measuring very tiny temperature changes. I thought that it was ingenious and in fact, he produced some very nice research from it.

Since one of the reasons that I was made department head was because of the research that I had been doing in the area of chemical carcinogenesis, I tried as much as possible to continue this in the time that I had available. So, when we got approval to offer a Masters in Biological Sciences, I kept my eye open for a graduate student who might work with me. One of my main objectives was to set an example for the other faculty. So, when a student came along who was interested, I had him work on another chemical carcinogen that produced liver cancer in mice. This worked out well and we ultimately published a paper on the project. In 1965, several faculty members from the department nominated me to receive the MTU Faculty Research Award. I'm sure that this was based on all the research I had accomplished since coming to Michigan Tech, not just during that year, as it had been quite minimal. My real accomplishment I think was to encourage several other faculty members to become involved as well.

As soon as they began working on the new building, we began receiving some of the new equipment for the new laboratories and when the Olivetti Programma 101 arrived, I had it moved to my desk since I had shown the most interest in it. Thus, I began reading the instructional material and typing in some of the canned programs that it provided. These included such things as average, mean, standard deviation and standard error. Each program was stored on a magnetic card so that it could be called up again when it was needed. Such programs are available today on simple calculators that one might buy in a drug store for less than $100, but at that time it was a remarkable machine that none of us had ever seen or used. (1967).

Even before we moved into our new building, we could see that things were going to be a little cramped. I went to Ray Smith and tried to talk him out of another floor in the new Chemistry-Biological Science Building. But he said, "Jim you should have asked for more right from the beginning. There is nothing that we can do now." This is one of the few things that he blocked me on, and I think that he was already looking forward to the time when his old department of Metallurgy, would be moving into the Chem-Bio Building, as well. In fact, it was my fault for being much too conservative in planning the biological science's section of the building. Things were not too bad for the first year or so, but only a few years later the department had to move into the new Mechanical Engineering Building, which initially was considerably over-built.

For the first five years, I really enjoyed my duties as Head of the Biological Sciences Department. However, several things happened that caused me to start thinking of going back to research and teaching. One was my relationship to the other faculty in the department. This had been exceptionally good during the first years, although I would not describe it as being totally democratic. I did everything that I could to encourage the professional development of every faculty member and, at social events, would brag about the things that they were doing to the extreme. Meetings were rather informal discussions and what we did represented the consensus of the group, although not too many votes were taken. If nobody expressed an interest in something, I would just make a decision and do it. There were few, if any, committees. We all knew our jobs and we went ahead and did them. Most of the departmental routine I just went ahead and did with the help of the secretary. However, after five years, many of these jobs had become boring and I hadn't prepared anyone else to assume part of the load. However, one evening after Bob Janke had returned from Colorado, we had a meeting at somebody's house and something he said triggered a discussion that led me to believe that there was a lot of dissention in the department. I pretty much blamed Bob, but probably there were underlying problems of which I had not been aware. Things were never quite the same after that night.

Another factor that lead to my decision to return to teaching, was that during the first four years of Ray Smith's presidency, there had been no Dean of Faculty due to Frank Kerekes' death. This meant that the college had been operating under a structure in which department heads answered directly to the president. This was a very enjoyable situation where, if one wanted Ray's approval on anything, the head could simply give him a call, describe what was needed and he would typically respond; "Sounds good to me, go ahead and just send me a memo confirming what you have done." Man, you can't beat that. Then, somebody noted that the college was now called Michigan Technological University and decided that we needed a "university" structure, with colleges of engineering, sciences, and business, etc. Of course, colleges need Deans to handle the administration and the university needs an Academic Vice President to run it all. So, before you know it, I was answering to a Dean of the College of Sciences and Arts and he was answering to the Academic Vice President, who was answering to the President. So, before I knew it, I had been demoted two levels and nobody even apologized. So, the same decision that had taken one phone call and a memo to achieve, now required a memo to the Dean, a meeting with the Dean, probably a revised memo, which could be forwarded to the Academic Vice President, followed perhaps by another meeting and then without further follow-up, the idea might be filed in limbo.

So, it just wasn't fun anymore and I decided to resign from the Department Head position at the end of my sixth year. Probably for similar reasons, a couple of other department heads made the same move. I heard from somebody later that Ray Smith accused me of being a quitter. I think that he understood our problem but did not want to admit that he would have done the same thing himself if he had still been a Department Head. He remained a very good friend of mine and I had a great admiration for him. I hope that he understood my decision, although we had never talked about it. I feel sure that the many things I have done since resigning my headship has reflected more positively on Michigan Tech than anything I had done before.

Thus, my last major responsibility was to assist in the search for a new Department Head. I felt that we should take this opportunity to bring in someone from off campus who had a major research program already in progress. It turned out that our search brought in Jack Slater, from the University of California, who was participating in one of the early stages of the satellite program. He seemed like a personable type, so I was rather taken with him initially. Also, I guess that I was awed by the fact that he was working with the NASA program, so with the approval of the Dean of the College and the Academic V.P., he was hired to fill my position.

It really didn't take long to realize that things were not as they seemed before his appointment. Apparently, he didn't get along with the administration, because by the fall of 1970 he was replaced as Department Head by Dr. Robert Stones.

CHAPTER 14

LIMNOLOGY AND OCEANOGRAPHY

(1968-1978)

After my six years serving as department head, I returned to teaching and research and had to decide what area of research I was going into. My major experience and research credentials were, of course, in cancer research. However, I was burned out in that field and after six years in administration, felt that I would pretty much need to start over again. So, it seemed that the effort involved might just as well be directed into a new area of study. To pick the area, I sought to answer two questions: 1) Which area of research would be the most fun for me? 2) What would be most appropriate to the needs and resources of Michigan Tech and the Biological Sciences Department? The answer to both of these questions was to study Lake Superior and the connecting waters that surround MTU, as the Keweenaw Waterway is, in essence, a freshwater estuary of Lake Superior.

The Keweenaw Waterway is a river-like body of water which stretches from the north side of the Keweenaw Peninsula of Lake Superior to the south side, at Keweenaw Bay. This waterway was, for the most part, formed naturally as a result of an early stage of Lake Superior, at least 10,000 years ago, that was trapped on the west side of the Keweenaw Peninsula by an ice dam that developed during the melting of the glacier. In part, this lake was cut off from the east by the range of mountains that went down the spine of the peninsula. When the level of water in the western portion of the lake got high enough to break through the mountain chain, it burst through cataclysmically, washing away the mass of rock and dirt that made up the range of hills where the towns of Houghton and Hancock are presently located. There is some evidence that this break occurred along a fault that ran perpendicular to the range, as the valley that makes up the central portion of the Keweenaw Waterway is extremely straight and narrow.

During the Colonial days of the French Voyagers, the waterway was called the Portage River, as it was open only at the southern end and was blocked by sand dunes at the northern end, thus requiring a portage of the canoes that attempted to make this crossing. After the beginning of the copper business on the Keweenaw some dredging was done to open up the lower entry to facilitate commerce to the towns of Houghton and Hancock. Later, it was opened up by short canals built at both the northern and southern ends to facilitate entry of large ships through the waterway.

The idea that the entire Keweenaw Waterway was constructed by man is a misunderstanding that continues to this day. The major river entering the Keweenaw Waterway system is the Sturgeon River. Other rivers include Coles Creek, Boston Creek and the waterway that connects to Torch Lake. For a map of the waterway and additional pictures, see Keweenaw Waterway in Wikipedia. Clearly this is a complicated system which is open for both investigation and further description.

The Keweenaw Peninsula is very nearly at the geographical center of that Great Lake, making Michigan Tech an ideal place to conduct lakes research. Despite these obvious facts, no significant research in either biology or chemistry of this great resource was being done at MTU. Lake Superior research was being carried on at the University of Minnesota, Duluth, and a few exploratory projects by the Universities of Michigan and Wisconsin. So, it was obvious that great potential existed in a very interesting study area.

Limnology is the application of physics, chemistry, and biology to the study of lake systems and is directly analogous to oceanography, which is the application of science to the study of oceans. The first step was, of course, to study the literature to gain some knowledge in this area. I found that to an extent, it was simply a matter of applying basic chemistry, primarily analytical chemistry, to a new area (I was going to leave the biology to somebody else).

The big difference was in how one collects his samples. In order to see what our competition was doing, Ken Kraft and I made a trip to Duluth to meet with the major researchers at UMD, where Ken had previously served on the faculty. We found these men to be the most congenial colleagues that one can imagine. My first thought was that the difference between limnology and cancer research was like night and day. Later encounters with limnologists served only to confirm this view, as after being treated to lunch and a tour of their lab, we left Duluth with all the pertinent literature that they could muster and encouragement to launch our studies in this exciting new area.

One of the obvious requirements of lakes research is to have a platform for collecting samples, which generally means a boat. Some of our earliest studies were done using our family craft, the *Pat-Sea*. Ken Kraft and I, with a couple of students took an exploratory trip to Keweenaw Bay. I remember particularly the trip to Rabbit Island in Traverse Bay. One of the things that we wished to see was the Great Blue Heron rookery that was said to be there. We approached the island very gingerly, as the shores were covered with boulders. We finally found a small bay that appeared to be fairly safe to enter. So, we tied the boat to a tree that was close to the shore and headed off into the interior to make our search. There was no one living on the island and little evidence that there ever had been. The woods were largely deciduous, mainly maple. One thing that stands out in my memory was the impressive mounds of moss that we observed. This moss was a couple of feet deep in a few places. We walked for about an hour without finding any evidence of the heron rookery and so we headed back to the boat, rather disappointed at the failure in our major objective. However, as we began to untie the boat, we heard a loud "squawk" and looked up to find a heron perched in the top of the tree our boat was tied to. Then, our noses confirmed that we had indeed found the heron rookery. It was not large, consisting of only three or four nests. Apparently, we had been so anxious to begin our search that we failed to notice what we had come to look for. In the end, our exploratory trip was a success. I would continue to use the *Pat-Sea*, particularly when we needed to go some distance from the university, or we needed a fast boat to get to our area of investigation.

Bob Brown led our first attempt at construction of a lakes research vessel with the aid of an NSF grant for student summer research. His design was a raft; constructed of polystyrene logs held together with 2x4 lumber, which the students constructed on the porch of the Hubbell School building. This raft was used by the students to make some initial investigations in the vicinity of the MTU coal dock and also at Dollar Bay. The research was probably limited to collections of bottom organisms and use of the Hach Kit to measure various chemical constituents. Because of its rather flimsy construction, this first craft lasted only a couple of years.

After I began devoting my research time to limnology, about the first thing we did was to put together an NSF Undergraduate Equipment proposal. In order to broaden our credibility and to justify the large budget proposed, we decided to make it an interdisciplinary grant involving Geology, Civil Engineering, and Forestry, in addition to Biological Sciences. The interdisciplinary concept was fairly new at the time and so NSF was easily sold on the idea, with the result that we received a very large undergraduate equipment grant. With this money we purchased a number of basic limnological research tools and built a 20-foot steel pontoon raft. The latter project was carried out by the MTU Physical Plant Department, based on our specifications. Since it consisted of a raft with an 8x8 foot pilot house/lab on its deck it was called the *Monitor* after the so called, "cheese box on a raft" of Civil War fame. The name had a double meaning in that our initial investigations were to monitor the pollutants of the Keweenaw Waterway system. Since the Physical Plant had constructed the *Monitor*, I had no trouble getting them to designate a docking site at the east end of the coal dock. They also provided about 800 sq. ft. of storage space in the green building nearby and also provided some workspace and running water. Thus, we had a Lakeside Lab that as far as I know was still being used until it was replaced by the three-story Great Lakes Research lab was completed in 2013. With the aid of the Physical Plant, we also set up an automatic water level recorder. This was sufficiently sensitive to monitor the seiche activity in Keweenaw Bay, thus we got some interesting data over the years it was in place.

On another project, I was able to interest one of the engineers on the National Parks Service's ship, *Ranger III,* to allow us to place a temperature recorder on the intake water supply during the voyage back and forth to Isle Royale. He also agreed to turn on the recorder when it left the dock, mark the time when the ship left the waterway, again when it entered Rock Harbor on the north side and turn it off when it docked. He also added other tidbits of information when noted. At the end of the summer I had some very interesting data that tied in nicely with the studies on the thermal bar that we did later and that other researchers have done since.

After writing some applications, I was able to get two small grants for the support of MS graduate students. One of these grants was from the Ontonagon-Huff Paper Mill and the other was from Michigan DNR. With this money I was able to hire two graduate students who were ideal for the work that we were doing. They were both from Superior, Wisconsin, with fathers who had worked on the ore boats. Thus, they were able to provide a lot of common-sense boating knowledge to support my initial forays into this field. We had two main projects. One dealt with the investigation of the Keweenaw Waterway system from Lake Superior on the north to Keweenaw Bay on the south, including Torch Lake. The other project covered about a mile of water in and around the mouth of the Ontonagon River (about 60 miles away). The objective of each was to find out anything unusual about the chemistry and biology of these two bodies of water that would have a bearing on future management strategies. Both students participated in both projects, but Dave Drown was responsible for the Ontonagon project and Jim Yanko was responsible for the Keweenaw Waterway project. I went on most trips, primarily directing the chemical aspects of the projects. Ken Kraft consulted on the biology of both projects, which consisted primarily of bottom invertebrates.

In the Keweenaw Waterway, the most interesting chemical feature was discovered more or less by accident. Not having much of a research plan, we began to measure most anything that was easy to measure. This included phosphate, nitrate, oxygen, and chloride. One constituent, we hit upon more or less by accident, as we were going to carry out a dye tracer experiment by dumping fluorescent-dye into the lake and measuring the dye in various downstream locations using a fluorometer. However, we discovered that the background concentration of fluorescence was so high that it obviated the tracer study and thus we became interested in the source of the fluorescence; was it natural or was it a pollutant? It turned out to be the result of the tea-colored tannin-like substances in most of the streams and thus natural. Oxygen depletion and the nutrients, phosphate and nitrate, were only found in significant amounts in Dollar Bay, which suffered with runoff from the local milk processing factory. So, it ended up that we routinely began to study the concentrations of chloride ion and natural fluorescence. Here we found that the chloride concentration varied from 300 ppm in Torch Lake to about 10 ppm in Portage Lake to about 1 ppm in Lake Superior. The high chloride (salt) content was later traced to the dewatering of a mine called Osceola #13, which drained into a creek, which fed Torch Lake. Other rivers had only a 1 or 2 ppm. We also found some interesting variations in the natural fluorescence of the water. It was high in rivers, relatively low in Torch Lake and almost zero in Lake Superior waters. When we tried to study bottom invertebrates, we found that most of the waterway was covered with a fine clay-like material that was so dense that it was largely devoid of invertebrates. This material was found to be the result of finely ground copper-ore waste that had been dumped into the system over a period of almost a hundred years. These results seemed to be sufficiently interesting that Jim Yanko had a thesis topic and I had at least something to report at the upcoming Great Lakes Research Conference.

Our Ontonagon study yielded somewhat less of a concrete nature. There were little significant changes in chemistry and the bottom was so dynamic because of the river flow that not much was found to be growing there. This latter fact led to the major discovery, or I should say invention, of the project. Ken Kraft had the idea of forming an artificial invertebrate environment to see what might be collected. The students decided to make this device by gathering up some small rocks from the shore of Lake Superior and wrapping them with hardware cloth to make a container with dimensions of about 12 x 8 x 2 inches. The result was what they called a "rock pasty" because of the similarity to the local Cornish meat pies that are a Copper Country specialty. When these "rock pasties" were placed at different locations (such as under docks), allowed to remain for approximately a week and then sloshed up and down in a baby bathtub (a common tool for invertebrate study), a measure of invertebrate populations was obtained. The question is: what does it exactly represent? So, several studies were done exploring the applicability of the "rock pasty" for invertebrate analysis. This became one of the major topics of Dave Drown's thesis.

Serendipity is often an important component of research. It has happened to me more than once in my years of study, but never more so than on the Keweenaw Waterway project. As I was working on my introduction to the pollution paper for the Great Lakes Research Conference, I wanted something to support my contention that the waterway could be considered an estuary of Lake Superior. So, I went to the library and began perusing the topic of estuaries. As I began pulling books from the shelf, and thumbing through pages, I ran across a book called "The Estuaries". On flipping through the pages, looking for studies on freshwater estuaries, my perusal button* was still on and I ran across a very interesting paper that dealt with using two conserved chemical constituents to mathematically study water mass movements in the mouth of the Hudson River. Wow! I realized that all the data that we had been collecting for the past year concerning chloride and natural fluorescence concentrations would allow us to do exactly the same thing in the Keweenaw Waterway!

I checked out the book from the library and rushed back to my office to conduct a more intense perusal. Using the same mathematical equations, I was able to show that our system contained three kinds of water: Lake Superior water, Torch Lake water, and tributary water. To my knowledge, this oceanographic technique had never been used with freshwater systems before. Thus, our research had just jumped from the high school science project level to something at the Ph.D. level or beyond. We even had winter data, collected through the ice, which showed layering of the three kinds of water similar to what is seen in the Atlantic Ocean. For several reasons, the results were only published in a minor journal, the Great Lakes Research Conference Publication by Spain, Drown, and Yanko and by Spain and Andrews.

It was while writing the programs needed for the above conserved constituent analyses that I became more involved in the Programma 101 computer that we had purchased for the department. One thing led to another and I became convinced that I needed to learn more about the capabilities and applications of a computer to research. (1969)

We had some interesting experiences with the *Monitor* during the years we were working on the Keweenaw Waterway. One occasion stands out in my memory that has some barring on other lake experiences. This resulted from the raft-like design of the vessel. It first occurred when we were headed out on one windy day to take some samples in Torch Lake. The wind was blowing out of the north and we were on a southerly barring. As with other trips, we had the engines wide open to try to get there as quickly as possible. Even then it took the better part of an hour to get from the MTU coal dock to Torch Lake. Things were going along fine; I was in the pilothouse at the wheel and the guys were sitting outside on the lab bench that went across in front of the pilothouse. As we went down the lake and the fetch increased, the height of the waves grew larger and larger. Suddenly, we went down the front side of a wave and the bow of the flat deck raft went under the surface of the water. Suddenly, our surface craft tried to become a submarine and began going into a dive! This maneuver, which is like stubbing one's toe, threw my two students off the lab bench into a foot or so of water, which was now on the deck. Fortunately, they hung on to something and I pulled back hard on the throttle, so that the raft slowly backed out of this awkward position. Happily, there had been no equipment sitting on the lab bench (just two unhappy grad students). Wow! Nothing like this had happened before. So, we stood around for a few minutes considering the situation. Eventually, we decided that it had been some kind of a fluke and began to proceed down the lake, with the two guys at my side in the wheelhouse. We were so convinced that it had been a fluke, that we put the speed right back to where it had been. It wasn't more than five minutes and it happened again. There we were with the bow under the water standing at what seemed at the time to be about a 45 degree angle (actually it was probably less than ten). What we finally had to do was to maintain a speed of no more than that of the waves, which was very hard to do since we wanted so much to go faster. Eventually, we made it around the point and away from the waves. As you will note, in the chapter on the *Pat-Sea*, I ran into this situation again with even more startling consequences. I discovered that this is a general response of boats to waves when headed in the downwind direction. However, even experienced sea captains can be caught in this situation. The *Edmund Fitzgerald*, one of the last ships to go down in Lake Superior, was rushing downwind to get into the safety of Whitefish Bay when it disappeared below the surface with 36 souls aboard. There has been a lot of controversy about what caused this accident, but there is no doubt in my mind that it was the same phenomenon.

In addition to research, I often had the opportunity to instruct classes in limnology, both on the undergraduate and graduate level. In both instances, since I had never taken a course in limnology, it was much like the many other courses I had taught over the years. It required me to do a lot of studying prior to class and depend heavily on other areas of study that I had taken in chemistry, physics and geomorphology, as well as just fundamental knowledge of science, all of which impact on the study of lake systems. The only aspect of limnology that gave me problems was biology, because of my limited knowledge in that area. But that's what books are for and I had plenty of them. When it came to the laboratory portion of the class, the *Monitor* served as an ideal outdoor laboratory and we had two extreme examples of lakes to study. Only about a mile from the MTU coal dock was Dollar Bay, which had most of the characteristics of a nutrient-rich (eutrophic) lake, with high concentrations of phosphate and nitrate and low concentrations of oxygen, while on the other hand, we had Lake Superior, having all the characteristics of a nutrient-poor (oligotrophic) lake. We also had interesting populations of organisms living in Dollar Bay, while the waters just outside the Bay were almost devoid of life, although, there were nice examples of sediment layering. One time I had a class of high school teachers on the deck of the *Monitor*, probably more than I should have for the number of life jackets available. We were right in mid-channel studying the layering in a bottom-core that we had taken. I was down on my knees, with all these teachers clustered around looking at the layers we were finding, when one of the teachers, who was standing calmly asked, "Do they call that a ship or a boat?" Whereupon I looked up to see an ore-carrier less than a mile away and bearing down on us. About that time, he let loose with his air horn and I leaped over to the anchor rope to pull it up, so we could get the heck out of the way. Ah, those were the good old days of teaching limnology.

During this period, we had an opportunity to participate in a somewhat larger limnological investigation, as we received an invitation to join with the University of Michigan's work on the Inland Seas research vessel, when it entered Lake Superior at Sault Ste. Marie. Since the ship was supported by an annual grant from the National Science Foundation (NSF), we were able to participate without cost. So, Dave Leddy from chemistry, my two graduate students and I drove over to the Soo to board the ship for a two-week cruise. We made two trips like that. It was a great experience for us all, but particularly Dave Drown and Jim Yanko. My justification was to study the chloride content and natural fluorescence at various locations around Lake Superior, to provide background data for the conserved constituent research described above. The two trips sort of run together in my mind, so I will just describe it as one trip. First let me describe the ship. The *Inland Seas* was a 114' wooden-hulled minesweeper that was constructed during WWII. After the war, it was used by the National Park Service to ferry people to Isle Royale for several years under the name *Ranger II*. It was obtained as surplus by U.M. after being replaced by the steel-hulled *Ranger III*. U.M. outfitted it with oceanographic gear and had a full professional crew.

The research people, except for a few chief staff, were housed in the forecastle.

We sailed out of the Soo about noon and ran headlong into a fairly heavy sea coming out of the northwest. Since it was due to continue for most of the day, the captain decided to head into Batchawana Bay, where there was a sturdy T-shaped dock built by the Canadian government near the Indian reservation. The *Inland Seas* was tied up along the end of the dock and no sooner did we arrive, than the little Indian kids began climbing on the spray rail that went around the ship. They had lots of questions about this and that, but eventually invited the crew to play baseball with the Indian team. The crew accepted the challenge and walked over to the playing field, a short distance away. After a few minutes, the Indians arrived in an old car with spinning wheels that were spraying dust and dirt in all directions. It quickly became apparent that the Indians had prepared themselves by imbibing in a drink or two. The game progressed and rather quickly transformed into a "massacre", as the Indians were much better at baseball than our crew. After we returned to the ship, some Indians began a game of intimidation by driving their cars down the length of the dock and screeching to a halt, just before running into the side of the ship. The crew began moving all the equipment on deck to a safer location and guards were posted for the night. We were due to depart at 5:00 am the following morning and when we got out on deck, one of the guards said that they just quit with their intimidation. As we

272

sailed out of the harbor, we could hear the doors slamming shut as the Indian village settled down for the "night".

Lake Superior was fairly calm as we headed north for Michipicoten Harbor, near Wawa, Ontario and so we reached it sometime before dark. Since this was an interesting outpost town at that time, several of us hitched a ride into town to visit the local bar. I, apparently, had a few too many beers, as the following morning when we headed southwest to Michipicoten Island I was suffering from a hangover, which combined with the choppy seas caused me to have a case of mal de mar that was not fun. We were going to Michipicoten Island because the people studying algae wanted to make a collection at a much undisturbed site. The fog arrived there about the same time that we did. This was unfortunate because a Z-shaped channel characterized the entrance to this rock-bound harbor. With the help of radar and everybody watching from the rail, we slowly wound ourselves through the maze of the channel and into the harbor. Since this was a trying situation that the captain was not about to repeat until the fog lifted, all were given the remainder of the day to explore and collect geological samples. Off we went and later returned, everyone with more than their share of the local geology. How some of the rock samples were carried back is hard to believe. However, there seemed to be plenty of room on the ship, so rocks of all sizes began to accumulate at various places around the deck. The following morning the fog had lifted, and we headed for a spot called the Lake Superior Shoals, a shallow spot in the middle of the lake between Michipicoten and Isle Royale. Again, we were looking for algae. However, all we had for navigation at that time was dead reckoning, Loran, and depth sounder, so when we thought we had arrived there, we hadn't, because of the large probability of error. So, the captain circled round and round looking for this shallow spot. This went on for as much as two hours. All the time, I was lying in my bunk reading a book, while the sunbeams coming in the portholes circled round and round the forecastle. Finally, the captain gave up and with some disgust, headed off for Isle Royale.

We were late arriving in Rock Harbor, so I remember little until the following morning. It was a beautiful day and we left for the north point, as we were planning to go around to the northwest side to see Five Finger Bay, one of the most pristine parts of the island. Isle Royale is a 45-mile long island that runs in a southwest to northeasterly direction. It consists of a series of ridges, some of which run the length of the island. These ridges extend out into the lake to become shallow reefs, which on the north side of the island form five finger-like projections called Five-Finger Bay. We arrived there at about 11 am with clear blue sky and gin-clear water. Most of us had never been there, so we were all on deck soaking up the scenery, as the captain slowly guided the ship into the complex of reefs. For some reason he was cutting from one bay to another, when all of a sudden, there was a slight grinding noise as the *Inland Seas* slipped slowly on to a reef! We couldn't believe it. Everyone had been looking. The water was perfectly clear. But there we were, with about one third of the ship stranded on a rock. I think that there must have been a few choice words mumbled in the wheelhouse, but then the captain used the radiophone to contact Ann Arbor. Yes, the insurance was paid. Next, one of our scuba divers went down to see the impact on the bottom of the ship. It appeared that only a few bolts had been disturbed. The ship had slipped on so easily, it seemed like there should be no problem getting it off again. But that was not to be the case. Even after all of the geological samples were moved to the stern of the ship and the engines cranked up to full reverse, she would not budge. After an hour or so of this, the captain called the National Park Service to ask that they send a tug to help haul us off. They arrived in about an hour and the combined effort of the tug and the ship in full reverse was tried. But still it wouldn't budge. The next plan was to use the tug to yank her off. The first attempt at this caused the hawser to wildly whip lose from the cleat. It became obvious that we were dealing with a very dangerous procedure, so most of the observers began to back out of the way. The next attempt was even worse, as the hawser parted somewhere between the tug and the ship and came lashing back, crashing the full length of the deck! Fortunately, no one was standing in the way, but we all now knew that this was no longer child's play. After searching in the rope locker for a new nylon hawser, this was rigged up and the process was repeated one more time. This time there was a little nudge as the ship moved backwards a few inches. The next time brought full success. After further inspection of the hull, it was deemed safe enough to proceed. I don't know if there was any sample taking or not, but I rather imagine that we headed on down the backside of the island to the harbor at the southwest end. We spent the night at Windigo, the park service station at the southwest end of Isle Royale. The following morning, we headed for Houghton into about a 10-15-foot sea. I spent most of the morning standing on the lee deck of the ship trying to keep my digestive tract going in the right direction. Jim Yanko decided that he was not going to allow all the good food to go to waste (he was the only one who showed up for lunch), so he ate everything, proceeded to get sick, then went back and ate some more. I don't believe there was a soul on board who wasn't wondering a little bit about the impact of our recent visit to Five Finger Bay on the ship's hull.

From the above comments, you might wonder if any serious research was done during these trips. The answer, of course, is yes, as sandwiched somewhere in that trip were several stops at research stations. Each time, the ship would come into the wind, ship's bell would clang, and everybody would move to his or her workstations. My guys would help where they were needed as they had a powerful work ethic and picked up the ship's routine before the end of the first station. I helped with water sampling and took my samples to the small portion of the lab that had been assigned to me. Actual analysis was conducted later; usually when we were tied up at a dock somewhere. The data obtained from these trips didn't contribute much to my research, but the experience we gained was immeasurable. Some years later, the *Inland Seas* was sitting in port down in Lower Michigan when one of the stabilizers dropped off the side and the following year, she was replaced by a smaller ship that was specifically designed for U.M. Lakes Research.

After using the *Monitor* for about one year, MTU was fortunate to receive a gift of a 30' tugboat that had been used by the man who ran the small marina at the lower entry of the waterway. This was a lovely little tugboat called the *Lake Breeze*. Shortly, we had it outfitted for research, using some new equipment and a few things off the *Monitor*, which was subsequently used primarily for teaching limnology class, etc. My two sailors were much happier with the *Lake Breeze*, as this was a real boat, with a real engine and a great boat smell. We had it outfitted very quickly and used it for all the Keweenaw Waterway research from that point on. It was a significant step up in morale as we now felt that we were doing real limnological research not unlike that which we had experienced on the *Inland Seas*. By this time, we had an engine for hauling sampling gear up from the bottom. This was especially valuable for hauling up some of the larger dredges that we were now using. Ah, but with more power, you have greater opportunity to get into trouble.

Our biggest goof on the *Lake Breeze* resulted from several factors. The most important was that we had been experiencing some difficulty getting the engine to start for some reason. This caused us to keep the engine running when we were on station. On one particular day, there was significant wave action, so we decided to put out the anchor to keep the boat from drifting away from our assigned location. Then we put the engine in an idling mode and set the gears into neutral. Then we got to work to get the samples collected as rapidly as possible. Everything seemed fine until we finished and began to pull up the anchor. Right away, we discovered the anchor line was hooked on something and the something was the propeller shaft! What had happened is that the gearshift had slipped just slightly out of neutral and the propeller was slowly turning over, wrapping the anchor line around the propeller shaft. Well, there was nothing to do, but have someone get into the water and try to untangle it. Dave Drown volunteered and went over the side to see what needed to be done. What we finally had to do, as I remember, was to slowly put the propeller into reverse, while Dave freed it from the tangle of line. This was a very dangerous maneuver that I probably should not have allowed him to try. It took a lot of trust in the man gently nudging the reverse lever. What made it even more dangerous was that it was late in the year, when the water was already very cold, and the wind made it even worse. Fortunately, we were able to get it untangled and get the anchor up before we drifted ashore. I think, at that point, it's likely that we made do with whatever samples we had already obtained and headed back to the dock.

As I indicated above, some of our water sampling was done through the ice. To accomplish this, we needed a means of getting to the primary stations on Portage Lake that were several miles from our Lakeside Lab. My initial effort in this direction was a six-wheeled amphibious vehicle that was purchased with the initial NSF grant. This proved to be almost worthless for everything. It barely moved in the water; it had no traction on ice or snow; and it was so low-slung that it could get hung up even driving on dry land. So, we managed to get rid of it somehow and do our work with an Evinrude Snowmobile that the university had obtained through one of its testing programs. This was a heavy machine and thus was able to carry my son, Will and me, as well as pull a sled full of equipment. Everything went fine until one day we went out on the ice-covered lake after a reasonably heavy snowfall. We moved along well on open ice, but about halfway to the key station we were headed for, we hit some heavy snow and the Evinrude bogged down. When we got off the machine, we discovered that under the snow was a good four or five inches of slush. This commonly occurs when the ice is weighed down with snow causing it to crack, so that water comes up over the ice. Our weight and that of the snowmobile were not helping. To make things worse, slush had gotten in under the snowmobile tracks. Before we could do anything, all this slush had to be cleaned out. Then, dry snow had to be piled up to provide a base to get the snowmobile on so that the engine could be started. This operation took fifteen minutes, or more. Our objective was to get the equipment out of the slush field

279

back to the solid ice. So, we got the machine revved up and Will jumped on it to drive it away. It only went a few yards and it was bogged down again. It became obvious that it was not going to hold anybody's weight, much less pull a sled. So, I hauled the sled to the safety of the clear ice, while Will worked on cleaning out the slush. We piled up the snow again and lifted the snowmobile into place. After revving it up, Will tried running along beside it for as long as he could go. This time it went perhaps ten yards before it bogged down again. This process was repeated about five times, until we finally got it out of the slush field onto firm ice. By that time, we were both about dead, so the sampling trip was canceled. We just could not face the possibility of getting into another slush field. This was particularly bad because I was counting on the sampling of this trip to provide winter analysis data for the paper I was hoping to complete on water mass identification by chemical constituents.

I was invited by Wisconsin DNR to do an analytical chemistry study on Oscillatoria Xanthene, a pigment that is given off by the blue-green algae, called Oscillatoria rubescens. This happened because one of our students had gone on to work with the Wisconsin Natural Resources Department and he asked if we would be interested in carrying on the analysis of cores taken from Lake Winnebago. This became a very interesting project to me because of the beautiful red color that Oscillatoria Xanthan had when purified and that the process of analysis involved purification of pigments by chromatography. So,

I hired my son to work on this project. Without going into detail, it all turned out very well and I was able to get a paper that could be presented to the conference on limnology and oceanography

After Dave Drown and Jim Yanko graduated, my lake research diminished somewhat until I got together with Davis Hubbard of the Chemical Engineering Department. Davis was a specialist in hydrology and the peculiar aspects of fluid flow. Somehow, he became interested in a special feature of large lakes called the "thermal bar" (TB), probably as a result of comments that I had made to him. The thermal bar is a feature that occurs during the warming of lakes in the spring, where inshore water warmer than 4 degrees C comes in contact with offshore water that is colder than 4 degrees. Since water is most dense at 4 degrees; it tends to sink to the bottom to be replaced by both inshore and offshore water, which mixes to make still more 4-degree water. The result is a curtain of descending water that traps inshore water within the 4-degree line. Hence it becomes a thermal barrier or "bar". Unlike the thermocline, which is a horizontal barrier that occurs in lakes during the summer, this is a thermal barrier that occurs in the spring. As far as we could find, no one had studied the fine structure of the TB and no one had studied the TB in Lake Superior.

Our first study of the thermal bar was near Eagle Harbor, in the northern end of the Keweenaw Peninsula. Here, it is so clearly demarcated that one sees a line of flotsam at the surface of the bar and distinctly different colored water on each side - a beautiful blue offshore and green on the inshore side, all within a space of 10 feet. Although the thermal bar undulated as we watched it, we failed to realize how this would impact the research we carried on the following year. These observations fascinated both of us, so I was able to recruit a fellow scientist for the following two years.

Davis had a graduate student who was interested in studying this phenomenon with a special computer analysis program. First, we needed some data on the fine structure of the TB. We decided to get 100 meters of polypropylene line, marked it off in 10-meter units and put floats and anchors at each end. We also set up two pieces of plywood to serve as a range marker on shore. Then, when the weather was appropriate, we took a series of 10 vertical water samples and temperature readings every 10 meters across the thermal bar. All this was carried out at the upper entry to the Keweenaw Waterway. We believed that this must have been the most intensive set of transect samples ever taken in lakes research.

Since each location took about 20-30 minutes, it took hours to complete and was done at least two times during the spring. The water was analyzed for both natural fluorescence and temperature, which were higher in the inshore water because of the runoff. All the data was subjected to the computer analysis. Despite the general pattern that confirmed the thermal bar concept, there was no distinct line of demarcation. We were very disappointed in the results because we had hoped to answer the question of whether the line leans inward toward the shore or vice versa. Then it became clear that undulations in the long-shore current that flows inside the thermal bar had caused fluctuations in the pattern during the time that we were taking the data.

So, the following year, Davis and I tried a new "snapshot" sampling technique, this time by taking a transect of Keweenaw Bay. His graduate student had finished up and gotten his degree by that time, so we were all alone. We started at one shore near a big old barn that served as our range marker and driving the *Pat-Sea* at about 20 mph, trailing a temperature probe about 10 meters behind the boat. I drove, while calling temperature readings into a tape recorder, and making sightings of special features as we passed ("we are now in line with the entry light", etc.). At the same time, Davis was taking surface water samples and calling sample numbers into the tape recorder. Again, we felt that we must be making limnological history of some sort, with our high-speed sampling procedure. The results of these kinds of studies were very striking. We found a very clearly demarcated thermal bar on each side of the bay. But it was evident that to see the fine structure, we needed a vertical array of thermal sensors and a very fancy recording device. However, we were operating with no financial support and no platform that could carry it. So, the next step was to use the data obtained to get that sort of apparatus.

Unfortunately, the following year, Davis went on sabbatical leave, to Venice, to work on the water problems in the Venice Lagoon and I became involved in working on the computer. After he returned, we never got back to the project, as he was working on some research that was more appropriate to the Chemical Engineering Department.

During the period of Davis Hubbard's absence, I had become more and more interested in the applications of the computer to teaching and research in both bioscience and chemistry. At the same time, Tom Wright had joined the faculty and taken over the responsibilities for limnology instruction and thus, I never followed up on the thermal bar research. As a result, the remarkably interesting thermal bar study that was performed on Keweenaw Bay was never published.

Chapter 15

Computer Pioneer

(1965-1994)

As earlier stated, while we were picking out the equipment for our new Chemistry-Biological Science building, one of the items that I chose was an Olivetti Programma-101. This was a programmable calculator that could be used for carrying out repetitive calculations, statistical analysis, and data analysis in general. I had little difficulty convincing the faculty that it was something the department needed, as they recognized that this was the direction of the future. When it arrived, perhaps a year before we went into the new building, I moved it into my office to learn how to use it. It turned out to be a large, heavy piece of equipment, at least twice as big as an IBM typewriter. It could be programmed by typing in a series of two-character commands, such as A^, B+ and C<. These commands caused numbers to be moved from storage "registers" (B, C, D or E) to the accumulator (A), where one would carry out some numerical operation based on the contents of some other register, then exchange the result with what was in one of the other registers. The memory would hold 32 such commands.

These commands and the contents of the registers could be stored on an 8-inch card with magnetic backing. The output consisted of a paper tape printout, which could list the program, print input, or data output. Since it behaved somewhat like a computer, it was called a "microcomputer". This also might have been called the first desktop computer, however that term was not prevalent at the time. The only computer otherwise was the "mainframe" that was being used by the engineers at Michigan Tech, but few people on campus otherwise. One other computer that was popular in the Math Department was the Analog Computer, which one wired up to solve differential equations. There was no Computer Science Department until about 1976.

After copying a few canned statistical programs into the P101, I began to try programming a few things for myself. Basically, I was perusing the capabilities of the programmer 101. Soon, I discovered that it had the capability of looping around and carrying out repetitive operations. I then asked myself if it could carry on an exponential growth process, by taking a fraction of a number, adding it to the number and repeating the operation again and again, printing out the results of each step. Since it did this with no problem, I began to try various other things observed in chemical kinetics, or in population growth. Amazingly, everything I tried seemed to produce data very similar to real systems. "Wow." I said. "I wonder if other people know about this?" Well, I looked in the literature and couldn't find any

286

mention of it, even in the journal *Simulation*. However, it turned out that they were about to have the *First Conference on Computers for the Undergraduate Curricula* at the University of Iowa, so I submitted an abstract for a paper on my simple simulations and it was accepted. Low and behold, when I presented my paper, I was the only person representing anything in biology and one of the very few in chemistry. Suddenly, I was rubbing shoulders with the "movers and shakers" of application of computers in the basic sciences. One of the people I was to meet was Hal Peters, the director of CONDUIT, an organization of universities to increase the transfer of software between different mainframe systems. Little did I realize how important our friendship was later to become. As a result, I was invited to be the chairman of the session on "Computer Applications in Biology" at the following convention, to be held at Dartmouth College. The work that I had presented in Iowa was subsequently written up and accepted for publication in the *Simulation* journal. It is amazing, in retrospect, that I was able to go so far as a result of a few hours exploring this primitive computer.

In addition to the determinative simulations on processes such as population growth, I also became interested in the simulation of random events by using random numbers, or at least what I had invented to serve as random numbers. Initially, these were produced by using a sequence of mathematical operations on a seed number to

287

produce a product that one was unable to predict. I was later to find that this is true even for the most sophisticated random number generators, the only difference being in the sophistication of the mathematical operation. Initially, I wanted a random number simply to determine the occurrence of a particular play during a simulated football game I was trying to develop. One of my initial interests was to devise ways to determine how random my "random numbers" actually were. At first, I did this by writing down long lists of numbers and counting how frequently certain digits were repeated. Later, I wondered if anyone else had been interested in this sort of thing. It was then that I discovered a thick black book in the library published by the Rand Corporation that consisted of page after page of computer-generated random numbers, not unlike those that I had produced, and a list of tests that had been applied to them. This led me into the application of statistical analysis to the testing of random numbers. I was later to discover that the generation of random numbers and their testing could all be done much more efficiently using the computer. And, that computer models based on random numbers make up a significant field of simulation in all fields of science. Much later, my interest in random numbers would grow and I would find that they could also be used for the encryption and decryption of data.

Long before the age of Google or Wikipedia, I became involved in the development of the Lake Superior Basin Computerized Bibliography, which made use of a mainframe program that was developed at the University of Wisconsin. This was done in conjunction with a consortium of schools in the Lake Superior region and supported by money from the Federal Government. The controlling board for the consortium defined a group of tasks that should be done to make the region more effective in protecting Lake Superior from potential problems in the future. One of the tasks was to develop a computerized bibliography to assist any researcher who wished to work on Lake Superior. Presumably, because of the availability of computers at Michigan Tech, we were given this assignment and I was selected as the leader of the project. Since the computer program was already available from the University of Wisconsin, all that was needed was to define the keywords to be used and assign them to each of the individual publications that dealt with the Lake Superior Basin. Despite my lack of experience with the bibliographical science, I forged ahead by hiring a group of part time students and getting the MTU Library to assign us a room not far from the main stacks. They were also kind enough to have library personnel gather all the books and journals that they thought dealt with Lake Superior in one way or another. These publications were brought to our evaluation room. The first weeks were spent in setting up the procedures that we would be using and getting to understand how the U.W. Bibliography Program worked. All the data was to go on IBM punch cards for entry into the program. All we had to do was to define the data, someone else was being paid to punch it into the cards. Perhaps you can understand this better if you picture it as sort of a crude Google-type system. However, this was years before Google was available. Our responsibility was to anticipate the keywords that one might use to search for information about Lake Superior. Our funding was for two summers and the first summer was spent largely in defining better and better keywords to cover the available publications. The second summer was spent trying to apply these to all the publications that were available in the MTU library, plus those that were in other bibliographic listings. This work was carried out on the large conference table. We would write down the bibliographic information on the card that we had developed and check off the appropriate keywords from the list on the card, based on a quick perusal of the publication. If the students had any questions, they would pass the book to me for arbitration. Consequently, I reviewed a heck of a lot of material during the summer, of course spending quite a bit of time on those things that caught my interest. The final product worked quite effectively and was used for several years at Michigan Tech and the other schools that had the necessary technology to make use of it. Whether it really was as effective as originally intended or not, I don't really know. Of course, it was not too many years before it was supplanted by bigger and more effective computer systems. We hoped that our bibliography played some role in laying the groundwork for the later systems. For a while I felt that these two summers had been a waste of my time in the larger sense, however in retrospect, I think it might have been very valuable as it may have contributed significantly to my skills in the area of perusal.

In the meantime, I was so convinced that computer applications should be an important component of the biology curriculum that I submitted a proposal for a new course. This was approved for the following year and for several years, I taught a course using the two P-101 machines that we now had in the department. Shortly, Olivetti came out with the P-602, and we obtained one of these as well.

After several years of teaching students programming of Olivetti computers, I decided that they would be better served if I were teaching them a language that was more broadly applicable, although I did hear from one graduate who had gotten a job specifically because he could use the P-101. However, I decided that we really ought to be using BASIC programming language, on the mainframe. So, during the next summer, I began learning IBM BASIC Programming Language, using the UNIVAC (mainframe) that Michigan Tech was employing at that time. Program input was accomplished by IBM cards generated by a Punch-card Machine about the size of a desk. Each single line of BASIC code was punched into an IBM Card, using a typewriter keyboard, each character producing a loud chunking sound, as the hole was punched into the card. A program consisted of a stack of such cards. This stack was preceded by a couple of header

291

cards that included your password and ID. This was then submitted to the service desk, where they would put it into the processing queue and wait for it to be processed, perhaps coming back the next day if they were very busy. On returning, you would receive a large printout, listing your errors, etc. Then, you would redo the necessary cards and resubmit the revised stack of cards. This could take several repeats to successfully get a single program to run. This was especially bad if it didn't run and wouldn't tell you why it didn't run, such as when the Computer Center changed your ID or their mode of operation for some reason. Sometimes, after an exasperating discussion, you would find that your password was no longer valid, and they would say, "We explained that in the October Newsletter, didn't you read it?" Of course I hadn't read it since most of it was unintelligible to me. Despite these difficulties, it was clear that I had been hooked into the whole concept of using computers as a scientific tool (1975). Eventually, I worked up to using Time-Sharing Terminals for running my programs, which saved considerable time. Despite all this, I spent a major portion of my time at the Computer Center for a couple of years.

In 1978, I felt confident enough to offer a College Teacher Workshop on Computer Modeling in the Life Sciences. This was arranged by the Continuing Education Department and came off very well, using the course materials that I had developed for my department course. It was attended by 12 faculty representatives from various parts of the country. The whole operation was set up in a classroom in the computer center. One of the people who came to this initial workshop was Brian Winkel, an applied mathematician from Rose-Hulman Institute in Terre Haute, IN. This fortuitous meeting changed both of our lives, as he has made the copper country one of his favorite places and his support helped me realize several of my ambitions, including my first textbook. He became so interested in what we were doing that he came back for a sabbatical year at Michigan Tech, teaching in the math department and becoming a friend and colleague for the remainder of my life.

About this time, several companies were beginning to introduce small computers that had significant memory and video output. One that particularly took my fancy was Radio Shack's TRS-80. This had 8K of memory, a cassette recorder for storage of programs and a black and white screen. Best of all, they were designed to be programmed in BASIC which included a command for generation of a random number. In addition, some low-resolution graphics, including crude curves, could be displayed, as they were being generated. Somehow, I was able to get one. Now, I had total control of my programming, right on my own desk. I was no longer hassled by passwords, ID numbers, changes in operation, etc. As soon as I was able, I discontinued my relationship with the MTU Computer Center. I set about transferring all of my simulation programs to this platform. Every day was a new thrill, as crude curves were generated on the screen with so little effort. One day during Christmas Break, when I was in the building alone, I set about transferring my curve-fitting program to the TRS-80. When it got close to lunch time, I called Pat to tell her that she better go-ahead and eat lunch, as I had a few more things to do. However, everything that I did, suggested something else that would make the program just that much better. On and on I went; adding this; checking that; when all of a sudden, I looked up and discovered that it had gotten dark outside my window. It was then that I realized that I had been sitting at my desk, first turning to my computer, then turning back to my scratch material, then back to my computer, etc., <u>while never having once gotten up to eat or go to the bathroom for the entire day</u>! I had never been so absorbed by anything in my entire life.

The following year, with the help of Brian Winkel and a student, we set up two workshops, one for college faculty and one for high school science teachers. These were supported in part by NSF, but also by Radio Shack, as they loaned us 30 TRS-80s for use during the workshops. These were described in the brochure as *Microcomputers and Modeling in Undergraduate Life Sciences*. On the weekend before the workshops were to commence, a truckload of boxes arrived and in only a couple of hours, we had a complete computer center, with 30 workstations, up and running. These were fun sessions, as the three instructors learned as much as the students, due to the many computer tricks that participants brought with them. During this period and in subsequent years I was writing programs at what seems like one a day (but probably, more like one a week). These, of course, were simple programs; things like using random numbers to describe the path of a worm moving around the screen; a simple AI program to play a game of paper-rocks-scissors, analysis of a pendulum, describing a path of a satellite orbit, firing a cannon, etc., etc. My conclusion was there was nothing you could not do with a computer, if it had any basis in mathematics. And, that the computer was the all-purpose toolbox for making things that behaved like the real world and testing ideas about real-world scientific behavior.

In 1979, I submitted three interdependent proposals to the National Science Foundation. The main one was to carry on a project to develop 20 simulations that could be used for undergraduate biology instruction. This was called the *SUMIT Courseware Development Project*. The word SUMIT stood for Self-contained Undergraduate Modular Instructional Technique, which was sort of meaningless, but gave a salable acronym. The second proposal was for 10 TRS-80s that would be used for testing the material in biology classes. The third proposal was for three undergraduate workshops that would be used for dissemination of information about the completed simulations. Although, these proposals were submitted to separate divisions of NSF, each mentioned the other and apparently met with the approval of all three reviewing committees at NSF. Subsequently, the project director at NSF called to negotiate a change of computers from TRS-80s (B &W screens) to Apple IIe (color screens) and further required that I have a commitment from CONDUIT to publish the materials before the combined project would be approved. The conversion to the Apple IIe was an obvious advantage and since I had previously gotten to know Hal Peters, Director of CONDUIT, we didn't have any trouble arranging the commitment from them. When all the requirements were met, all three projects were approved, and Michigan Tech was awarded approximately $250,000, one of the largest educational grants given out by NSF during the 1979 academic year!

Soon after the SUMIT project was begun in 1979, I obtained three excellent graduate students named Ted Sohlden, Cathy Leece, and Mark Shaltz. The other faculty member was Ken Kramm. The 20 proposed projects were parceled out to the five staff on the project and we began working on them. The funds were used to provide summer salaries for the two faculty and stipends for the three graduate students. Unfortunately, Ken Kramm left the department after the first year. However, he had completed much of his assigned work and so he was not replaced. During the following two years, we were able to complete about a dozen modules. My graduate students wrote master's theses describing the planning and development of these projects to complete the requirements for the MS degree in Biological Sciences. The students assisted in the 1980, 1981 and 1982 workshops. About 10 modules were submitted for review by CONDUIT and the following year, I went on sabbatical and spent the majority of my time getting the modules ready for publication. In the end, eight instructional modules were published. The remainder of the simulations were made available to workshop participants and the general educational community on computer disks available from Michigan Tech. The eight modules developed by SUMIT made up the bulk of CONDUIT'S biology offering between '84 and '90. Unfortunately, all but one of these was available only for use on the Apple II computer, which was beginning to be supplanted by the new IBM-PC. It is only hoped that in addition to being used for instruction, they played some role in future developments in instructional computing. Although this sounds like we fell far short of our goal, it was exceptionally high productivity compared to most NSF projects, which were typically designed to produce a single product.

Ironically, one of the published modules, called BAFFLES, was not among the original 20 proposed. However, it was a game that had significant application in teaching students the principles of scientific inquiry and deductive reasoning. It was based on a physical game called "Black Box", in which one discerns the location of objects in a closed box by probing it with sticks. With Baffles, all of the objects are reflectors that can either deflect a beam to the right or to the left when "laser beam" probes are directed at one of forty points around the perimeter of the box. By analyzing the place where the beams exit the box, one is to deduce the location and tilt of each "Baffle". This becomes quite challenging when the number of baffles is increased to a point where almost all exit beams are the result of multiple hits. The score was based on the number of beams that were required to correctly locate all the baffles. The amount of time required was not a factor. This was sufficiently popular that it was made available for both the Apple II and the IBM-PC computers. It also led to some spin-off games of a similar nature. This serendipitous outcome turned out to be the most important result from the SUMIT project.

I decided to use the same principles in a reverse fashion in the design of a computer game that I called "Lazer Maze". In this game, the player was allowed to see the location of a bunch of reflective baffles that were randomly placed in an open box. Then a beam was fired into a randomly determined location. The objective was to predict, as rapidly as possible, where the beam would emerge from the box. This produced an exciting game that I tested on several students and friends. It appeared to be much more interesting to females than males. Up to that point, computer games were mainly based either on sports or war games and hence were mainly enjoyed by males. Was

Lazer Maze perhaps the long-sought computer game that appealed to females? Somehow, I had gotten the name of a company called Avant Garde, in Portland, Oregon and knew that their president was named Mary K. Smith. So, I sent them the disk and waited for a response. Shortly, I got a call from some computer nerd who said that the program worked fine, but they really had no interest in it since it just wasn't the kind of game they published. I asked if the president had reviewed it and he said that she hadn't. So, I asked if he would get her to do so. He grudgingly said, "OK" and hung up. In about 30 minutes I had a call from Mary K. Smith, who was really enthusiastic about the program, saying that she thought it had the potential of starting a "whole new genre of computer games." and that they definitely wanted to publish it. Then, she put the programmer back on the phone and he said that he would soup it up a little by putting in some "laser sounds" and making it so that an alien was killed when the laser came out the other end. I wasn't crazy about the alien aspect of it, but in about a month, the revised product came back for my approval and even though it had lost some of its feminine mystique, I wasn't going to argue at that point, so I signed the contract and returned it. Lazer Maze sold for a couple of years, during which time we went to visit them once. About a year later, I had a letter from LA, saying that a company that planned to distribute computer games by cable TV had bought Avant Garde. I gave them my permission to use Lazer Maze but have never heard from them since. Every now and then, I look through a display of computer games to see if there is anything that looks like Lazer Maze, but aside from that one call, the issue appears to be closed.

Meanwhile, we continued to offer summer workshops for both college and high school teachers. In 1982, Winkel and I were joined by Jim Randall, from Indiana University, who had written a text on Microcomputers and Physiological Simulation. In 1983 Winkel and I were joined by Tom Coleman from Univ. Mississippi and in 1984 it was Winkel, Randall & Spain again with 24 participants. Over the seven-year period '78 to '84, there were a total of about 120 participants representing 105 colleges and universities. There were also at least an equal number of high school teachers who were involved in high school workshops. It was gratifying to see the interest we had generated and to have played a role in the general application of computers to science education in both colleges and high schools.

During my own teaching in biological sciences I had gradually gathered instructional materials for students to use. These were printed up annually by the MTU print shop and sold to students at cost. After several years, I began to look for a publisher and in 1980, Addison-Wesley agreed to publish a book on the subject, if I could provide the camera-ready copy of the manuscript. About this same time, Brian Winkel and his wife, Phyllis, were in Houghton for the summer, so they agreed to produce the camera-ready copy for me. This was great as they already had experience publishing a journal called *Cryptologia*. This was a major undertaking as I realized that I really wanted something much more complete than what we had been printing locally. Fortunately, Brian and Phyllis helped me with the many mathematical equations and my colleague Ed Williams from Chemical Engineering agreed to go over the English and logic that I had employed. So, all in all, I had much more help than I would have ever gotten by sending a manuscript to a publisher. The result was that my 1982 simulation class had a real text to work from, *Basic Microcomputer Models in Biology*. Soon, I was receiving comments from faculty who had either used the text in their class or at least read it. Several years later, I had more citations in *Citation Index* from *Basic Microcomputer Models in Biology* than from the twenty-five research papers I had struggled to produce over the years previous. When I decided to go on sabbatical in 1983, I was able to get a position teaching at the University of British Columbia as a direct result of the book and used it in the instruction of a fisheries biology class. During my sabbatical, my replacement at MTU was Bob Keen, who spent the year writing an *Instructor's Manual to Accompany Basic Microcomputer Models in Biology* (this book was remarkable in that it was twice as thick as the original text it dealt with). So that in the year following my return, when I decided to take early retirement from MTU, Bob took over my course and subsequently assumed senior authorship of a revised text that was published in 1991 by John Wiley.

This text, *Biological Simulation Techniques, a BASIC Approach*, by Keen and Spain, is still being used at a few schools around the country.

CHAPTER 16

LIFE CHANGES

(1982-1985)

I. Sabbatical Leave

I was eligible for sabbatical leave from the Biological Sciences Department after I completed the major work on the SUMIT courseware development project, so I began exploring where I might go. I was to receive only half of my salary during my sabbatical year. We were interested in spending more time on the west coast. Since I had been corresponding with faculty at University of San Francisco and University of British Columbia, I wrote to these schools and a few others to see if there was any potential for half time employment. It turned out that USF was able to come up with some money for the fall semester and UBC was able to cover my spring semester needs. This sounded like a workable plan, so I sent letters of acceptance to both. Pat would accompany me for the fall term in San Francisco but would miss most to the spring term as she was continuing to manage the Hancock office of the UP-Tax Service until all the income taxes were completed on April 15. So, she would meet me in Vancouver, BC sometime after that.

Pat and I were thrilled with the fortuitous opportunity to return to Central California and spend some time together exploring San Francisco. When we arrived in San Francisco we were able to find an exceptionally nice apartment in a large complex in the Southwest corner of the city. It included beautiful views of the ocean, a nice pool, and exercise area including a racquet ball court, one of my interests at the time. Though quite far from downtown and the university, it was near the SF Zoo, Lake Merced, the SF Golf Course, right beside the famous Olympic GC. From our 7th floor apartment, we were able to see the hang gliders sailing out over the Pacific Ocean from bluffs at Fort Funston. Needless to say, we found more than enough activities to engage in and the weather that fall was absolutely beautiful. My responsibilities at USF were minimum and so I was able to spend almost all my time completing some of the SUMIT modules and getting them ready for publication based on the suggestions of my friend Hal Peters and other editors at CONDUIT. On several weekends we got together with my brother George and his wife Bev. We went places with them that we probably would not have gone to by ourselves. It was great fun. We were quite close to a small family owned Japanese restaurant which was very good and other times we went to a very good Chinese restaurant (Happy Family

Restaurant). Once, it was very crowded and we were the only "Round Eyes" in the place. Although I love the "City by the Bay", I will admit that there was probably not a time while I was there that I didn't think about earthquakes. We only had a minor shake or two, but I always had that strange feeling in the pit of my stomach. Our apartment was just not that far from the San Andreas Fault and it would have gone down like a stack of cards.

Before we went back to Houghton for Christmas, we drove up to Vancouver to find an apartment for me, for the spring semester. When we got close to the Canadian border, we spent the night in the border town and had dinner in a very special restaurant. It had amazingly good food and the owner/cook wandered among the tables, playing his accordion. The next day while waiting in line to go through Canadian customs, we reminded ourselves that we didn't want to mention that I would be working for UBC because of Canada's strict laws about taking jobs away from Canadian workers. The next thing I knew, I was responding to the custom's man question "What are you going to be doing in Canada?" with the statement; "I'm going to be working with UBC". Oh. mistake! "OK, sir, will you pull up there please." Then after an hour or so, assuring various officials that I wasn't taking anybody's job, etc. We finally got on our way and arrived in Vancouver after dark. My thought was that they must be constructing a lot of big buildings with huge cranes, suspended over the city, I found out later that I was looking at the lights of ski hills on the top of adjacent mountains that were not visible in the black sky. The next day we were able to find a small apartment that belonged to a couple of women who were going to be staying in southern California for the next four months. It was located just across the street from Stanley Park within walking distance of downtown. They, also, were leaving their furniture and a couple of bikes that I was free to ride. In addition, their garage was available and UBC was about six miles away. It looked like I was all set, so we headed on back to Seattle where I left the car with someone we knew.

When I arrived back after Christmas, I moved into my apartment and went off to see what things were like at UBC. I found that the man I was replacing was a fisheries biologist who wanted me to teach his fisheries course, using my text to teach his students the principles of computer simulation, emphasizing wherever possible, fisheries applications. I discovered that I had inherited an office with overstuffed furniture and a beautiful Asian secretary.

On top of that, every Friday afternoon the graduate students of the department held a TGIF party out in the back of the lab. The faculty at UBC had a huge Faculty Club with a grand dining room looking out to English Bay that was far beyond anything I have seen before or since.

Vancouver is a remarkable city. Despite its latitude north of that of our home in Houghton, there were flowering trees starting to show in January and it continued to get more and more beautiful as we went through the winter into spring. Rhododendrons were beginning in March, so that by May when Pat arrived, just about everything was in bloom. Because of the British influence (many people spoke with an accent), most people's yards looked like they employed a Japanese gardener. It was amazing driving back and forth to the university and there were several parks that were loaded with flowers. Stanley Park, across from where I lived, was a huge nature preserve, with many walking and biking trails weaving throughout. The weather was quite damp with misty, drizzly, rains, but about every 5th day would be sparkling sunshine, and everyone would seem to take off from work and would be out walking or riding all over the place. Even with the rain, I would usually take a walk downtown to explore the city. Often, I would find a neat little restaurant and have dinner. One disappointing thing was the number of homeless people in the city, typically pushing their belongings in grocery carts. Often these were indigenous people.

One weekend, I took the ferry over to Vancouver Island and drove north along the shore of Puget Sound. I encountered little, but a few Indian villages. I ran out of time before getting to the north end of the island, but I did manage to cross to the Pacific side and found a very flat and broad beach with the tide way out. It reminded me of the beach in pictures of Mt. Ste. Michelle in France and I was afraid to venture very far out on it. In another trip I drove north along the eastern shore of Puget Sound. This was fiord country with beautiful forests lining the shores. Another trip was across Lion Bridge to the north side of Vancouver Harbor. Here within a few miles I arrived at the parking lot at the foot of the mountain where people go to ski. One got to the top by cable car, where an active ski hill operated day and night. Around Vancouver it was literally possible to see cars with a full ski rack going one direction and cars with wind sails and other beach gear going in the other direction. It was a great place and I was ready to move in, but Pat wasn't so enamored and within a few years Hong Kong was taken over by Communist China and many thousands of rich Chinese moved into Vancouver. The cost of living went sky high and Vancouver became a very large city. C'est La Vie.

II. Early Retirement from Michigan Tech

During the year following my sabbatical, I had what you might call a terrible hangover. After spending a delightful fall in SF and a spring-like winter in Vancouver, the Houghton climate just left me 'cold', you might say. The tune "How ya gonna keep 'em down on the farm, after they've seen Paris?" kept going through my head. It was just not the same. The fun we had skiing, skating, watching ice hockey, etc. was just not there anymore and I began thinking more and more about going somewhere else.

Fortuitously, the Board of control approved an "Early Retirement Package", for which I was fully qualified. It was unique to my situation. Not only was this package available for just one year, but it was an exceptionally good package, and was later described as "the year of the Golden Parachute". When I looked back over the years I had been at Michigan Tech, I realized,

I must have taught a <u>record number of courses in</u> <u>my 29-year career at Michigan Tech</u>!

In the first six years, I taught all aspects of general chemistry, organic chemistry, lecture and lab, physical chemistry for metallurgists and geologists, introduced instrumental analysis and reintroduced biochemistry for senior chemists, radiological methods of analysis for nuclear engineering, and graduate course in biochemistry all in the Chemistry department.

Then, I transferred to the Biological Sciences Department, where I was responsible for biochemistry, animal physiology, histology, genetics, and micro technique. When I discontinued my administrative responsibilities, I added courses in biochemical lab technique, introductory limnology, graduate physical and chemical limnology, computer applications and computer simulations in biology. Many of these courses involved extensive notes as there was no text and one (computer simulation) involved the writing/publication of a textbook.

During these years I had started three technically challenging lab courses. The first was a senior level course, Instrumental Analysis in Chemistry. After I had moved to the Biological Sciences Department, I felt we needed a Biochemical Techniques Course and finally I decided that there should be a Computer Applications course in Biological Sciences. To my knowledge all three of these courses are still being taught in one form or another by appropriate faculty

My Favorite, all time, introduction to a lecture was for a course in limnology. I went into the lecture hall and used a piece of chalk to draw a straight line from one end of the blackboard to the other. Then, I said: "If that line represented the 350-mile length of the surface of Lake Superior. What line could we use to show the depth of Lake Superior if we use the same scale?" The maximum depth for Lake Superior is 1,333 feet and it comes about 1/3rd from the east end of the lake. After giving the students some time to think about it and nobody said anything, I said; "I think that you will find the depth of Lake Superior is shown by the width of the chalk line!".

The point of this introduction was twofold. First, there is damn little freshwater out there and we better take care what we have and second, all the pictures of lakes that you will see in textbooks are NOT drawn to scale. They are used to emphasize particular features of the Lake.

III Eastern Michigan University

Though, I had taught for thirty years, counting my year at Stanford, I still needed one-year to complete my thirty years in the Michigan Education System to receive full retirement benefits from the State, so I began looking for a college to complete my thirtieth year. It turned out that Dr. Ron Collins, whom I had met at some of the early computer conferences, was provost at Eastern Michigan University. He had been thinking about starting an Instructional Computing Center (ICC) for some time and asked me to come down to Ypsilanti (adjacent to Ann Arbor) to interview for the position. So, we turned out to be a good match and after a few formalities, I was appointed Director, with a joint appointment in the Chemistry Department. The first semester, I taught a biochemistry class, but the second semester was totally devoted to operation of the Instructional Computing Center, with me as its sole employee. This was great fun, as I interacted with people in various departments across the campus. The center was directed by a committee that included Ron Collins, whose background was in instructional computing in chemistry and John Moore, a chemist, well known for his activities in instructional computing and Editor of the Seraphim Project. He went on to become editor of the Journal of Chemical Education and Director of the Institute of Chemical Education at the University of Wisconsin. So, there were several top-notch people interested in having the ICC do something useful. While I was at EMU, I would also meet Bill Butler, an instructional software programmer at nearby University of Michigan. This would be an important contact, as I would ultimately carry on the programming of general chemistry software that he had initiated, originally for the Commodore Pet computer, in about 1975.

My approach as Director of ICC was to visit a department and give a presentation on what the potential was for use of computers in their discipline. This was generally followed by questions and answers, from which I was usually able to identify an interested faculty member with whom I could work. I would meet with the individual in his/her office, where we would explore an idea of what the instructor wanted to achieve. From this plan, I would return to my office and I would put together a rough computer program in BASIC that would achieve the objective. In a day or so I would return to the instructor's office with something that we could look at on his/her computer. I had five Apple II computers that I could loan out for this purpose. It was a lot of fun and I was able to come up with about ten different programs that at least gave the faculty an idea about the potential for instructional computing in their area. Several of these led to grant proposals of one sort or another to support the development of the completed product. One project of particular interest was done for a faculty member in Sociology. The objective was to write a program that answered free-form questions on sex education. The thought was that kids would ask questions from a computer that they would be too embarrassed to ask a teacher. I felt and still feel that it had enormous potential. The result was that I went to Washington to talk to the people at the Department of Education. However, we did not do the proper groundwork and so I didn't see the right people, with the result that the project died. In chemistry, I set up a drill and practice program for naming elements that ultimately became a part of the ChemSkill Builder system to be described in a coming chapter.

The weather in the vicinity of Eastern Michigan University was certainly milder than we had experienced at Houghton but was still cold on occasions. One time we had a particularly cold Friday and at about 5:30pm the wind was blowing about 25 mph when I was walking across campus on my way to the car. All of a sudden, my hat blew off and started cartwheeling across the open area that was covered with about six inches of snow. I found myself chasing it in my bootless oxfords with snow going in around my socks. I already had a bad cold starting, so I was not too happy when I finally caught up with my hat and jammed it down on my head. I got in the car and drove to the grocery, as I needed to stock up for the weekend. Pat was in Houghton, until April 15, as she was still managing the UP-Tax Service. When I got out of the car going into the grocery, I disgustedly pulled off my hat, flung it on the seat and slammed the door. On arriving back with a bag-full of groceries, I found the car to be locked

315

with the key still sticking in the ignition! So, I went back into the store and asked if any of the bag boys were able to help me get the car open. One volunteered, but on looking at the car, a Chevy Citation, he said; "You can't get into those horizontally sliding locks." So, we went back to the store to see if there were any other suggestions. "Why don't you call your wife." said the clerk. "She's 550 miles away, in Houghton." I said. Then I realized that the extra keys were in the apartment about a mile to the west. So, off I went jogging into the vicious northwest wind, through the snow, no hat, until I finally got to the apartment and got the janitor to let me in. The first thing I did was to collapse on the couch with a bottle of wine, where I stayed until I was ready to make the return trip. However, this was not quite so bad since it was downwind, and I was more prepared with a wool knit cap. With this experience to draw on, I was not very interested in spending more than one winter at EMU.

While I was at EMU, I received a letter from the Director of Instructional Computing at Stanford asking if I would be interested in interviewing for a position in their department. This was exciting as we always had it in mind that we would like to go back to that area. In my mind there was only one snag, which was that I would have to learn to use the language they were using to program on Macintosh computers. So, I responded in the affirmative and we received an invitation to come interview. Pat and I flew out to San Francisco, got a rental car, and drove down to Stanford. After meeting the director,

Pat went off to look around the area and I went to tour the facilities. Later that morning, I met with the advisory board and was asked questions like "How do you like directing staff members, programmers, graduate students etc." To these questions, I responded with comments like: "I really like working on my own", "I really enjoy the one-on-one interaction with faculty members" and "I like to write small programs to show faculty the potential of instructional computing", basically, drawing on my experiences at EMU. These comments, which I thought were quite innocent, elicited strange looks from the committee. Eventually, this awkward interview came to an end and I didn't think much more about it. However, the following day, I was walking across campus with the director and he said; "Well, I'm very disappointed that you are not interested in the director's position!" I must have said something like "Say what!" or "Come again!" Whereupon he explained that he wanted to step down as director and that they were looking for a replacement. Unfortunately, they had failed to communicate this concept to me. I guess they had assumed that since I was a "Director" at EMU that I would only be interested in such a position at Stanford and it wasn't necessary to explain that to me. Obviously, I didn't get the job. However, it was much too expensive to live in the Palo Alto area and it had become very crowded since my student years. In retrospect, if by some quirk, I had gotten that job, we would not have had the opportunity to go to South Carolina and thus would have missed out on all of the interesting life experiences that follow in the next several chapters.

317

CHAPTER 17

CLEMSON

(1985-1994)

While I was at EMU, I had gotten to know Joe Allen, who was on sabbatical leave from Clemson University in South Carolina. We often ate lunch together, as we were both new to the EMU scene. He would tell me about the "mountain brook" that ran through his back yard and of the neighboring college, Western Carolina University, which I knew to be deep in the mountains. Since I had always loved the mountains, I began to wish I could live in such an area. Pat and I went out to dinner several times with Joe and Doris, his wife, and we became quite good friends. At the end of the fall term, Joe and Doris moved on to complete his sabbatical year at Clarkson Univ. We subsequently decided that one-year would be enough in the Detroit area where EMU is situated and began looking for employment to supplement my retirement income. Low and behold, I found that Clemson University was looking for a sabbatical leave replacement for the coming year and so I applied for it. Could this be a place for us to retire – at least, it looks like the first place to start looking.

We spent the summer back in Houghton at our home in Royalwood, wondering if I had a job or not. Finally, I made a call to Dr. DesMarteau, the Dept. Head at Clemson, and he said: "Oh, yes, I guess you do have the job. I meant to give you a call. Can you get down here by August 17? That's when the fall semester starts." This led to some real scrambling, but by August 10 or so, we had most of our traveling furniture and other stuff loaded in a U-Haul trailer and I was on the road south. Pat was to stay behind to finish up loose ends and drive down to join me in about a week. My trip took me on I-40 through the Smoky Mountains and then on I-26 from Asheville, south. According to the map, I was to get off I-26 onto US-25, which would take me to Greenville, SC. Well it turns out that US-25 crosses I-26 many times and I took one turn too early and ended up going through downtown Hendersonville and then through East Flat Rock, all on mountain roads. Finally, I made another bad turn and ended up on a one-lane road going up into the mountains. I managed to get the car and trailer turned around and back on the right road, which turned out to be a four-lane divided highway. However, no sooner was I over the South Carolina line, when the road turned abruptly downhill, with the beautiful mountains of North Carolina in my rear-view mirror. I was thinking: "NO, there must be some mistake. Clemson is supposed to be in the mountains." Eventually, I got into Greenville and on the road to Clemson, which after passing through a "strip-city" called Easley, and finally turned into a beautiful four-lane parkway honoring John C. Calhoun.

On arriving at Issaqueena Trail, I turned off and went directly to the apartment that Doris Allen had arranged for us. It turned out to be somewhat less than we had hoped, so I looked at a couple of others in the same complex and finally took one on the agreement that they would replace the carpet. This allowed me to unload the trailer and get it returned to U-Haul. All in all, it was pretty discouraging, as I knew that Pat wouldn't be happy with the apartment. The next day, I went about 30 miles into Greenville to check on furniture rental and found some stuff that I thought we could be happy with. After that, I drove around a bit, getting to know the Clemson area and found that the mountains were only about 50 miles away. The next morning, I was walking in the neighborhood that surrounded our apartment and discovered that a really nice apartment complex was just across Issaqueena Trail from the one I had moved into. It included a beautiful pool and other amenities that we were looking for. I went into the attractive clubhouse and talked with the lady in charge. She said that they did have an apartment that I could look at. It turned out to be nice and new, so, I said; "I'll take it". Now the question was how to get out of the other contract, as they were already working on the new carpet. That night, after the workmen had departed, I began moving our stuff out, loading it into the car and hauling it up the stairs of the new apartment. I think it took two evenings to do this, but finally, I was done. I felt guilty as hell but knew we wouldn't have been happy in the original place, even with the new carpet. I called the furniture rental place and told them the new address and they delivered the furniture about the time that Pat arrived. The apartment was quite well laid out, with two bedrooms and two baths on opposite sides of the living room. There was a dinette with a pass through to the kitchen and a balcony-porch big enough for a couple of chairs. It looked like we should be quite happy there. The next day, I went back to the rental office to settle my account on the original apartment. I told the owner that my wife was just not happy with his apartment and asked if there was any chance of getting some of down payment back. He smiled at me and said, "That's fine, I understand. Let me write you a check for the full down payment." He then proceeded to write out a check for the total amount with no rancor at all. I couldn't believe it. If this had been any other place I'd ever lived, he would have laughed in my face. That was our first experience with Clemson's southern hospitality.

When I arrived at the Chemistry Department, Joe Allen was happy to see me. Other faculty members welcomed me, as well. The first semester, I was assigned only a single general chemistry lecture and the only meetings that I had to attend were the department meeting and the general chemistry meetings, where Joe was the chairman. I also participated in running the computerized instruction center, that consisted of six or eight Apple II computers and some assorted programs that students looked at, some of which Joe had accumulated during his sabbatical. Students got credit for just looking at the programs and writing up a short report. Since we were in the old chemistry building at the time, I was sharing an office with an analytical chemist and the lecture hall was of the old style. It took me a while to get myself back into the mode of teaching general chemistry, as I had not taught it for 23 years. The biggest thing was building up a set of notes, which really consisted of drawing up a set of transparencies, as that was the mode of teaching, I had developed during the last ten or fifteen years. I almost never used the blackboard, largely because my writing was so bad. I also had to do a lot of reading in the text and doing all of the assigned problems to try to stay ahead of the students. It kept me busy for the first year. However, I still had time to work on the computer and at that time, I was interested in the "bootstrap" technique that I had read about in *Scientific American*. It consisted of repeatedly sampling from a simulated set of data, using random numbers. Since it had to be done an enormous number of times, I would set up the computer to run all night. The object was to see how much sampling was necessary to achieve a certain level of confidence about the data. For me, it was just a curiosity thing, but it kept me busy for quite a while.

We enjoyed our stay in the Clemson area, as Pat and I soon joined a small par-three golf course called Woodhaven that was run by a young man named Clint Wright, who had come from Florida and graduated from Ferris State College in Michigan. We enjoyed playing once or twice at an 18-hole golf course called Boscobel. We also joined a group of couples called the Newcomers, who played bridge about once a month. Here, we met several new friends and generally had a good time. We also enjoyed the swimming pool, since it was just across the street from our apartment and we could go over at about ten in the evening if we wanted to and have the pool all to ourselves.

My disappointment at not living in the mountains was ameliorated when we would hear about the icy roads and school closings in the mountains on our TV channel from Asheville, NC, while we were enjoying the bright sunshine of South Carolina. So, all in all, we had a good time that first year and as the year began to draw to a close, I was not so interested in looking for another place to work. My discussions with Dr. DesMarteau suggested that they might find a place for me, but there wouldn't be any money for a salary increase.

The second year, a fairly loud couple moved into the apartment below us, so things were not quite so sublime. However, after a month or so of these conditions, we found that there was an apartment available on the backside of the complex, which had a balcony that overlooked a wooded valley. So, we moved to this new apartment, which proved to be an excellent choice. It was basically the same arrangement, but because of the location, was much quieter. As I said, the balcony looked out toward a stream valley with large trees, partially obscuring a fairly new housing development on the opposite hill. We also had less sunshine as it was facing east. We remained in this location for a couple of years and found that it was almost ideal for having guests, because of the location of guest's rooms on the opposite side of the living room and dining area.

We only had one problem there. We had noted that there was evidence of mice in the kitchen around the refrigerator. Then one morning, I was eating breakfast while Pat was working in the kitchen, having just put some bread in our open-front toaster. When suddenly, I smelled something like burning fur and Pat began screaming. I looked through the pass-through to the toaster and saw a mouse running around in circles on top of my still-cooking toast! After about three turns, he dove over the side of the toast into the red-hot grill, to his ultimate demise. Pat came running out of the kitchen gagging, as she proceeded toward the bathroom. "Get that toaster out of here!" she screamed, as I doubled over with laughter. I put the toaster out in the breezeway, came back to open the sliding doors and turn on the fan to get rid of the smell. It took an hour or so for her to recover from this trauma, then we went to Hardee's to get some breakfast. On the way home, we picked up some traps to get rid of our mouse problem and bought a new toaster. We gave the old one to the janitor to dispose of the mouse and clean up for himself. He was happy to get it.

The same morning as the mouse incident, I discovered something about Hardee's that I still find hard to believe. Because of the earlier activities we didn't get to Hardee's until about ten o'clock. I forget what Pat had, but I had biscuits and gravy, which I found to be so good that I decided to have another order. Before I got back to the counter, I had noticed something I thought was odd. They were dumping huge trays of biscuits into the trashcan. So, I got in line and finally got up to give my order. "I would like another order of biscuits and gravy" I said. To which, the girl replied, "I'm sorry sir, it is past 10:30 and we are serving the lunch menu now." "But I just saw you dumping biscuits into the trash!" I said. "I'm sorry sir", she said calmly. "This is ridiculous!!!" I said. Despite my red face and waving arms, I never got my biscuits and gravy. This apparently was a general policy of Hardee's at that time. However, we were having lunch at another Hardee's store when the manager came out and passed out free biscuits for everyone to enjoy. Apparently, the lunch policy does have some modifications.

About the end of the second year when I talked to Dr. DesMarteau about the possibilities of another year, he suggested that I might be given the responsibilities for all the general chemistry laboratories. The current director of labs was Melanie Cooper, who didn't exactly get along with DesMarteau. Enough was said to me that I began planning how I would handle laboratories in the future. My thoughts were that I would get rid of the "cook-book" approach, where all students were assigned to carry out exactly the same procedure. My idea was that each lab should be a mini-research project, in which the students would be given some objectives and they would select the means to achieve them. For example, in an electrochemistry lab, students would be provided a bunch of different metals and different electrolytes and they would decide which to use to produce a battery. Once the battery was formed, they would do some tests to determine the voltage and amperage under a given load. Such a lab would be very challenging to design, but much more valuable to the student than the procedure of simply following a series of directions. I spent a couple of weeks getting my preliminary plans together, but did not go much further than that, as Melanie went to the higher authorities and in the end, Dr. DesMarteau decided to back off. Melanie was given full responsibility for the lab and ultimately given tenure and a full Professorship. Over the years she developed a model lab and is well known around the country. She has held important positions in the Chemical Education Division of the American Chemical Society.

Somehow, the department found the money to keep me for another year, without much of a raise, of course. I didn't have much bargaining power, since Dr. DesMarteau knew I was receiving retirement income from MTU and that I really liked the Clemson area. I think that it was the following year that we moved into the new building and I was given my own office. This was a nice facility with an excellent lecture hall that was sloped so that you could easily see every student. We each had classes sometimes reaching as many as 200 students. About that time, I began trying to learn student's names. The way that I did it was to bring a camera on one of the first days and have the students write their names on a sheet of paper. Then I would take pictures of groups of about 20 students while they were holding the nametag in front of them. These prints were cut up into individual student pictures and glued to a file folder. I was able to learn some of them that way, but no matter how hard I would try, I couldn't call them by name, as I had hoped to do. I think my interest in names must have come from an awesome visiting freshman chemistry lecturer named Clark Bricker, who had the unbelievable ability to learn essentially all student's names in the first couple of weeks. He would be standing down in the isles as the students came into the room and have a conversation going with most of them, again calling them by name. His lecture was a conversation with the students, calling on them and asking questions to get them all involved in a participatory manner, totally at ease, as were the students. Remember, I'm talking about a class of 150-200 students. As I say, Bricker was a totally awesome teacher. When the exam grades came in, his classes were head and shoulders above the rest of us. He was simply a master teacher. Unfortunately, he was there only for a single year.

One of the good things that we did in the general chemistry program was to give a common exam to all students for both the midterm and the final. This was a lot of work preparing the exams, but they were new every time and as fair as we could make them. Each instructor would submit about ten questions and the director of the program would put them together to achieve as much of a balance as possible. Then came the hard part. We would discuss them in a group session. In some cases, this meant argue about them. Two or three times I got into some really bad arguments, once with Melanie. This didn't make any friends and I was to regret it later. Joe Allen was a good mediator and we always ended up with an exam that was about as good as anyone could expect. As I indicated above, we always were interested in how our results came out compared to the other five or six instructors. For a while, I was coming out on top (not counting Bricker), then Melanie Cooper began to pass me by, as she began to use the peer-group discussion method in her class. The college had an Instructor's Evaluation Form that we passed out at the end of each term. I was happy to do this, as you could always learn some interesting things.

One term, I was surprised to read my evaluation sheets and find that several students remarked that they liked me because I was so funny. This I thought very odd, as I never told a joke, or at least not a planned one. Of course, if I thought of something funny or interesting, I always threw it into my discussion. One time I really put my foot into it. I was discussing the "activity series" of metals that has to do with more active metals, like sodium, replacing less active metals, like copper, from their compounds, so I said that it was sort of like the "pecking order" in chickens. This comment was followed by dead silence and totally blank faces, so I realized that they really had never heard of the "pecking order". Thus, I explained that chickens naturally set up a pecking order in which one chicken will peck on a weaker chicken, but a stronger chicken will peck on the first. And then I said quite innocently, "And the top pecker, pecks on them all". With that, the class dissolved in laughter and my face became as red as a beet, as I realized what I had said. Fortunately, the period was about over, so I said; "I guess that's about it for today."

About this time, Joe was asked to serve as acting department head and indicated that he would not be returning to the general chemistry program. So, the department was actively looking for a new

329

Director of General Chemistry. As I now felt myself sufficiently experienced to handle this position, I submitted an application. Unfortunately, the reviewing committee had in mind getting someone considerably younger than I and they hardly acknowledged my application, other than to send me a thank you letter. At this point, my ego got the better of me and this obvious slight began to work on my mind. Unfortunately, I became so upset that I reported the affair as a case of age discrimination to the federal agency that handles such problems. In retrospect, I don't really think that I wanted this position, as much as I wanted the recognition that this position would have implied. As I have said before, I work best by working alone and not by directing other people to work. But my ego was running the show. Anyway, when I talked to the people at the federal agency, I was told that I probably had a pretty good case, but if I pressed it any further, I would end up losing most of my friends at Clemson and probably wouldn't accomplish anything. So, after full consideration, I decided to drop the whole thing and go back to doing what I really ought to do. In the end, the position was taken by Jeff Appling, a very likable young man who ultimately positively influenced me and made the suggestion that led to my next major career change. My being willing to accept the situation turned out to be very fortuitous and possibly one of the most important course corrections of my life.

When we moved into the new building, we had a special computerized learning center that had been designed by Muriel and Barnes Bishop, as well as by Joe Allen. However, because of my experience with computers, it was more or less being turned over to me. Just as we were moving into the building, the Instructional Technology people tried to talk the department out of the lab. It turned out that they wanted to put some computer terminals in there and give us a little dinky room at the other end of the hall. After some negotiation, they put about 15 IBM-PCs in the main room and took the little room at the other end of the hall for the terminals to the mainframe. Wow! We had come out smelling like a rose. As a result of the PC gift, we began phasing out the Apple II computers and changing over to PC software. We had been using *Computer Aided Instruction for General Chemistry* by William Butler & Raymond Hough, drill-and-practice software for freshman chemistry. About that time Bill Butler, whom Joe and I had met while visiting the University of Michigan, was changing his software to run on PCs. We could now assign the students to do specific programs and require that they obtain a grade of at least 80 to get credit for the work. The change did not cause much complaint, so we continued in that mode for the remainder of my stay at Clemson. The only problem with the Butler software was that it was lacking in many areas, particularly in the second semester. Initially, I thought I would augment this with some of my simulation programs. I had one that I had designed to teach kinetics, a topic that deals with speed of chemical reactions. I was very proud of it and had shown it to several faculty members, with what I thought were positive results. However, when used on the students, it fell totally flat! The general comment was "I liked all the instructional programs except that thing on kinetics! It didn't help me one bit." I then realized that what the students wanted and needed was something that would teach them information similar to that which was going to be asked on the examinations. Despite its utility, this type of instruction known as "Drill and practice" has a low reputation among educators. However, if this is something students need and want, then why not use it? Thus, I began to augment the Butler software by writing programs of a similar nature to fill in the gaps that he had left. This crucial decision set me on a new path, from 'simulation' to 'drill and practice' as my solution to computerized instruction.

About a year later, I wrote to ask him if he would be willing to send me his code on a particular program, as I wanted to use the same sort of procedure in a later chapter. He wrote back saying that he was sending me all of his code, as he had no further plans to work on the freshman chemistry software. Apparently, he had been given the word by the university that if he didn't develop a research program, he would not retain his position on the UM faculty. In effect, he turned the entire project over to me. About a year later, he was very seriously injured as a result of a fall from a tree-stand while hunting for deer. I believe he was in the hospital for quite a while and never really went back to work. A very sad ending to a great career in computerized instruction.

It was about that time that I made a serious commitment to myself to rewrite the entire series of programs using the approach developed by Butler, but greatly improving the format used. The language was to be BASIC, as was his, but I was going to change the font to allow for a full set of chemical characters and make use of color to the extent possible. Problems were going to check for proper number of significant figures and units in the answers submitted by students. Random numbers were to be used to vary problem content, so that students working next to each other would not get the same problems. Full explanations would be provided whenever the student submitted the incorrect answer. Subjects covered were to encompass the full year of general chemistry. In other words, the goal was to produce a collection of software that went well beyond that which was available at the time. Since we had Butler's software to use, the new units could be brought online as they were developed, without hampering student development. It took about four years to complete this project, working mainly during the summers while I was in Houghton.

During this time, I was managing the Chemistry Learning Center with four or five student assistants. Some were graduate student assistants, usually those with language problems that prevented them from teaching lab sections. The others were undergraduate work-study students, who usually turned out to be my best workers. After the first year, we obtained several more IBM PCs so that we usually had about 20 computers set up at all times. Sometimes, when a deadline for a particular assignment was due, we had as many as 50 students working away, sitting on boxes, lab stools,

333

etc. It was amazing to see that many students working on chemistry, all discussing what the answer to a question should be and how you should get it.

In order to compare the student input in response to numerical problems, which makes up approximately one third of the total problems, the computer was to analyze and provide numbers with the proper number of significant figures, as this is not provided as a component of any version of BASIC I had encountered before or since. Because the use of the proper number of significant figures (digits) is taught and expected by most faculty, it was essential that an effective subroutine for significant figures be developed. So, early on, I began working on this problem. I cannot remember how many times I thought that I had it solved. I would test for a hundred or so randomly generated numbers and it would appear to be working fine. Then, a problem situation would come along that did not work properly, and I would get a complaint from a student saying that the computer marked them wrong when in fact they were right. Many times, of course, the student **was** wrong, and they simply misunderstood how to determine significant figures. But sometimes they were correct. Since the computer is making a binary to decimal conversion during each calculation, there are certain numbers close to 1.00000, such as 0.99999 or 1.000001 that just don't work right. That is the sort of thing that can drive you crazy. The upshot was that the final development of a fully consistent significant figure algorithm required about 6 to 8 years to develop and was only finally completed when both Hal Peters and I worked on it together. My conclusion was that if a computer science instructor wanted a good project for a final exam, he or she could not do any better than assigning the development of a significant figure subroutine.

Almost all of the program development was carried on over the summer months, on an inexpensive IBM PC Junior that I had purchased. I continued to use interpretative Basic language, storing the resulting programs on 5.25in floppy disks, which were the standard at the time. This resulted in about 5 or 6 chapters of material per summer. I think that our ultimate goal, at that time, was to complete 20 chapters. It was only much later that we were to achieve the full 24 chapters. At that time there was no numbering of the chapters, simply named, as in "Molarity", "Gases", "Liquids and Solids", etc. The following year, these would be tested in the Learning Center at Clemson on the general chemistry students. It later turns out the importance of doing this work during the summer, on our time, is what resulted in the determination the software belonged to us and not Clemson University.

The more I worked with the students using our general chemistry programs in the Learning Center at Clemson, the more I became convinced that this was a very effective way to teach chemistry to large numbers of students. The learning center ran about 60 hours a week. The expense of operating it was minimal, as it was manned by graduate student assistants and undergraduate work-study students and me as director. All we had to do was to answer questions and sign the student record cards. By this time, the grade was based on the number of sections that were completed with a grade of at least 80%.

I learned a lot from this experience, as I could wander around when the Center was not so busy and listen to what students were saying. From this, I learned what was good about the programs and what was not so good. When I got better ideas or saw errors that needed correction, I could return to my office and make the changes on the program immediately. The next day, I would have the revised software up and running.

During this period, several other schools were using the learning center version of this software on a test basis. These included, among others, John Moore at the University of Wisconsin and Darrell Smith at the University of Georgia. The fact that John Moore was using the materials was particularly significant in that he had all the material he had collected from his Seraphim Project and, yet he selected my stuff for his class (of course, he was a good friend of Bill Butler, which didn't hurt). The use of the software at UGA was to develop into a significant relationship it turns out. I was getting some feedback from some people, but not as much as I would have liked. The most important result was that it gave me the confidence and encouragement to continue the development of the project.

The final year that I was at Clemson, I devised a way to have the record of the student's work printed out to eliminate the transcribing of records by hand. This made less work for the student assistants, but more work for me, as I had to review each report to make sure that each was a valid student record. However, this ultimately led to the next stage in this process, which involved an electronic means of recording and transmitting records. This part of the story will be discussed in the chapter on Electronic Homework Systems.

During the last couple of years at Clemson, several of my friends began to take retirement and since I was beginning to struggle a little with the teaching, I was beginning to think about retirement myself, as I was approaching 65 and was eligible for full retirement under Social Security. About this same time, I received a letter stating that I was eligible for an early retirement bonus from the state of South Carolina. The first letter I received, I just tossed in the trash, as I thought that cannot be for me since I was a temporary faculty member and they can get rid of me any time that they want. When I received the second reminder, I said, "What the heck, I will give them a call and see if I really am eligible". The secretary responded, "Just fill out the form and send it in. It can't hurt." So, I did and for a couple of months I had heard nothing from them and happened to run across the old correspondence again. So, I gave them a call and this time talked to the man in charge. I told them that I had sent in my form and wondered if I had been eligible. "Did you hear anything denying the application?" he asked. I said no, and he said: "Well, you must have been eligible then." So, I received a letter saying that if I retired by the end of the year, I would receive a bonus of over $8,000. Apparently, I hadn't been a temporary employee since my fifth year on the faculty. So, in 1994, at the end of 9 years on the faculty, I retired from Clemson and received both the early retirement bonus and the retirement benefits of the State of South Carolina. It had been a really good experience, where I made some very good friends, who for a while met once a month for lunch and enjoyed each other's company. I am even considered part of the Emeritus Faculty by Clemson University. During this period, we had also accomplished the other objective we had in coming to South Carolina – we had found the part of the country where we wanted to retire. As the Upstate area and Boscobel Golf Course has all the features that anyone could ever want.

* *Computer Aided Instruction* for **General Chemistry by William Butler** & **Raymond Hough** *Drill-and-practice software $40 (4-disk set). John Wiley & Sons, Inc. Copyright 1982 (?)*

CHAPTER 18

GOLF

(1949-2013)

It was not until I got to Michigan Tech, as a student, that I took golf as one of my physical education options and began to play on occasion at the Portage Lake Golf Course, a nine-hole layout that had been built in 1902 and later purchased by Michigan Tech. Apparently, I had a pretty bad slice at the time, as I distinctly remember the difficulty, I had on what is now hole #18. Almost every drive went over the fence out of bounds on the right into the farmer's field. This was before the trees grew to the size that they are now and so it was a wide-open space for slices. It was also "out of bounds" for students since the owner had some serious no trespassing signs. I remember little more than this, as most of my time was spent on campus some four miles away, and I had no friends who were golfers.

After graduating from Michigan Tech, there was a rather extended golf hiatus, as I was busy going to graduate school. This caused me to miss some great opportunities, as the Stanford Golf Course is one of the great golf courses in the country, which is one of the reasons Tiger Woods and Michelle Wie went there. As a graduate student, I could have played this course very inexpensively, if not for free. However, my head wasn't into golf at the time and apparently none of my colleagues were either. So, it wasn't until I got back to Michigan Tech as a faculty member that I took up the game again. After about a year, I joined the Men's League. However, this turned out to be too competitive for me and I only lasted a year or so. It was not 'til several years later that I joined up again, this time with Larry Lawrence, a retired Army Colonel, as my partner. Either I had gained confidence, or they had changed the rules of play, as I started enjoying the game.

Pat also started playing golf after Lisa was born. She took several lessons in a class run by Verdie Cox and helped by Evan Hughes and some of the other golfing volunteers. It was not long before she was playing with Ladies League every Tuesday. I continued to play in the Men's League with Larry as my partner for pretty much the remainder of my golfing career.

Pat and I had some great times playing with couple's groups. These operations were led for the most part by Evan and Eleanor Hughes, Jim and Shirley Tormala, Dan and Sandy Cooney and Warren and Joan Monberg. Beside the Friday outings, there was usually an annual Labor Day outing at the Keweenaw Mountain Lodge. At this time of the year, most of the summer tourists would have left the area, the bugs were gone, and the golf course was in good shape from

340

Summer operation. We were usually joined by a few other golfers who were not part of the regular group, as there was usually a "big money" scramble of some sort set up between the men on Saturday. It was all great fun, followed by a party at one of the cabins. Here, I would usually take some of my homemade wine and play guitar for a bit. After the post-golf party, we would all go up to the Lodge for a buffet dinner. As we got older, fewer people would participate and the last one was attended by only a few couples and finally stopped for us, when I took early retirement, because of our early departure for Clemson each year. The last of these outings, the men's foursome consisted of only Hughes, Tormala, Monberg and me. Because of the casual nature of the game, both Hughes and Monberg brought along their Golden Retrievers and they were bounding along with the foursome, chasing squirrels and other critters. When we got to the 5th tee box, Monberg began bragging about how well his dog would retrieve a stick no matter where it was thrown. So, he was tossing it around and carrying on. Finally, he said "I bet you ten bucks that he will bring it back even if it is thrown way back into the woods." Whereupon he threw the stick casually back into the woods. By chance, the stick lodged in the crotch of a tree about ten feet above the ground. The dog went over to the tree and began trying to get the stick, but to no avail, whining and barking all the while. After, a few minutes of this, it was obvious that the dog was not going to return the stick and we were all doubled up with laughter. Then, Warren said "Damn it dog, the next time I take you some place, bring a ladder!" As was usual on such occasions, there was no payoff on the bet.

Unfortunately, this round of golf managed to get our foursome ejected from the course for the rest of the year.

When we went to South Carolina, we first played at the Woodhaven Golf Course, just outside Pendleton. This was a par-three course owned and operated by Clint Wright, who came from Florida, but got his golf course management degree from Ferris State College in Michigan. So, we had a few things in common and we talked with him on several occasions. The course was convenient and only cost about $30 per month for both of us to belong.

It wasn't long however before we tried a full 18-hole course, down the road, that was called Boscobel. Wow, that was something! It was a homey course, but quite demanding, in that every hole was different. Gradually, we began going there more and more. One day, after living in the apartment for about four years, we were walking by a brick house on the 13th fairway and saw that it was for rent. We stopped in and after some negotiation with the landlord; we moved in and had a home right on Boscobel Golf Course.

Boscobel was the name of a plantation that went back to the early days around 1830, when low-country plantation owners used to summer in the up-country and settled around the town of Pendleton. In the early 1900s, Boscobel was a favorite spot for Clemson students to swim and meet the local girls. It had a beautiful spring-fed pond, in the center of the property. Adding a sliding board and dance pavilion further developed the swimming area. In 1932, a golf course was added, and the swimming facilities were allowed to decline. In 1949, the golf course was improved by the addition of a second nine and restructured to its present configuration. At this time, it was owned by a consortium that included Baseball Hall of Fame-pitcher, Whitey Ford and a local man named, Buck Hancock. Later, Hancock acquired sole ownership of it. A few years after we joined for about $500, Buck sold it to Joel (Joey) Herbert and a partner. It is strictly a public golf course that has been successful because it caters to the "good old boys" and encourages lots of group outings. Another feature that attracted many people was that there was no rule against five people playing together as long as they didn't hold up play. In fact, many of the guys in the big money games seemed to prefer to play as a fivesome.

After becoming residents, we were asked to join the Senior Couples group that was active at that time. In one of our first outings, husbands and wives were teamed together for 9 holes in the "Scotch Twosome" or alternate ball format, where first the husband hits the ball and then the couple goes to that point and the wife hits the ball. Amazingly enough, considering some of the other golfers involved at the time, Pat and I won the tournament. This group has since disbanded as most of the members began getting too old. But it was fun while it lasted.

Shortly after we moved into our rental house, the Hughes and Monbergs began stopping by on their way south. One memorable time was when both the Hughes and Monbergs spent the night with us and we played as a threesome, with the Clemson University Golf Team playing right behind us. A golfer named Patton was on the team and during that round broke the course record. He later won the US Amateur Tournament and was invited to play in the Masters Tournament. All of this added to the thrill of playing on our course.

We enjoyed living in the rental house and after a year or so, began inquiring whether we might perhaps buy it. Well, it turned out that the landlord, who lived up north, was planning to live there when he retired. Next, we inquired of Buck Hancock, the owner of the Boscobel properties at the time, whether he had a lot for sale. After looking at several locations, we decided to buy the lot across the corner from our rental house. Before long, we had built a beautiful house located adjacent to the 12th tee. Here we spent about 8 months of the year, from 1991-2011. Our summers were initially spent in our old home in Royalwood, outside of Houghton. After a couple of years, however, we decided to sell this house and move into an apartment adjacent to the Portage Lake Golf Course. So, for a period, we lived right next to a golf course during both the summer and the winter. That was convenient, to say the least. During most of this period, we were running the software company and on one memorable occasion, directly from the golf course. I had just finished putting on the 15th green, when Pat called to me from our bedroom window, which faced out onto the green. She was on the phone with a customer and wanted me to talk to him. I went up to the window and she held the phone to the screen, where I finished the conversation with the customer. This is not such a big deal now, but those were the days before cell phones (or at least I didn't have one, still don't). We were only in the apartment for about five years, when we got a hankering to live on the lake and bought a wonderful cottage on Lakeshore Drive in Chassell.

At Boscobel, what they called a Wing-Ding was a monthly tournament, held during the months of April to November. This was started by Joey Herbert who was the new owner and operator of Boscobel. He usually set up the teams so that each consisted of an A-player, a B-player, a C-player and a D-player or a woman, although sometimes there might be two women. It cost about $15 plus greens fee and cart rental for each person. Winning teams might receive up to $45 per person. This was played on a Sunday afternoon and ended with a free supper with beer. These were fun outings, as some of the A and B-players were quite spectacular and this was about the only opportunity for us to play with golfers like that. Several times, Pat and I were on winning teams and we piled up quite a bit of money toward the purchase of merchandise.

It was in one of these Wing-Dings that I got my first "hole-in-one". I was on a team that had just about completed the 18 holes and had not been doing very well. When we got up to the 7th tee box, someone said, "About the only way we will win anything is for somebody to make a hole in one". Well, I must have been doing pretty well, so that I had confidence in my swing. Anyway, I took out my five-iron and took a mighty whack and the ball sailed through the air, landed on the green and rolled into the hole. The unbelievable thing is that Pat, who happened to be playing in the previous group, came back to the edge of the green and said, "Who hit that?" Since the 8th tee box is very close, she had heard the ball hit the green and looked back to see it roll into the hole. Well, since the beer was free because of the Wing Ding, I was lucky all the way around. Joey even arranged to give me a special gift of a golf club traveling bag. But that is not the end of the story.

Joey reported the hole-in-one to the newspaper to be published in the usual 3-line format: name of the golfer, club used and names of the three witnesses. But in my case, there happened to be a cub reporter at the weekly paper in town, who decided to get the full story. So, a day or so later he came out to the pro shop and Joey called to have me come down and give the reporter an interview. On top of that, he wanted a picture, so we drove out to the hole and he took a picture of me taking a ball out of the hole. The result was a half-page article in the paper that included such details as where my mother lived. Never has so much been made of so little!

Picture taken by the Clemson Messenger Newspaper

Billy Taylor is a Legendary Boscobel senior golfer, who is indeed an extraordinary person. He is the most unlikely looking golfer, being rather pudgy in figure and having a ruddy face to match. However, Billy played on the golf team for a small church college and has been active in golf most of his life. He was a Baptist Preacher by profession. Ordinarily, his golf game is about as you would expect by looking at his figure. Except for one thing! He has made something like 37 holes in one! (I forget the actual number. It may be 48.) I have never witnessed any of these, but there have been several during the years I've been at Boscobel. What I have witnessed is even more spectacular… One day, Billy Taylor rode in my cart when I was playing in the Wednesday Seniors Tournament. He had not been playing very well, getting bogeys on the first four holes. But this changed when we got to the 450 yd., par 5, 5th hole, where he got off a good drive and then proceeded to hit his second shot into the hole! At first, we thought the ball was lost, as it's a blind shot, but on further inspection, there it was, *IN* the hole. He became so excited that he began to whoop and holler. His game from there on was like a different person. I doubt if he made another bogey. Because of this, our team won first place and, of course, he won first in singles competition. He is a great guy to play with and we often ride together. I think perhaps it reminds him of the day he got his "Double Eagle", the rarest shot in golf!

I began wondering about this many years later when I was rewriting this book, since I was the sole witness of this remarkable event. If he was not totally honest, as I had always assumed, he could have simply picked up the ball and dropped it in the hole when I wasn't looking, since I was quite busy trying to make a bogey. As a result, I called Joey Herbert to find out what Billy Taylor was really credited with. He said that he had died about a month ago and was "credited with 48 holes-in-one and that he made a double eagle, and on the same day had made a hole-in-one"! I knew that didn't happen, so I realized that Billy Taylor was something more than just a golfer. He had become part of the Legend of Boscobel Golf Course.

The Masters Tournament is played at Augusta, Georgia, about 70 miles south of Pendleton. I had always wanted to see it and when we first started going down there, you could just drive up and go to the "practice rounds" by paying $15 or $20, depending on the day, Monday, Tuesday, or Wednesday. I will always remember the first time we passed through the gates and walked out on to the first fairway. It was awesome! I felt like walking into the National Cathedral and just as in a cathedral, everyone was speaking in hushed tones because they are all experiencing the same awe. The fairways are cut so that every blade of grass is trimmed to exactly the same length. At the time we were first there, there was almost no rough, so fairways went from the perfectly placed pine straw under the trees on one side of the fairway to the same on the other side. The golf course was originally a nursery for bushes and trees, which is the original source of many of the flowering plants. Each fairway is planted and named with its own flowering tree. As you walk around, you soon find that the whole course is quite hilly, with the first nine holes generally going up and down hill to the right as you enter and the second nine going down to the famous "Amen Corner" on the far left. The best way to get to know the course is to follow along with one of your favorite golfers and see him tee off at each hole. With all of the walking, you soon begin to lag behind with other foursomes and end up finding a viewing point to sit for a while. It doesn't take long before you really appreciate how much work is involved in playing professional golf, as golf carts are essentially nonexistent at the Masters. Pat and her friend Marcia would take Masters Chairs and sit all day, just off the green at the par-3 hole #6, where you could see balls landing and watch all the golfers practicing different putts they expected to experience during the tournament. This also allowed them to see a little of hole #16 that was off to their left from where they sat. My strategy, on the other hand, was to try to experience all 18 holes on the course at one time or the other during the day, sometimes doubling back to catch some of them more than once.

One of the amazing things about the Masters, was the ancillary facilities that were provided for the patrons (what they call all visitors including members). These included large permanent toilets made of concrete blocks, strategically located around the course. The ladies' toilets even provided uniformed maids with towels, etc. Food and drinks were also dispensed from permanent facilities around the course. The price of sandwiches was an unbelievable $1.00 for pimento-cheese, $1.25 for sliced meat, etc. (in 1990-1995). Despite the fact that these facilities were only used by a captive audience for 7 days a year, there was never any attempt to take advantage of the patrons.

We soon discovered that Wednesday at The Masters was the best day to watch because it included the Par Three Tournament, an optional fun round, played by the pros that was independent of the main tournament that runs Thursday through Sunday. This competition is played on the small course that was designed for President Eisenhower. We didn't even realize that this other little course existed until we asked where the par 3 tournament was. It turned out to be down behind the cottages, to the left of number ten, where special guests are housed, for example, there is the Eisenhower Cottage and others. They also interview the winners there. The holes are designed to cross over several little lakes that dot the par-3 course, so that most shots are across the water. We found that by setting up our chairs just behind the sixth green, we could see the shots coming right at us across the water. Most of the players are just having a good time, because superstition has it that, nobody who has won the par-3 tournament would also win the main tournament that year. Consequently, we have seen lots of funny stuff happening. For example, once one of the following players thought they were leaving the green too slowly and hit on to the green while someone was still there, who then picked up the ball and tossed it back into the water.

Another time one of the spectators made a remark that a chip-shot was lacking in skill, whereupon the pro said, "OK, let me see you do it", and handed the spectator his club. We have even seen at least one hole-in-one made while we were watching.

Once as we were leaving the par 3 tournament, we saw Bernhardt Langer with two of his cut-up buddies, all teeing off at the same time and Bernhardt was counting down for the tee off, "Eins, Zwei, Trei...". Bernhardt Langer has always been one of my favorite pros, who is still wining tournaments in the Champions Tour.

In 1988, Pat and I were standing out near the practice range and happened to notice this pro from Scotland, named Sandy Lyle. Unlike all the other pros who were hitting away at the balls, Sandy Lyle was spending his time, coaching one of his buddies on his golf swing. The interesting thing about this was that when the tournament was all over on Sunday, Sandy Lyle was the winner!

So, for several years in a row, we would go down and enjoy the beauty and spectacle of Augusta National. We took several roles of pictures that were later saved in a scrapbook. However, the practice rounds began getting so crowded that the course put the tickets on a lottery basis, and we have had only one opportunity to attend since, despite submitting our names for several years after. We went back to enjoying The Masters every year on TV like most everyone else. Our experience there made it even more interesting since we had walked all the fairways and know it much better than most people.

Buck Hancock was fairly well known in Anderson County. Unfortunately, most people didn't seem to like him. He and Margaret, his handsome wife, lived in a big house overlooking the 9th fairway and a pond that is called "Boscobel Lake". Apparently, he grew up in one of the mill towns in the Anderson area, became a boxer and then went north to make his fortune. He wanted to learn to fly and so took lessons from Margaret, who had been one of the lady pilots who ferried planes across the Atlantic during WWII. They got married and he became a contractor, building shopping malls in the DC area where they made enough money to return to Pendleton and become part owner of Boscobel. He was the sole owner of Boscobel when we joined in 1986.

There are some interesting stories about him and Harvey Brock, his golf pro for over 30 years. It is said that one time Buck dressed Harvey up as a chauffeur and they drove his limousine to a golf course over at Myrtle Beach, looking for a big money game with a couple of guys. After the stakes were set and the game decided, they started looking around for a fourth. Buck suggested "I think my chauffeur has played some golf." and of course he had. The rest of that story is pretty obvious.

The story was that he had sold the golf course to Joey on a "land contract", believing that he would not be able to make the balloon payment when it came due and the golf course would revert to him. But Joey did such a good job running the course that he made the payment with no problem.

Buck had always been honest with me and we had gotten along very well. Maybe because one time I'd gone over to his house and played my guitar. When we asked to buy the property just off of the 12th tee box, we were able to get it for $25,000, which was probably pretty good for eight tenths of an acre right in the middle of a golf course. He and Margaret often drove by and admired our yard, often telling us what a good job we were doing keeping it up. I often think that he thought that we were just taking care of it for them. I will always remember him driving his old limousine out across the fairway on #13 even years after he had given up the ownership of the golf course to Joey. I guess Joey just accepted him for the way that he was. Buck died in 2005. He was quite a character.

After purchasing the lot across from our rental house, we looked through a book of typical plans to see what sort of layout would best fit our needs. A plan that featured a hexagonal great room attracted our attention, partly because it had the shape of a benzene ring. So, Pat began to see how it might be modified to fit our needs. She designed a wing-shaped plan with the hexagonal great room with a wing containing the master bedroom and two guest bedrooms extending in one direction and the kitchen, dining room and shop extending in the other. A large screen porch wrapped around the sides of the great room, dining room and one guest bedroom facing the fairway. After figuring the dimensions the best we could, we turned the plans over to the architects of a construction company to complete the process. We were able to move in by Christmas, with only a few errors in our plans and were quite happy with our wonderful new home.

After a few years in our new "digs" we realized that because of the construction of the house and nature of the golf course, we had an ideal setup to host small golf tournaments. I believe the first outing was for the golfing group at church, most of whom lived in a golfing community about 10 miles away. I talked with Joey to see what kind of a deal he could give us for green's fees and golf carts, and it turned out to be fairly economical. Our groups would tee off after all the regular groups got underway and finish up before the late afternoon people arrived. I would collect all the greens fees and turn the money over in a lump sum to Joey at the end. Our house was situated on the 12th tee box where we could put out a cold box of liquid refreshments for the final six holes. At the end, all the players would meet back at our house for further refreshments, awarding of prizes, and pot-luck dinner. The real enjoyment was to sit out on the porch and watch the other golfers go by. We had about six of these tournaments during the years before my retirement from Clemson, about half with the faculty and graduate students in the chemistry department and half with members of our church community. These were all great fun, but we had to give it up because of Pat's health.

As I got older, the quality of my game slowly declined. It helped quite a bit for a while when, after 70, I moved to the forward tee box, which initially allowed me to get to most greens in regulation. But, that didn't last too long and I was back to scrambling for par's again. However, my luck still seemed to be holding. On April 1, 2004, I got my second hole-in-one on the 12th hole at Boscobel. It was one of those things where it felt good and it looked good leaving and so I reached down to pick up my tee. Then, about seven people were hollering at me that the ball had gone in the hole. It was my three partners, Al, Bob, and John, plus the foursome behind us who had finished putting out early on hole #11 and were sitting in their carts behind us. The group ahead of us saw it. Even Pat saw it from our porch! I was the only one that missed it. I bought my buddies lunch and beers for some of the other guys who saw it. I decided that if it ever happened again, I was going to see it.

Well, I didn't have to wait long, because on April 9, 2004, it happened again on hole #7. What happens when you have had a hole-in-one is that you begin to imagine the possibilities, every time you tee off at a par 3 hole. Particularly when the hole is in an ace position, not too close to the front, etc. That proved to be the case that day on hole #7. So, I concentrated on keeping my head still and hitting the ball right in the sweet spot. So, off she went arcing right on track, hitting the green in just the right spot, and then rolling right back to the hole. Plunk! When it works, it is so easy it's ridiculous. So, within the space of eight days, I had made two aces and the final one I had seen all the way! This made it three and my poor partners who had been playing more regular than I, had yet to get their first. What a crazy game!

On reviewing this round of golf many years later, I realized I had been playing the game all wrong. Whereas I had been in pursuit of good scores, I should have been perusing the golf course, looking for really good opportunities to score big, as I had been doing in the above instance. There is a subtle difference, but I think an important one. It is just a little late for me to take advantage of.

Summer-time golf gave me a chance to play at Michigan Tech's Portage Lake Golf Course with a whole new set of buddies. The golf course changed over the years as it went from 9 holes to 18 holes because of adding an additional nine holes on the back of the original nine. These were quite different as they had been designed by different architects. Initially it was called the back nine because it was in the back. Then they renumbered it so that it went from 1 to 9, so now, by tradition, it was called the front nine. For several years it was hard to call it the front nine as it was in the back. Finally, we got used to it. During all the years of play at Portage Lake, I never had an Ace, despite the three Aces I had at Boscobel and the Aces collected by my partners at Portage Lake. I did go below 80 only twice in my career, once with a 79 at Portage Lake and once with a 79 at Boscobel.

Our foursome initially consisted of Larry Lawrence and I with Paul Shandley and Rollin Keeling. Then, Rollin died, and we had Paul Swift joining the group for several years. Then Paul Shandley died, and Paul Swift got older, until he reached 90, when he decided he was too old to join us anymore. In the meantime, Ross Johnson, had been playing with Bob Leonard and Jim Tormala for a number of years, but

Jim got disgusted with his play and quit all together. About the same time Bob Leonard died in a car accident.

Since Ross knew us from way back, he joined our group, as did Dave Uitti, my old college buddy, who had moved up to Hancock about the same time. We kept this foursome together for a couple of years. Usually it is Larry and I in one cart and Ross and Dave in the other. Ross is the top dog in the group, as he had played for many more years than any of us, including being on the golf team at Michigan Tech and holding the Portage Lake Club Championship on several occasions. So, we felt honored to have him in our group. We generally met each day during the working week to play 9 holes during the afternoon. Larry often met his lady partner, Marion, to play an additional 9 holes after that, while I would go home and have a nap. For many years, Larry and I would play as partners in the Portage Lake Men's League, where we took the division championship one year. Of course, you have to understand that our division was the "old geezers" and Ross helped by substituting until I arrived from South Carolina. In 2008, Larry and I decided to terminate our membership in the Men's League, as it was no longer much fun. Then, Dave moved back to California and we added John Sustarich until the fall of 2011, when our group broke up for good. Ross had been slowing down and was more and more unhappy with his play. About a week after the golf course closed for the season, Ross was found seated in his chair looking at a golf magazine. He had apparently died of a heart attack. The following year, the spring of 2012, my buddy, Larry reached the age of 90 and decided that he would quit golf. Without having a partner and lacking Ross to play with, I only went out to the golf course three more times, playing parts of nine holes with my daughter, Lisa, and her husband, Gary.

It has been a great life, belonging to two golf courses, having the best of both climates and a wife that let me play whenever I wanted to. Who could ask for anything more?

CHAPTER 19

GUITAR PICKER

(1948-2010)

One of my interesting hobbies began when I was in high school in New Orleans. My mother got me started playing the ukulele on some of the old songs that she played as a teenager and young woman. I enjoyed it enough to carry it on for a while. But I became more interested in the rhythms of more contemporary songs. One of the shows that I went to see while in N.O. was Louis Armstrong returning for one of his periodic concerts. Another memorable show was Hank Williams performing the free Hadacol show (Hadacol was a patent medicine, with a high alcohol content). Unfortunately, I didn't have any chance to go down to the French Quarter, as this was taboo for all of the guys I went around with. However, just living in New Orleans was a great stimulus to one's music interests. Some of the guys I ran around with got together a little band and I played the "gut bucket", made from a 10-gallon paint can and a cord. However, one of the defining moments of those years was when I went to a party and Stumpy, one of Dad's coworkers, sang on a professional quality ukulele. He did a fantastic job playing "Five Foot Two" and "You are My Sunshine", songs I still sing today. I didn't have my gut bucket, so I made rhythm by banging on a trash can or something. This impressed Stumpy, who said I should get a snare drum, which eventually I did. From that point on, my main interest was in piano rhythm music and Dixieland Jazz. Consequently, I would play the snare drum in time to various phonograph records in our collection, including Dad's Dixieland jazz records.

When I went to Michigan Tech the only "musical instrument" I carried with me was the pair of brushes from the snare drum. But, my interest in jazz was one of the things that led me to become friends with Dave and Paul Uitti. Actually, they were more interested in the Chicago style jazz of Lionel Hampton, and similar music, but this was close enough. We used to go down to the lounge in the basement of the dorm. They would play Boogie on the piano, while I played my brushes on the brass ashtray. However, they knew only a few tunes, so our interests began to turn in other directions. When we went off to the local hangouts, polka music and country music were played on a 50/50 basis. Since I was familiar with country music and had actually seen Hank Williams, the Uitti brothers and I began to listen to this with more and more interest. In the Town Club, music was sometimes provided by Lucille and Helen, a couple of gals from Lake Linden, who had been in a few country groups. After I got to know them a bit, I was able to "sit in" on the drums every now and then. By the end of the first year, my main music interests had switched from jazz to country. Clearly, I needed a guitar. This was reinforced by the fact that the kids called me "Tex", as my folks lived in Dallas and I was registered at Michigan Tech as a Texan. Those who knew this would say "Hi Tex, where's your guitar".

Following the first year at Tech, I spent the summer living at my grandmother's on Jackson St. in Arlington and had gotten a job at the Arlington Trust Co as a cashier's assistant. I think that I made something like $30 a week and fast became convinced that this was not the kind of job I wanted for the rest of my life. But I enjoyed my grandmother's cooking and I made one of my infrequent contacts with Pat Mann, who was home from her school in New York for summer vacation. I think that was the summer that she had a party up at the Country Club around the swimming pool. It was also the party where I met Lelia Buck, whom I was rather taken with for some time. Lelia was the sister of Henry Buck, who Pat was dating at that time.

The other memorable thing that happened was that I went down to the pawnshop in Roslyn and bought my first guitar. Its name was "Stella". Since I had already learned to play the ukulele, I had little trouble picking up the basic guitar cords. Once I got calluses on my fingers, so that I could stand pressing down the steel strings, I would sit out on my grandmother's porch and play by the hour (well almost). My gramma's favorite song was "Hey Good Lookin", (what cha got cookin'). By the time I returned to Michigan Tech, I knew most of the common Hank Williams and Ernest Tubbs songs. My favorites were "The Lovesick Blues" and "Walkin' the Floor Over You".

Jim and Paul Uitti around 1950

When I returned to Tech for my junior year, Dave Uitti had gotten married over the summer and Paul Uitti became my roommate. Shortly after getting together, I bought a Gibson guitar at the Dover Music House in Hancock and Paul eventually got an electronically amplified "f-hole" guitar. So, we would practice our guitar pickin' on

364

a daily basis for about a half-hour after lunch and maybe an hour after dinner (to the consternation of some of our dorm buddies). And, after we became more adapt at playing, we took the guitars down to the Town Club and played for beer, or to some amateur show where we could further develop our skills. I remember on one occasion, we actually played on the stage of the Italian Hall, site of the 1913 disaster, where 70 or more people died during a panic after someone called, "Fire!" and they were unable to get out the front entrance. Fortunately, our audience wasn't large enough to cause a panic, but it was a good experience.

During the spring break of our senior year, we took a tour down to Nashville, in Paul's '36 Chevy. This was a great trip, as we went to the Grand Ole Opry at its original venue, the Ryman Auditorium. We followed this by going to Ernest Tubbs' music shop, where the show continued to well past midnight. The following morning, we were driving through some great country and were inspired to stop on the edge of a beautiful field to sing "Mockingbird Hill". We continued on down to Harlan County, KY to soak up the real hillbilly atmosphere.

One time later that term, a friend with an accordion got together with Paul and I out on the back steps of the dorm. We were having a great time playing all the local music until I heard someone in the room above us playing some polka music that really sounded great. I said: "Stop, stop, I want to hear that." So, we stopped to listen for a few minutes and finally asked who was making that music. The fellow upstairs said: "It was you guys. I recorded it." What a wonderful feeling that was. By the time we graduated, we were sounding pretty professional, or at least we thought so.

When I went to graduate school at the Medical College of Virginia, I of course, took my guitar with me. I lived in the city of Richmond within walking distance of downtown, although most of the time I took the bus. On Saturday night, they regularly had the Old Dominion Barn Dance. They would have two shows every Saturday, one of which was broadcast over the radio. The show featured Grandpa Jones and some of the other stars that later were featured on the TV show "Hee-Haw". So, it was great fun for me and often I would go up in the balcony and hide down below the seats when the first show let out. That way, I could enjoy the second show as well. Often, they told the same corny jokes, but that didn't matter to me because the music was usually different.

As you can see, Richmond was a minor center for country music and several radio stations in the downtown area would have local country groups playing on Saturday morning. I began going and watching these guys through the window between the lobby and the broadcast area. After a round of songs, some of the players would come out into the lobby for a smoke and I began to gab with them. About the second time I did this, I was asked to come on in and play along on one of the extra guitars. The next thing that I knew I was singing as well. At one of the studios, I was asked to join the group and meet with them when they practiced at somebody's home. Besides singing on the radio, they had a gig singing the leadoff before a wrestling match. This turned out to be somewhat less than wonderful, as the microphone was on a wire that dangled in the middle of the ring and if somebody didn't hold it down, it went up out of reach. This required someone to stand in front of the singer to hold the microphone down. Another disadvantage, was that the leader was a bossy type guy who wanted me to sing songs that I didn't know, causing me to spend time learning songs that were not necessarily my favorite. I think I left that group shortly after the wrestling match gig.

My first year at Richmond was spent mooning over Margaret Ann, the good-looking gal that my roommate and I had the good fortune to share the breakfast and dinner table with. So, I was always looking for an opportunity to impress her with my prowess as a country music singer. However, the opportunity rarely presented itself, as she usually had a date in the evening and often went home to Farmville for the weekend.

One Friday, the members of the boarding house got invited to a party downtown and I was asked to bring my guitar. I was especially good on a song called "Mississippi" and all of a sudden, I had the interest of a cute little gal from outside of the house (I'm not even sure Margaret Ann was at the party). Anyway, this gal and I were hitting it off pretty good and she invited me to come home with her after the party. However, when it came time to leave, a couple of my female housemates took me aside and said, "Jim… You don't want to mess around with that! She's not the right kind of girl for you." So, we all got back into our cars and I went to sleep in my own little bed.

At Christmas of that year Pat Mann and I got together and from then on, I had almost no time to devote to playing the guitar other than a few songs for my own relaxation. This was the way that it was until my second year at Stanford, when we moved into the apartment in Menlo Park. Here, we would have patio parties every now and then and I would play a few songs for group singing. In fact, from that point on, I began shifting away from country music and learning more and more songs that people could sing along with, such as, "You are my Sunshine", "I've been Working on the Railroad" and "Five Foot Two". I still sing the old country music for my own satisfaction, but at any outing, one country song is usually enough. This usually turns out to be "Bessie the Heifer", or Hank Williams version of "The Lovesick Blues".

When we moved back to Michigan, tape recorders came into vogue and I was able to record some of the country songs. After stereo taping was developed, I set up one microphone to tape the guitar and the other for the voice. I found that with most of my taping sessions, only about one song in four could be done without some kind of goof-up, either in the singing or in the playing of chords. After collecting several tapes of this type, I was able to put together one, called "The

Best of Spain Country", that was almost good. In all this taping and re-taping, one of my favorite places to set up my studio was the men's room of the Biological Sciences Department. This room had an echo that made it sound like I was singing in an auditorium. Of course, this sort of thing was best done on Sunday afternoons when I was not likely to be disturbed. Those people who happened to wander in were sometimes rather surprised at the source of the music, since I was head of the department during some of these years.

When we moved to South Carolina, I expected that my country music would go over in a big way. However, I never received much response from various Chemistry Department outings, either for the country music or the sing-along music. This was somewhat of a disappointment. The only good sing-a-longs have been at the New Year's Eve parties that we had for a while and at the Boscobel Homeowners Christmas Parties that we have had up at the clubhouse.

We still have some nice sing-a-longs at various summertime parties in Michigan, but even this is beginning to wear thin, as my voice is beginning to give out on me. One song that I rarely sing anymore is the "Lovesick Blues", despite the fact that it is still my favorite. The main reason is that I have not been playing for myself like I used to. I keep saying that I'm going to practice more, but good intentions just don't do it. However, before it's all gone, I want to pass along a little of what I've learned.

Through the years, I've learned some easy ways to play chords on the guitar that I would like to pass along to young guitar players. Usually, one starts by learning the chords in C major key, as this key is easy for most people. Thus, the three chords that I first learned were C, F and G7th. If you are lazy, as I am, you simplify this to C, F and G. These work for many simple songs like "Red River Valley". If the song is a little more complicated, like "You are My Sunshine", you can add C7 between C and F. The next more complicated song, still in the key of C, would be "Home on the Range". This requires that you include D7 before going to G. If you examine the simple chord progression that I have included below, you will see that all of these chords are accomplished by ONLY TWO chord shapes, being moved up and down the keyboard.

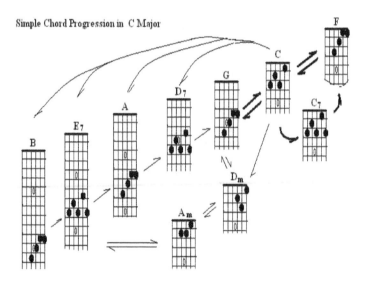

Simple Chord Progression in C Major

370

So, this is not hard to learn. More complicated songs like "Five Foot Two" and "Shanty in the Town" simply involve more chords of the same shape but moved farther down the keyboard. For these songs the chord sequence would start in C, jump down to E7, A, D7, G, and back to C. Other songs might go from F to A, to D7, G, then C. Only very fancy songs involve the minor chords, such as Am and Dm, both of which require different chord shapes. The point that I'm making is that you can play a very large number of common, old-time, campfire-type songs by the simple chords that I have described and are shown below. Of course, if you want to play songs in another key, you are on your own.

Another important point that you should understand is that the guitar is a rhythm instrument, at least in my hands it is. One of the tricks that I learned by listening to country music is that there are two ways to make rhythm. The most basic is to pluck one of the base strings of the chord then strum the rest. But this is the hard way. The other way is to strum all of the strings of the chord, while holding it properly, then strum all strings while holding the strings more loosely. This causes a BLUUM-bluuk sound. This is modified for various songs to give BLUUM-bluuk-bluuk, or bluuk-BLUUM-BLUUM, etc., depending on the rhythm, waltz, polka, etc. The main thing is that you are holding the same chord, without worrying about plucking specific strings, so it is a lot easier to play. Some songs I play one way and some songs I play the other. After a while, don't even think about it. Whatever sounds good, you do it, more or less automatically.

The whole thing is enjoyment. I can play for myself and enjoy it and I can play for other people and enjoy it. There is nothing like the zing that I get when I play a song for people and see that they are really getting into it. You can see it in their face, and you can see it in their eyes. There are only a few songs that really turn people on, but when it happens, there is nothing like it. The important thing is to be able to do it automatically without having to look at the chords and the simpler the chord structure, the easier this is to do.

Back when I was in college and was playing a lot, I found that I was able to write a few songs. This was really only song lyrics, as I was only changing the lyrics on a song that had already been written. One example was the "Bosch-Bosch Boogie".[5] The verses were all about local bars, such as "At the Sportsman's Bar in Wolverine, they play their boogie on a music machine, It's the Bosch-Bosch Boogie, It's the Bosch-Bosch Boogie, It's the Bosch-Bosch Boogie, and they Boogie-Woogie all the time". As you can see, this is really high-class stuff. A similar example was my song called the "Copper Country Limited", that was about the local train that came in every day from

---

[4]This title will require some explanation. At the time I was in school there was a local beer, called Bosch Beer (no relation to Anheuser-Busch) that was sold both in the U.P. of Michigan, where it was called Busch, and also in the Lower Peninsula, near Detroit, where it was called Bausch. So, all the radio advertisements said "Up here we call it Busch and down there we call it Bausch"

Chicago. This was sung to the music of "The Orange Blossom Special", which again was of interest mainly to my college buddies.

Somewhat later in life when we were living in Royalwood, we lived next door to Fred Lonsdorf, the ski coach. One year, Fred was directing the Central US Ski Association (CUSSA) Tournament at the Michigan Tech's ski hill, Mount Ripley and he asked me to come sing a couple of songs at the Awards Banquet at the end of the tournament. So, I decided to write a song for the occasion. This was titled "Johnny Olsen, Hero of the CUSSA", which was sung to the tune of the "Wreck of the 98", an old railroad song. I was able to put together a couple of verses by the time I was supposed to sing and of course I saved it for last. It seemed to be well received by the attendees and that's all that mattered. Since then, I have "written" very little, but on occasion, when I'm diddling around on the guitar, I put together a few chords that sound different and original (one never knows whether they are or not). But, since I don't read music, neither do I write it, so these interesting chord combinations and the accompanying notes are soon lost to posterity. However, I am satisfied that if I really wanted to, I could write music and that's all that matters, since I have found much easier ways to make money by other means.

So, that is my history as a "guitar picker". I think you can see that I recommend it highly as a hobby. It launched my interest in other forms of music, including the keyboard, which occupied many hours of enjoyment.

CHAPTER 20

ELECTRONIC HOMEWORK SYSTEMS,

INC.

(1994-2010)

During my final year or so at Clemson, we had set up the computer modules in the Learning Center so that scores were printed out on a sheet of paper that the students turned in for homework credit. These modules had been modified to deter students from producing bogus credit sheets, but they still had to be examined by someone to make sure that they were not fake. The person who did this and gave them credit on the master record was me, as only I knew the distinguishing features of the valid printout. About the middle of my final year at Clemson, Jeff Appling, the director of the freshman chemistry program, came into my office and looked at the five-foot-high stack of printouts and said; "Isn't there some way we could do this record keeping electronically?" And, of course, the answer to that question was yes, it was only a matter of doing it.

Thus, I began work on what was to become the first *Electronic Homework System*. The basic idea was to retain the scores in some sort of a computer file along with the name and other identification data, so that it could be transferred to the instructor. The instructor would use this information to provide credit for the student's homework. It had been found over the years that unless the instructors gave the student some credit for homework, only a few good students would bother doing it. But, without obtaining the practice of homework, students would learn little about chemistry, as I had discovered, it is not a subject that one can learn by simply listening to a lecture.

Doing problems and answering questions about chemical logic is a skill that can be learned only by *doing*. Assigning homework problems has a long history in chemistry, second only to that in math and physics. The problem has always been to find someone who would take the time to check the student's answers and provide the necessary credit. With Electronic Homework, where the homework was already corrected, the problem was to find a simple way to store the record of student response in a <u>secure form</u> that could be easily transferred to the instructor.

A typical data file consists of an array of individual chunks of information that would be transferred sequentially and then formed back into an array after it arrived at the destination. Considering that there were 1200 students in the freshman chemistry program at

Clemson, the use of standard data transfer methods would seem rather cumbersome. Thus, I decided to incorporate all data for a single student into a single string of characters that would be transferred as a single unit. The conversion of the array into a data string would occur as a subroutine within the homework program. I don't know if I had employed this technique in any earlier program, but it seemed the logical thing to do at the time. I decided that to save space, grade scores as well as times and dates could all be converted to single alphanumeric characters. Those of you familiar with computers will know that each character is associated with a number called the ANSI code. In fact, this is the only way that alphanumeric characters can be retained in a computer, as a computer only deals with (binary) numbers. Therefore, each character in the (ANSI) code for a 16-bit computer is represented by a number between 0 and 255. The first 32 characters include control characters that have various controlling effects on the computer and therefore would be unacceptable. However, this leaves 223 characters for use in our number-to-character conversion process. This saves a lot of space, as a three-digit number may be represented by a single character and no separators are required. Thus, the total data for a student may be retained in a string of only 311 characters. These early decisions proved to be very fortuitous when I later went to more exotic data transfer methods over a network.

One of the thoughts that should have crossed your mind by now is, "What happens if the student attempts to make changes in their recorded scores?" This, of course, crossed my mind as well. It was evident that the data must be encrypted in some way that even the most knowledgeable students could not decipher its code, in order to change their grades. Clearly this is a challenge that every 'would be hacker' is inclined to give a try. Encryption means changing the characters of the record string in some organized way that would allow it to be changed back again after the file reaches its destination (their instructor). I knew from previous experience, that the random number generator provided in the BASIC programming language is organized in such a way as to provide the basis for an encryption engine. All random number generators only seem to be random. Given a certain random number "seed", they will always generate the same sequence of "random" numbers. If you have some way to provide a unique random number, seed, for each student, the encryption would be different for each student. Thus, I took two characters from the student's last name and two numbers from his/her ID number to form the seed. For the most part, this would give a different sequence of "random" numbers for each student. From this sequence we formed a conversion array for transforming one character to another. This made up the encryption engine that was used during the first year of operation and is the basis for all encryption that I have used since. The homework programs encrypted the data before it was stored on the student's record-keeping medium. Initially, this was the 3.4in disk. An identical procedure was used in the reverse manner by the in data analysis program to transform the encrypted code back to provide the grade information for the instructor. This all sounds like a complicated business that must take a lot of computer time. However, the entire encryption-decryption process takes only a fraction of a second, even in the older computers.

So, it turned out that by the end of my final semester at Clemson, I had a system that worked reasonably well. While this was all going on, something else happened that opened the door to the commercialization of the chemistry programs developed during my years at Clemson. The question that must be answered was; <u>did Clemson University have any rights to my work?</u> I didn't think that they did, because most of the design and programming had been done in Houghton, while I was on summer "vacation". It had all started with the development of a new font that allowed for both subscripted and superscripted numbers, as well as numerous special characters that are unique to chemistry. This was done with a little help from Ted Sohlden, one of my ex-SUMIT graduate students, then working for the Computer Resource Center at Michigan Tech, who gave me a program for designing special fonts. What I had done at Clemson was to test my programs on chemistry students and make changes when required on a computer that belonged to Clemson. However, all the design work in Houghton had been done with my own PC-junior computer. So, I filled out the necessary forms for the Intellectual Properties Committee and after some time, they sent me a letter saying that they had reviewed my situation and had concluded that Clemson University had no interest in the commercial development of the software. This was a major decision as it allowed me to develop the product as I wished.

The main marketing strategy was something that I had already described in a paper about software development, published in *J. Chem Education*, with Joe Allen as co-author. The point that I made in that paper was that the development of computer software for chemistry instruction was inhibited by the lack of remuneration that was available for such work. Rarely if ever, did software development get rewarded by salary increase or academic advancement. In fact, there was some evidence that it had often been detrimental to the faculty member's advancement (Bill Butler, personal communication, and others). The sale of such a product in the present mode was not likely to yield much reward, as few universities or colleges were willing to pay much to buy computer software. Also, the book companies that had been interested in computerized instruction a few years earlier, had lost money and consequently lost interest in buying or licensing software. Given all this history, my suggestion was to adopt a textbook marketing model and sell the software directly to the student at the bookstore. For example, if each student in a class of 1000 students, was encouraged to purchase a computer package that netted $10 profit, the income would be $10,000 per year, whereas that same university would be unwilling to license the same software for $10,000 per year. There would be no point in even asking a professor to go to his department head to request such a financial outlay. Whereas, the same professor would think little about asking his students to spend an additional $20 for purchase of the software at the bookstore, as this would be less than a problems manual or workbook, he may already be asking them to buy. It seemed clear to me, which marketing strategy was correct. I already had some potential customers among the ten or so instructors across the country, who had been receiving my software free during the years of its development. So, the more I thought of it, and the more I discussed it with Pat, the more it seemed the thing to do. There wasn't that much that we could lose, and it seemed better than the alternative of running a motel or a bed and breakfast after I retired (especially to Pat). Besides, I was already committed to providing the product for Clemson, so, selling it to someone else's students was just another small step in the same direction.

By the end of May, we were ready to make a trial run with a class of about 150 students during the summer semester at Clemson. The homework program for the first semester was small enough to get on a single floppy disk. We had this duplicated at the Print Shop in downtown Clemson. We may not have charged the students anything, as it was a beta disk and we were more interested in how it would work than in making money. I had programmed an early version of the grade management software and was available in case something went wrong.

During the summer, we discovered that my encryption scheme was not as good as I had envisioned, as one of the students at Clemson found out how to crack it and passed the word along to a few buddies. However, they were not very smart about it, as they all gave themselves grades of 100 on all sections, a grade that was not achieved by any other students. They even gave themselves a grade of 100 on sections that did not yet exist!

On questioning by Jeff Appling, the students admitted to cheating and they, unfortunately, received failing grades for the course. Well, this was not something I wanted to happen again, so I set about improving the quality of the encryption process. One of the things that the students had found was that the first five characters were grades for the five sections of the first unit, then came a character for time, then came grades for the five sections of the second unit, then the time for the next unit, etc. So, if they reset all characters to the character representing 100, it was done. So, I decided to use the randomly defined encryption array to not only vary the nature of the character, but also the location of each character. This way, they wouldn't know if they were varying grades, times, or dates. Finally, I maintained some redundant records of certain grades so that we could check for correspondence between redundant grades to see if anyone had been altering grades. If the program discovered that the grades had been altered, the file was scrambled, and the student had to revert to the backup file.

If they altered the grades twice, the backup file was deleted as well. Under these conditions, they would have to re-register the disk.

In other words, the program policed itself so that no other student would be trapped into thinking that they were getting away with altering the grades. After these measures were added to the encryption process, there have been no more proven instances of student tampering in well over half a million sales, although I'm sure many of these students must have tried. There were reports of corrupted files that at first, we thought might have been tampering, but all proved to be the result of a programming glitch of mine that we subsequently corrected.

With these corrections, we set about developing something that could be sold in the bookstore for the fall term. This entailed getting some packaging designed. These initial packages were in what are called jewel-cases. The initial color printing was done at a print shop in Anderson, SC and assembly of packages was done on our dining room table. These packages were not very pretty and were not something that the bookstores liked to sell, as they were too small to stand on a shelf. The original price was $6 per disk, good for one semester.

After we got some of the product together, we began thinking of broadening our sales area. So, I made a trip down to the University of Georgia, which had been using the original learning center-based programs for a couple of years. It turned out that they were interested in trying the new Chem-Skill-Bildr, which was the logo I had adopted for the new electronic homework product. I got to know Joel

Caughran, the manager of the UGA Chemistry Learning Center. He was to work closely with me in making improvements to the product over the next few years and in the course of the next 6-8 years, UGA purchased well over $100,000 worth of Chemi-Skill-Bildr and subsequent products. Ultimately, they would develop courseware of their own and discontinue CSB use. But I'm happy that we played a role in contributing ideas to that development.

During the first year, one of the problems that was reported at UGA by Joel Caughran, where a number of good students were coming up with corrupted disks. We didn't have a clue as to what was causing it to occur. Being a small business with an 800 number for technical support, the calls came directly into our home phone. One night at about 1:00 am, I got a phone call! I don't usually answer these, but fortunately, I got out of bed and answered the phone this time and I received the clue I needed. On the line was a young lady who said, "Oh! I didn't expect to get a *person* on the line!" So, I said; "Well, I'm up now, so I might as well help if I can." She said that she had been working along with CSB when suddenly the program indicated that her record file was corrupted. We talked for a while and I asked her why she was working that time of night. She said that she often did, as it was quiet in the library. I began thinking that there might be some connection between working at night and the problems that some students had been experiencing. The next morning, I got on the phone with Joel and asked him if he thought it had anything to do with working at night. He said he would check and was shortly back on the phone confirming that all of the students experiencing the corruption problem had been working late at night. Then, it began to hit me that there might be something wrong with my time calculation subroutine. Sure enough, when I checked, I had not considered that at midnight, the computer's clock would be set back to zero. This caused my simple equation:

total time worked = final time - initial time.

...to give a negative value for time, whenever someone worked through the midnight hour. On checking, I discovered that during the encryption process, if there was a negative number, it simply left that character out and all the following characters were shifted out of position to the left. The result was that all characters past that point were totally out of place and redundant scores no longer matched, causing the program to scramble the record. The short-term solution was to tell all students to stop work just before midnight, go back to the main menu, have a Coke or something and then start again about 12:05 am. The long-term solution was to add one line to the time calculation subroutine saying:

if final time is less than initial time, add 86,400 seconds to the final time.

Those of you who were involved with computers in the year 2000 should recognize this as being much the same as the

"Millennium Bug" that cost millions of dollars to correct in computer programs around the world. In my case, it was simply a matter of correcting the next master disk that went out for duplication.

By this time, we had a disk duplication company that was up in New Hampshire, near the Canadian border. This did not last long, although I don't remember the problem that we had with them. However, we next went with a company called Midwestern Diskette, in Creston, IA. This seemed to be a reputable company and so we shortly had them not only duplicating our disks, but also carrying on what is called fulfillment. This included in addition to duplication, putting together our packages, warehousing the product, accepting orders, shipping to customers, sending invoices, receiving payment, and sending us the money. In other words, they took over much of the work we had been doing, which left us with responsibility for product design/correction, programming, marketing, technical support and keeping track of finances. In our naïveté, we had made these arrangements with no bonding or any other financial protection. If we had training in business, we might have realized that it was unwise to put so many eggs in one basket, particularly eggs that involved money!

However, this was a much more manageable company, which by now had been formed into an S-corporation called *Electronic Homework Systems, Inc.* This corporation did not pay any IRS taxes, but could make charges that would not be taxed on our personal income.   These would include such things as travel, phone, advertising, equipment purchases and professional meetings.   The company paid a small salary to Pat, who, as CFO, did the bookkeeping and office management.   The rest of the company profits were paid to Pat and me, as main stockholders.

The first year I stopped off at the University of Florida on the way down to visit my mother.   The director of the freshman chemistry program was Gardiner Myers, who showed immediate interest in *Chemi-Skill-Bildr*.   While we were chatting about the program, I described the architecture and he suggested switching to Quick Basic, as a means of making the programs a bit more compact and more efficient in the use of disk space.   He indicated that UFL would like to try using *CSB* the following fall.   When I returned from my vacation, Gardiner also sent several suggestions for improvement of CSB pedagogy.   So, by the end of the first year, I had picked up two major customers (UGA and UFL) in addition to Clemson.   Unfortunately, John Moore at the University of Wisconsin, decided to discontinue use of *CSB*, even though he had used the free programs I had sent him over the years.   It turned out that some UW faculty members were in the process of developing a similar product.

I believe that it was during the first year that we began planning a summer workshop at Michigan Tech.   This was handled through the MTU Conferences & Institutes Department, much as my earlier workshops.   They sent out the brochure to about 1000 people on their mailing list. The first summer, we ended up with less than ten people attending. However, almost all became customers, one being the Director of Freshman Chemistry at the University of Kentucky, and one was to become my programming partner, Hal Peters. Hal had been retired for several years from CONDUIT, because of disability and was interested in developing a Visual Basic version of *CSB* that would run on Windows. Up to that time, my programs had run on DOS and were sometimes described as crude or "clunky" by more discriminating clients, i.e., most of the students.

Before arriving at the workshop, Hal called to renew his acquaintance and describe his interest in working on the product. Consequently, I had sent him the BASIC code for *CSB* and before arriving at the workshop, he had programmed a prototype of the "Electrochemistry" unit (chapter). It looked great and worked much as the original. So, I said if you are willing to work on this, I will be happy to work with you. I then planned to come over to his home in Iowa City and work out the details of our agreement. So, about a month or so later, I joined him at his beautiful old home in Iowa City and discussed how it might work out. Part of our activities while I was there included going to visit with a friend of his at W. C. Brown Book Co. in Dubuque. This was an up-and-coming company that had started with lab manuals, but was now publishing several full-scale science texts, two of which were in chemistry. They examined my product and Hal's prototype of the Windows version and became very interested in handling the publication of the Windows product. With that in mind, we returned to his home and put down a rough agreement for our future relationship. In that, he was to receive 50% of the royalties accruing from the courseware published by W. C. Brown. At that time, we thought that we might make $20,000 profit, so that he would get at least $10,000 which would make it worth his time to do the conversion to Visual Basic. It was clear to me that if he didn't make the conversion, that most of my customers would soon lose interest.

After returning home, I continued the process of negotiating with W.C. Brown and in about a year, the agreement was completed. All it took was my signature to make it complete. Fortuitously, W.C. Brown was about to be bought out by a giant conglomerate called Times Publications (not to be confused with Times-Warner), which at that time included McGraw-Hill as its main book company. This raised some major questions about going with W.C. Brown. Would we be lost in the confusion of it all? Finally, we concluded that it could have some positive value as the sales force would be dramatically increased and so I signed, but with an escape clause that allowed us to cancel the contract if we were not happy after nine months. So, Hal and I worked very hard to get the new Visual-Basic version of *CSB* ready for the fall of 1996. In the meantime, the merger of W.C. Brown and McGraw-Hill went off as predicted. The amazing outcome of this was that the W.C. Brown group with which we had been working, became the Higher Education Division of McGraw-Hill Company and the people we knew were advanced to significant positions in that division. Unfortunately, this took about a year to occur and this was the same year that our new version of *CSB* came on the market. The result was that they only added two small colleges to our list of customers during that year. In the meantime, I had been hearing from my customers that they were unable to buy product, as the salespeople in New Jersey, or somewhere, hadn't even heard of *CSB*.

I was still providing the technical support of course, as I was the only one who could answer such questions. Consequently, I decided to exercise my option to terminate the contract at the end of nine months. The McGraw-Hill people were not too upset, and we left the door open for future relationships, should they develop. We did agree to sell them *CSB* at a discount rate so that they could package it with some of their texts. Thus, the following summer we were back in business as a publishing company and spent a goodly amount of time letting our old customers know that all orders should be directed to the people at Midwestern Diskette. At that same time, we changed the name of our general chemistry product to *ChemSkill Builder* and adopted a new logo. Part of this process was instigated by my daughter Caryn, who made a strong recommendation that we get new packaging. Thus, I used PowerPoint to design new inserts for both the front and back of the plastic binder in which the disks were now packaged. The color printing was done by the Book Concern in Hancock, Michigan.

ChemSkill Builder

New ChemSkill Builder Logo

Now that we had more confidence in our future, we worked harder at getting new customers by sending out major mailings to a large mailing list that I had been developing. This was largely based on names from the *ACS College Faculty* listing. Unfortunately, this service was discontinued in 1996. We also attended national conventions, such as the BCCE, the semi-annual chemical education conference, where we put on workshops and made presentations. We also "manned" a booth in the exhibition hall. One year, Hal helped us. Another year we received help from Josh Van Houten, one of our customers. And still another year, our daughter, Caryn joined us at the BCCE meeting in Bellingham, WA and helped us refurbish our booth to make it more attractive. Each year led to growth in customer base. One year we picked up Oregon State University by just talking to someone in the convention hall. Another year we attracted the attention of one of the chemistry faculty at the U.S. Naval Academy.

In the 1st year or so someone suggested that it would be possible for students to buy a disk and then simply sell it to someone else who was coming into the course either the same year or the following year. Therefore, I became convinced that we should have a password that changed every year and began working on the whole process of making passwords. After a few calculations, it became evident that one could make a password that consisted of 8 letters which would give a huge number of possibilities at any one time, with no repeats within one year and from one year and to the next. The students were warned that the password became part of their record file, so they should not be used by any more than one student. The passwords were printed on individual slips of paper that were included with the disks, with instructions for use.

We began adding product lines in 1997 when we developed a product for introductory chemistry courses called *ChemSkill Foundations*. This consisted of a mixture of the introductory topics from *CSB* and the addition of some new sections of introductory material with more graphic questions and simulations. We had a few Clemson students assist in programming of the simulations, based on some experimental material that I had given them. After this was released, we began working on an updated version of *ChemSkill Builder*. This was instituted because we had several complaints from schools saying that they liked the first semester material, but that they thought that the second semester materials were a little weak. So, we decided to change the grade management so that all units had a maximum of six sections and to basically add a new section to each unit. In the first semester units, we added some of the introductory material that we had developed for CSF, especially the simulation

392

materials. For the second semester we added a section of more rigorous material to each unit, much of which was developed from mid-term and final exams contributed to us by the University of Kentucky chemistry program. This took the better part of a year, but was completed by the fall 1999, so we named it *CSB/2000*. With only slight modifications this pedagogical format remained even though the grade management aspect of the program had been upgraded to become *CSB/3000* for the 2005-2006 academic year.

For a while, Midwestern Diskette worked quite well. Then, one year they encouraged us to open a bank account in town to facilitate the transfer of funds. Not knowing anything about banks in Creston, IA, we left it up to them to set up an account for us in the Creston National Bank, which, it turned out, was the same bank that their company used.

Later that year they asked us if they could have a deferred payment on one of the monthly checks, since they were having some cash flow problems. They made the payment on the following month's collections, but we began to worry a little. So, I thought it was about time to go to visit them, as all our actions up 'til then had been by phone. Anyone with any business sense will realize we had been compounding our errors!

So, even though it was the middle of the winter, I hopped on a plane and flew to De Moines, IA. It turned out that they had just had a major snowstorm, but I rented a car and drove the 50 miles, or so, down I-35 to Creston. With many cars and trucks in the ditch, it was hard not to remember that these were the same hills that I had spun out on during a Christmas trip back when I was a Tech student. However, after thirty years' experience in Houghton, I got to Creston without a hitch.

The next morning, I met with the president, the sales manager, and the financial officer, and found them all to be nice people. Apparently, what had happened was that they had done a big job for some cereal company and had failed to get paid. I enjoyed my visit with them, had a beautiful drive back with the pink sunrise highlighting the beautiful countryside, but in the end, the company went bankrupt and we lost about $40,000.

Part of the problem was that the same bank that held our account also owned Midwestern Diskette. But, the president of Midwestern honestly wanted to help us, so he intercepted some checks before they went to the bank and we got back more money than we would have otherwise.

That same year, we lost another $10-12,000 from the Wallace Bookstore chain that went bankrupt, as well. This was an outfit with headquarters in Lexington KY, where ironically, our friend, Peg Foster, had warned us several years earlier that the owner was a little questionable. Fortunately, our company was doing well otherwise that year, so we still made out all right in the end. However, losing Midwestern Diskette, left us without a major component of our company (about 60%).

I set out looking for both a duplication company and a fulfillment company to handle our product. After working about a week, I was beginning to make some tentative agreements with a couple of companies, when I got a call from Terry Nichols, my ex-sales representative at Midwestern Diskette. He informed me that he had made arrangements on his own with a large duplication company in Minneapolis, to take over all of the responsibilities that Midwestern Diskette had previously assumed and that he would continue as our sales rep.

I was not very happy that he had done this for two reasons. First, I was upset that he had gone off and done it without consulting me and second, I had not been too crazy about him as a sales rep for our company in the first place. He, of course, was just trying to salvage his job. But the package was just too good to turn down and so we decided to go with it. Isn't this amazing? However, this was the best deal I had. So, within a week, we were back in business again and all I needed to do was to let our customers know. Even this did not require much, as Terry had been able to keep his same phone number.

It turned out that despite our complete lack of business acumen, that this arrangement worked out well for a number of years, with only a few minor changes. Actually, it was not long before Terry retired and his job, including phone number, were taken over by a very nice young man called Ernie Ellies. For a year or so, we went without a written contract, just a phone agreement that they would continue "doing what Midwestern Diskette did". After a couple of years Pat and I were passing through Minneapolis and dropped in to meet the officers of the company, which was called Advanced Duplication Services (ADS). ADS specialized in duplication of CD-ROM type disks using very modern equipment. We discovered that EHS was the only customer for whom they provided fulfillment activity, pretty much on an experimental basis. However, our experience with them had been good and they did not appear to have any financial problems, so we decided to continue indefinitely.

Our success led us to think that this might be a good time to sell the company. I spent some time with Dwaine and Lucy Eubanks, two chemists who were beginning to think of retiring from Clemson. They prepared a proposal that was not exactly a sale, but involved taking over marketing, distribution, and sales of EHS products. Since much of this was being handled quite well by ADS, I rejected their proposal and they decided to work on other projects for the next couple of years.

Up until that time, our main markets were colleges and universities. But there was a growing interest in high schools particularly by the AP chemistry instructors, who used *CSB/2000* to provide experience doing college level homework. We were also getting some interest in using *ChemSkill Foundation* (CSF) courseware for regular senior level high school chemistry. This really began to grow, after a few AP chemistry workshop leaders began requesting CSB/2000 for their workshop participants. So, after a year or so, I was sending off cartons of as many as 50 packages on a gratis basis to five or more workshop directors. This procedure was particularly effective in Texas, where after a couple of years, we had 60 or so high school clients, some of whom were using both *CSB/2000* and *CSF/2000*. Trinity High School in Louisville, KY, had been a particularly good customer for almost ten years. After a couple of years of this activity, it began to sink in that this might ultimately be our major market overall. Because of the number of high school students, the potential is certainly much greater, in addition, we found that another advantage is that high schools pay on time, whereas some college bookstores are difficult to deal with, especially those belonging to big chains like Barnes & Noble. The disadvantage is that most high schools require more technical support, so that the technical support, per unit sold, tends to be greater.

As you probably know, high schools use their textbooks year after year and simply require that the students maintain them in as high-quality as possible. Hence, many high schools requested to use the same disks over and over and I would simply send them a listing of passwords for their use at a price of $5 a password. They seemed to be happy to do this as it saved them a good deal of money

As I said earlier, we continued to be involved with the Higher Education Division of McGraw-Hill Book Company (MGH), as they were one of our major customers, amounting to about one fifth of our sales. At one of the BCCE meetings we had breakfast with Kent Peterson, the main man in the publication of chemistry texts for MGH. Since many of their customers had been requesting an internet version of *CSB*, he suggested that Electronic Homework Systems (EHS) license the code for *CSB* to MGH, so that they could have some commercial programmers design internet software. According to Kent, "this would allow Jim Spain to retire and collect the vast royalties that would accrue over the years."

As we had also had some clients requesting the internet version, I decided it was just a matter of time and we would lose these customers if we didn't somehow meet their demands. We might as well lose them to an MGH version of our product and at the same time give them what they had been asking for. In short, we signed the necessary agreements with EHS to receive a royalty of $4 for each unit sold or used with MGH texts. MGH hired an educational programming company from Chicago to begin work on the project. Since this was fairly close to Iowa City, Hal went to a couple of meetings to help get the project going. What the programmers failed to understand was that the Visual Basic code produced by Hal was complicated by the fact that it incorporated the Quick Basic code by me. Also, the homework questions were further complicated because they were not questions, but question shells, into which were inserted the randomized question components. In short, the Chicago programmers were unable to make the conversion and consequently gave up after one year, costing MGH something upward to $100k.

Amazingly, MGH did not give up and subsequently, a second group of programmers was selected. This group was based in Atlanta, so that I would be able to go down and help if necessary. Although the second group produced a working version after about one year, it was filled with errors. So, Hal and I went to work proof reading and helping to identify the cause of the errors. Unfortunately, the process of correcting errors was not very successful. It seemed as though they did not believe that correcting the errors was necessary, or that what we said were errors were in fact, errors. Finally, they got a beta version up and running, which MGH allowed some schools to use for free. Then they were receiving lists of errors from the instructors, some of which were passed along to me. After a year of including the software with all text orders, with no extra charge, there were still a significant number of users. During this period, one programmer was assigned the responsibility for errors and began working effectively with me to solve the errors as they were reported. However, important customers such as the University of Iowa were complaining that many of the reported errors were never acted upon. I knew that this was not because of me, because all errors that I received were transmitted directly to the programmer in Atlanta and quickly corrected. My strong suspicion was that the weak link was in the MGH office. Although there was some talk of producing an internet version for *CSF*, MGH had spent so much on the *CSB* version that they had lost their enthusiasm for further development in that area. Surprisingly enough considering the problems, I received word from Kent Peterson that MGH has sold a total of over 170,000 units.

In the meantime, EHS has continued to compete with MGH and publish individual student packages, designed for sale in the bookstore although EHS had lost a significant number of users to MGH. During this time, the gross income fell approximately 50% each year due in part to the internet version despite the introduction of additional products, such as the network additions of *CSB*.

In the meantime, I had been developing another product, designed for General-Organic & Biochemistry courses, taken by allied health students, is called *GOB-ChemSkills*. This product took the better part of three years to design and program, with the help of Dr. Lucille Garmon, a GOB instructor, at the State University of West Georgia, Carrollton GA. The product was to be the epitome of my work in electronic homework, as biochemistry was the climax of my career in chemistry. However, the marketing of this product became a long sad story, primarily because I was in too much of a rush to get it into the hands of the students. The result was that three initial runs of the product were scrapped and redone at a total cost of over

$30,000. At each run, I would find numerous additional errors. The result was that the co-author had so little confidence in the product that she never asked her students to purchase it, perhaps it was too advanced for a typical GOB class. Clearly, I should have been much more conservative in releasing the product to the user. In the end, I gave most of it away. What should have been the peak of my effort, became my greatest disappointment.

Meanwhile, our relationship with Advanced Duplication Services (ADS), our duplication/fulfillment company had been going along reasonably smoothly for several years, when I received a call from Ernie Ellies on March 28, 2005. He asked how my day had been going and I told him that several rather traumatic things had happened. Then he said that he wasn't going to do much to help, as there had been a meeting of the officers of ADS, during which it had been decided that they were going to limit their operation strictly to disk duplication and product building. In other words, they were no longer going to provide any fulfillment services! And, that I would have to find other means of accepting orders from my customers before April 15, 2005.

Since these activities (warehousing product, accepting orders, shipping, invoicing, receiving payment and accounting) made up a major portion of our company, it meant that once again I had to get busy finding other means of carrying on these activities. I think Ernie's call came in at a little before noon and by 5:00 pm I had three companies that were willing to make offers for our consideration. One idea was to re-examine the proposal that had been put forth several years earlier by Dwaine and Lucy Eubanks. It turned out that their proposal seemed a lot more attractive now, than it did several years earlier when ADS was providing very inexpensive fulfillment. So, I called Dwaine and asked if he was still interested in the EHS business and it turned out that he was. The project they had been doing for McGraw-Hill was about over and Lucy was now fully retired from Clemson. So, after looking into a fulfillment company to handle warehousing and shipping, they agreed to take on the full responsibilities for marketing, sales, and distribution of EHS products. That is, they became our distributors, in that we sold them our product at a discount, and they sold it to individuals, bookstores and high schools. They seemed ideally suited for this, as they had many years of experience handling the ACS Exams Service. And as a result of this, they had many contacts in the chemical education business. Only time would tell if the full potential market would be brought to fruition. After some initial problems picking a poor fulfillment house, they then settled into a very effective mode of operation, using the internet for most of their sales.

Since the name *CSB/2000* was several years out-of-date, we decided to change the name to *CSB/3000*, with comparable software for *CSF/3000* and *GOB-Chem/3000*. The emphasis of this change was on a grade management system that no longer depended on the floppy disk for record storage. Thus, the 3000 software switched emphasis

402

to the use of USB-drive (Flash drive, etc.). The system also facilitated the use of transfer by e-mail. At the end of the fall term, *CSB/3000* was further modified to include the wireless transfer capability of CSB network system and renamed *CSB/3000+*.

Because of the cost of building the standard package had crept up to over $5 per unit, due to the hand insertion of all components, the cost of the vinyl folders and printing inserts, Ernie Ellies had suggested that we begin using the DVD-type of package. It would cost only about half what the plastic binder package had because of machine packing. I also came up with a way to initiate the registration process using the password process, also used by the network software. The difference was that this Password needed to be entered only during registration, instead of every time, as with the network password. So, with the encouragement of Dwaine, we had made four significant advances in our software. First, we got rid of the floppy disk. Second, we moved to a much more economical packaging system. Third, we modified the grade management software to make it much easier to use. And, finally, we had taken on a much more modern name for both the instructional software and the grade management software. Only time would tell how these four changes would impact the sale of *ChemSkill Builder* and our other Electronic Homework Systems.

In January 2007, Microsoft released their new operating system called Vista. This impacted us, as virtually all computers sold from that point on would be supplied with Vista. When we first became aware of this during late 2006, we assumed that our software would have little chance of being supported by Vista. Both Dwaine and I set about trying to learn to program in a 32-bit language called REALBasic, with the idea that we would try to re-program *CSB* in that language. Dwaine felt confident that this could be done, but from my experience with the problems MGH had in translation to the Internet *CSB*, I was very skeptical. However, after Vista came out, I was delighted to find that if all the available Microsoft downloads were applied, our software worked fine on the original Vista computers. We later found out that this was not entirely true, as the Vista font did not recognize four of the characters essential to our work. However, after about two weeks, we had redefined the location of the four characters and modified the units where they were used. By the end of two more weeks we had made these units available to all the instructors so that they could pass them along to the students who had purchased Vista computers. Because of the Vista problems and some additional problems of my own doing, the fall of 2007 turned out to be the worst technical support nightmare of any year so far. However, by making the technical support problems and solutions available to all instructors, in a way that we had not previously done, I ultimately reduced my workload. Amazingly, despite all these problems, we still had a cadre of instructors who think that our software is the best available, at least from the pedagogical standpoint.

Things carried along in this manner until the beginning of 2009 when I discovered that Microsoft had come out with a new version of Vista that was based on **64-bit architecture**! Up to that time the computer architecture was 32-bit which could be adjusted to make it compatible with our original 16-bit (Visual Basic, Version 3.0) software.

But there was nothing that we or the student could do to make it compatible with the new 64-bit Vista. We were not alone in the effects of this disaster, as this change impacted perhaps as much as 50% of all software production.

That, of course, was the objective of Microsoft's change in operating system architecture! Old software needed to be replaced by new software and Microsoft was able to provide this New Software. Since 64-bit Vista was provided on essentially all computers purchased after fall 2008, we were finally <u>dead in the water!</u>

Thus, in spring 2009, Dwaine Eubanks conceded that he was going to be unable to reprogram the *CSB* in REALbasic and thus, that he was no longer planning to serve as the distributor of EHS software after fall 2009. On hearing this I decided to discontinue further development of a product that was to be released with the software on a USB-drive (flash drive). And to stop all operations other than technical support of existing products and completion of existing contracts.

I was actually able to talk Dwaine into continuing as distributor until the beginning of 2010, in the hopes of getting rid of all remaining inventory. Although considerable inventory remained, I took it over on January 1st and started reducing it in both the spring and fall. We finally gave away much of the remaining product and signed the papers to dissolve Electronic Homework Systems, Inc on December 31, 2010.

One solution to keeping the company going was to either sell the company or hire a competent programmer to make a 64-bit translation to Visual Basic. But, by 2010, I was 81 years of age and both of us were ready to enter full retirement and there was no interest expressed by either The Eubanks, or Hal Peters.

At that time, I had assumed that customers still wishing to continue using *ChemSkill Builder* would have the McGraw-Hill *Internet-CSB* product to use, however by the end of the 2011 academic year McGraw-Hill had decided to discontinue providing that product and I began receiving numerous e-mails such as the following from one of my remaining customers.

November 22, 2011
Dear Dr. Spain,

I was very sad to see that McGraw-Hill is discontinuing your ChemSkill Builder on-line program. Your software package has done more to help my students learn chemistry than any lecture or textbook assignment ever did. ChemSkill Builder develops confidence for students who have been terrified of chemistry. The ability to continue to work problems until the student is comfortable is a big plus that I don't see with newer electronic homework systems.

I am very interested in finding a way to continue to use ChemSkill Builder with my students. In my brief internet search, it appears that you are still offering ChemSkill Builder as a stand-alone package. If you are still distributing ChemSkill Builder I would be grateful if you could send me a link to your website. Thank you for your help.

Best Regards,
Caleb Arrington
Wofford College, Spartanburg, SC

In June of 2013, I sent a letter to Kent Peterson, Vice President, McGraw-Hill Publishing, asking him if he had any insight as to why MGH had discontinued publishing the online version of *CSB* and received the following:

Hello Jim,

I am not surprised to learn that you are still receiving "fan mail" related to Chem Skill Builder. From an instructional perspective it is a great product. Unfortunately, it is also not surprising to me that we have decided not to continue to support it. We have moved into the platform era of our business. This where education companies like ours focus their development time and money on platform-based solutions that run across the entire curriculum. Our platform solution is Connect. Connect products are available for nearly every course we publish in. The reason for focusing on one platform is scale. By having all customer using one platform we can scale our infrastructure both to make sure the software is reliable (99.9% up time is the industry standard) and that we can provide the necessary user support. Scale also helps us from a selling perspective. Instead of reps having to learn a software solution for each course, once they learn in general how Connect works, they can have a conversation with any instructor. We now offer very few course specific software applications like Chem Skill Builder across our product line.

`I am sure you will ask the question "Are these platforms pedagogically better than course specific programs like Chem Skill Builder?" The answer is "in some areas 'yes' and in other areas 'no'". It is likely that the design of some questions in Chem Skill Builder is superior to what we currently offer in our Connect for Chemistry. It is hard to beat the approach of a master teacher like you. The overall design of the software however is something that Chem Skill Builder simply can't compete with. The new adaptive LearnSmart aspect of Connect is really very good. This is the direction education software is heading and again by concentrating on one common solution, companies like McGraw-Hill can scale their investment to cover the most courses possible. This is a major benefit to the student population and something that we could not achieve by continuing to publish stand-alone applications like Chem Skill Builder.

Kent Peterson

Vice President, National Sales Region

McGraw-Hill Company

From the educational standpoint, this had been, without a doubt, my greatest accomplishment and at the same time had provided me an intriguing and enjoyable occupation following my retirement from classroom teaching. I feel that it was a major achievement from several points of view. First, it was a challenge from the standpoint of simply developing and programming computer exercises for a complete course in general chemistry. This, because of the randomizing nature of the exercises, took significant portions of about 8 years overall. Although the technique employed was originated by Bill Butler of Univ. Michigan, the project far exceeded that which he had published earlier and extended to many additional subject areas. To this I developed a means of retaining student records in an encrypted form that defied the best minds of over half a million students. Second was the reach of my teaching; When I taught in the classroom, I had a limited number of students I could reach each year. Through this product I helped 750,000 students strengthen and retain their understanding of chemistry.

Finally, between us, Pat and I ran a publishing company that was commercially successful, selling over three quarters of a million units during the 16 years following my retirement from Clemson. The fact that a computer-based product survived for that period of time was itself a remarkable feat. The fact that it was done by a couple of retirees, with essentially no training in either business or computer science, makes it phenomenal. Clearly, running the *ChemSkill Builder* company was a culmination of the fortuitous nature, a financial success, and a fulfilling enjoyment to both of us.

However, after a year or so, Microsoft Corporation failed to support any software previous to the "64 bit revolution". Thus, there is no *Chem Skill Builder* Visual Basic software that continues to operate! It is possible that the Quick BASIC version of *Chem-Skill-Bildr* written before 1997 still operates on an early PC computer, otherwise I am totally unable to look at one bit of the work I carried out during the years 1990-2010. This is one of the saddest aspects of this whole portion of my life.

During the winter of 2010-11, we closed out our company and began getting our house in South Carolina ready for sale, as We planned to move back to Houghton, Michigan, to spend the remaining years of our retirement.

Pat and Jim voted Classiest Couple at the Bluffs Retirement Community in Houghton, MI. (2013)

Chem Skill Builder 3000+

Minimum System Requirements
CD-ROM-drive, 256 color VGA monitor,
16MB RAM for Win 98 to Vista
USB-Removable-drive compatible

Contents of CD-ROM

Introduction to Chemistry
Units and Measurements
Nomenclature
Molar Relationships
Chemical Reactions
Molarity of Solutions
Properties of Gases
Thermochemistry
Atomic Structure
Oxidation and Reduction
Periodic Properties
Polyatomic Structures
Covalent Bonding
Liquids and Solids
Properties of Solutions
Chemical Kinetics
Chemical Equilibria
Acid-Base Equilibria
Buffers and Hydrolysis
Solubility Equilibria
Thermodynamics
Electrochemistry
Nuclear Chemistry
Organic Chemistry
Polymer Chemistry
Appendix

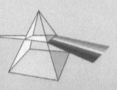

ISBN 1-89080354-5
53500
9 781890 803544

Back cover of the latest version of CSB

CHAPTER 21

CONCLUSION

(2020)

The title of this book would seem to promise that it would provide the means by which one would pick a pioneer pathway, so perhaps I should get about doing something of that sort.

The first time this book was written, it was primarily for my children and grandchildren as a Christmas present and so, when my daughters and I were looking for an objective, we decided that it should emphasize all the good luck that my wife and I had during our lifetime, so my title was *My Fortuitous life with Pat*. However, good luck is not something one has much control over, so is not much use in developing a strategy for one's life.

So, when I began rewriting the book primarily for students who were trying to decide on their future course of study, I decided to emphasize that it didn't matter where you started, although, I found that chemistry was the most effective start for me. Then after wandering about a bit in my career I ended up in the application of computer science to education, even though I had never taken a course in ether "Computer Science" or "Education". Consequently, I changed the title of the book to *Our Circuitous Pathway to Prosperity*.

However, on reading this book, my friend James Mitchell, a Michigan Tech Alumnus and Board of Control Member, said: "The book was very good, except that the title was wrong." He suggested that it should point out the various pioneering approaches that I had employed during the course of my career. Initially, my use of the word "pioneer" was limited to the one chapter dealing with my early efforts into computer science. On reviewing my life history, I found several other instances where it might be construed that I had played the role of a "pioneer".

The word pioneer is derived from a French word that means one who goes ahead. It is used to describe the soldiers who precede the main body of troops to carry out whatever jobs need to be done to make the main assault possible. Note the connection with the word "peon", meaning a person of little value and "pawn", the piece of little value with which one usually begins a chess game. However, Americans have used the word "pioneer" to connote a person, like Daniel Boone, who was willing to go ahead of the group to find the way forward. I would like to think of myself as the latter-type pioneer.

414

When the American pioneers were looking for opportunities they naturally went West, in part because of a famous quotation, attributed to Horace Greeley; "Go West, young man, and grow up with the country." It's almost as simple with science. Because the opportunities are found at the interface between one science and another! This is what led me initially to go into the field of biochemistry, which is obviously the boundary between biology and chemistry and one only needs to look at the ACS magazine, *Chemical and Engineering News*, to see that this is where the growth has been over the last 50 years. Again, When I was selecting a field of research for my PhD thesis, I selected the field of Histochemistry which is at the boundary between Histology and Biochemistry and it is at that point I believe that I got my start as a pioneer researcher. Thus, the rule is simple: "Go to the Science Interface, that's where the action is! And, if there is no interface, better yet, MAKE A NEW ONE!" As I go back to the first instance where I seem to have been playing the pioneer role was when, I discovered the technique called Precipitation Chromatography.

In this case, I was teaching a freshman chemistry lab and happened to notice that when ammonium sulfide solution mixed with some metal ions spilled on a paper towel, there appeared a series of colored bands such as one sees in chromatography. This attracted my curiosity and I attempted to duplicate it. The result, I called "precipitation chromatography" because the separation of ions was based on the solubility equilibrium. What followed were three papers in the journal, *Analytical Chemistry* and one in *Economic Geology*.

I think it is also interesting to note how it was that I happened upon this new technique. I was not in the laboratory with the intention of finding a new type of chromatography, but rather was going about my everyday occupation of teaching freshman chemists to analyze for metal ions and simply "perusing" my environment, watching for opportunities that might arise. This is much the same as any beachcomber would use when searching the beach to find valuable shells, shark teeth or agates. That's why I chose the word "peruse" to describe the way that I happened upon this new technique and is not unlike the original pioneer perusing the back woods, looking for nice pieces of land for farms and towns. As I look back at my life, that is what I seem to have been doing in many instances of pioneering that I displayed.

I had also presented a paper at the American Chemical Society meeting in Chicago, in which I was able to successfully carry out an unplanned demonstration. Following the paper, I met with several people who were active in the field of chromatography. With this encouragement, I returned to the chemistry department with increased interest in the field of chromatography and proposed a course on the general phase distribution techniques to Dr. Makens, the department head. However, he suggested that instead, I should develop a general course in Instrumental Analysis for senior chemists, and thus I became involved in a totally new pioneering project.

My first interest in computers came with the purchase of the Olivetti P-101 Programmable Calculator, which was bought initially for routine statistical analysis and other mathematical calculations. However, I found that it could be programmed to do repetitive operations, which allowed me to do what I called "simulations" of rate processes. (I later found out that what I was doing was really called "numerical integration of rate equations."). Since this technique is very important to chemistry, biology, physics, and biochemistry, I thought it would be important for people to know about this capability. So, I decided to give a paper at *The 1ˢᵗ Conference on Computers in the Undergraduate Curricula*, to be held in Iowa City. When I arrived, I found that I was the only person who was prepared to make a presentation in biology. While I was there, they were planning *The 2nd Conference on Computers in the Undergraduate Curricula*, to be held at Dartmouth, and I was selected as the person to lead the section on "Biological Applications of Computers". After returning from the conference I prepared a paper to be submitted to the *Simulation* journal, and had it accepted. This sudden success in the area of computer science led me to believe that I was, indeed, a pioneer in the biological applications of computers, even though, my "computer" was really just a programmable calculator. In other words, one can go a long way on guts.

I consequently started a course in "Biological Applications of Computers" that initially used the programmable calculator. This history wouldn't even be worth mentioning except that it led me to decide that the programmable calculator-based information was not of much long range value to my students. Unless I began using a programming language that had general applicability, they would leave the course with nothing more than a few ideas. Therefore, I obtained a book on *BASIC Programming Language* and changed all my programs to that language. I became fascinated with the new power that it gave me and wrote new programs one after another. After writing up a new set of notes, I was prepared to do all my programming in BASIC and start developing real exercises for my students. By the end of the year I had enough material that I thought I could present a summer workshop on the subject of mathematical modeling and simulation. This workshop brought in about ten college faculty from around the country that included Brian Winkel, a mathematician from Rose Holman Institute of Technology. He became so interested in what I was doing, that he joined us for a sabbatical year. The outcome was that between the two of us, we presented two faculty workshops the following summer. Later, I developed enough material to write a 350 page textbook, *BASIC Microcomputer Models in Biology*, that Brian and his wife helped me to get formatted and typed for publication by Addison-Wesley. The book was based on the material developed over about seven years teaching the computer modelling course, containing about a hundred exercises in microcomputer

418

BASIC. At some point, I realized that the book had the potential to become something more than just a text for my class and began putting significant effort into its composition.

In the end, the book received positive letters from several faculty around the country and more indexed citations than I had received from all my previous research papers. About ten years later, a second edition of the book was published by Wiley-Liss under the title *Computer Simulation in Biology: A BASIC Introduction,* by Robert Keen and James Spain. As I write this conclusion in 2020, Michigan Tech has recently added a degree program in Biological Informatics, that involves computer applications in Biology, most of which weren't even conceived at the time my first book was written. Many major universities now have Departments of Biological Informatics and last Christmas when I looked to see how many books there were about "modelling and simulation" there were at least a dozen with modifications of that title. Clearly, I had been on the right path.

After some work with instructional simulations that were prepared for national publication, and spending a year initiating the Instructional Computing Center at Eastern Michigan University, I was ready to move on to something more significant at Clemson University, where I had moved since my retirement from Michigan Tech.

The major project of my life came about when I concluded that chemistry instruction needed a full system of computerized homework exercises that would prepare students for exams and understanding of chemistry. Because of a fortuitous meeting with a person who had worked on such a project, I developed a major strategy that could be used to financially support such a project. I also switched from using simulations as my primary teaching method, to using the drill and practice approach that he had used. The Clemson Chemistry Faculty and I then began thinking of the homework exercises as being a form of quizzes, for which students would receive some credit towards their final grade. The final decision was to cause the results of student quizzes to be sent electronically to instructors, using secure means. That is, the results of quizzes needed to be encrypted so that the smartest students in the country could not change their outcome. These decisions were made over a period of years, based on discussions involving several faculty members and my experience running the chemistry learning center at Clemson. It became more and more obvious that I was planning to develop a national project for computerized instruction in chemistry, not just a project that was designed for Clemson students!

The product was tested at Clemson and was not released for sale at other schools until after I retired from teaching, and formed the company: Electronic Homework Systems, Inc. We decided to call our first product *ChemSkill Builder*, which in the next few years was sold to students at Univ. of Georgia, Univ. of Florida, Univ. of Kentucky, Oregon State Univ., Clemson University, and numerous smaller schools. All told, it was sold to over 750,000 students during the 16 years of the company's operation. It is clear that if you want to go big, you've got to think big!

I have come to believe that this might be the key to becoming a pioneer and may even be the answer to the question; "How do you become a Pioneer?". At some point, you have to <u>switch from thinking locally, to thinking nationally</u> because, it's at this point that you begin acting like a PIONEER. This switching was crucial in each of the three examples shown above and I believe occurred in each of the other cases where I might be construed as having been a pioneer.

As indicated above, this book was initially intended for family consumption, then modified to be useful for students at Michigan Tech, finally modified again to make it more attractive to a national audience. So, if you are part of the latter group and are still reading this book, it would seem that I have another pioneering publication to be proud of.

ABOUT THE AUTHOR

James D. Spain was born in Washington, D.C. and grew up in Arlington VA. At a young age he moved to Florida, and later to New Orleans, LA., where he graduated from High School.

He earned a BS degree in Chemistry from Michigan Technological University (MTU) in 1951.

He then went on to earn his MS in Biochemistry from the Medical College of Virginia Commonwealth University in 1953.

He earned his PhD in Chemistry from Stanford University in 1956. He did Post-Doctoral research at M.D. Anderson Hospital.

Jim's first teaching position was as Assistant Professor of Chemistry at MTU (1956-1962).

He became Professor and Head of the Department of Biological Sciences (1962-1968).

Professor of Biochemistry, while carrying out research in Limnology and Oceanography (1968-1978).

His interest changed with the development of microcomputers and he carried out research in Computer Simulation and Instructional Computing (1978-1984).

Following an Early Retirement from MTU in 1984, he was appointed the first director of the Instructional Computing Center at Eastern Michigan University, Ypsilanti for one year (1984-1985).

The following year, Jim moved on to Clemson University where he was a lecturer in General Chemistry and director of the Chemistry Computerized Instruction Laboratory (1985-1995).

He retired from teaching in 1995 at the age of 65 to start his personal business with the help of Pat. He was owner and CEO of Electronic Homework Systems, Inc. (1995-2011)

Major Publications:
James D. Spain; *BASIC Microcomputer Models in Biology* 1982

Robert E. Keen and James D. Spain; *Computer Simulation in Biology A BASIC Introduction* 1992

James Spain and H. A. Peters; *ChemSkill Builder* Electronic Homework in General Chemistry 1995-2010